# Moving Lives

# Moving Lives

*Twentieth-Century Women's Travel Writing*

## Sidonie Smith

University of Minnesota Press
Minneapolis • London

To Julia, with whom I've traveled distances

Copyright 2001 by the Regents of the University of Minnesota

A longer version of a section in chapter 2 appeared as "Isabelle Eberhardt Travelling 'Other'/wise: The 'European' Subject in 'Oriental' Identity," in *Encountering the Other(s): Studies in Literature, History, and Culture*, edited by Gisela Brinker-Gabler (Albany: State University of New York Press, 1995), 295–318; copyright 1995, State University of New York, all rights reserved; reprinted by permission of State University of New York Press. A longer version of a section in chapter 3 appeared as "The Other Woman and the Racial Politics of Gender: Isak Dinesen and Beryl Markham in Kenya," in *De/Colonizing the Subject*, edited by Sidonie Smith and Julia Watson (Minneapolis: University of Minnesota Press, 1992), 410–35. Parts of chapter 3 also appeared in "Virtually Modern Amelia: Mobility, Flight, and the Discontents of Identity," in *Virtual Gender: Fantasies of Subjectivity and Embodiment*, edited by Mary Ann O'Farrell and Lynne Vallone (Ann Arbor: University of Michigan Press, 1999), 11-36; reprinted by permission of the University of Michigan Press.

The lyrics at the beginning of the Introduction are from the song "Vehicle," words and music by Jim Peterik, copyright 1970 Bald Medusa Musa ASCAP. Reprinted by permission of Jim Peterik.

All reasonable efforts have been made to obtain permission for illustrations included in this book. If any proper acknowledgment has not been made, we encourage copyright holders to notify the University of Minnesota Press.

Published by the University of Minnesota Press
111 Third Avenue South, Suite 290
Minneapolis, MN 55401-2520
http://www.upress.umn.edu

**Library of Congress Cataloging-in-Publication Data**

Smith, Sidonie.
  Moving lives : twentieth-century women's travel writing / Sidonie Smith
    p. cm.
Includes bibliographical references and index.
  ISBN 0-8166-2874-2 (alk. paper) — ISBN 0-8166-2875-0 (pbk. : alk. paper)
  1. Travelers' writings. 2. Women travelers—History—20th century.
I. Title.
  G465 .S627 2001
  910'.82—dc21                                00-011804

# Contents

# Acknowledgments

When I began this exploration of women's travel narratives and technologies of motion in the early 1990s, the number of books and articles on the gendering of travel and on women's travel narratives more particularly was relatively modest. But in the early 1990s, books and articles began appearing regularly; and now the field is robust with work. Thus, I am indebted to scholars whose work has provided the basis upon which this study builds, among them Eric J. Leed, Mary Louise Pratt, Georges Van Den Abbeele, Dennis Porter, Chris Bongie, Sara Mills, Caren Kaplan, and Frances Bartkowski. And I am indebted to those scholars of technology and culture whose work prompted me to focus on modes of mobility and narrative practices, among them Wolfgang Schivelbusch, Virginia Scharff, Robert Wohl, Wolfgang Sachs, and Gerald Silk.

The staff of the Clements Library and the Labadie Special Collections of the University of Michigan libraries provided invaluable support in locating visual materials for inclusion in this book. I wish to thank specifically John Dann, director of the Clements Library, for facilitating my search of the early-twentieth-century archives, and James Fox at the Labadie for helping me peruse the remarkable Transportation History Collection. I thank Frances Bartkowski for referring me to the work of Tamara de Lempicka and to the cover image.

The editorial staff at the University of Minnesota Press has maintained enthusiasm for this project through many changes in personnel. I thank particularly Biodun Iginla and William Murphy, both of whom are no longer at the press, and Doug Armato. Here at the University of Michigan I owe special appreciation to Sherri Joyner and Caryn Burtt, whose research assistance proved invaluable in the last stages of preparation.

Several sections of this book have derived from previously published articles. Thus, I express my gratitude to the University of Minnesota Press, the University of Michigan Press, and the State University of New York Press for permission to reprint versions of those articles. I also express my gratitude to Jim Peterik, who wrote the words and music for "Vehicle," performed by the Ides of March, for permission to cite lyrics from the song.

Finally, I thank Gregory Grieco for his unflagging support and his willingness to keep traveling, and Tony Smith-Grieco for traveling in bookstores and finding me fascinating studies of such road phenomena as service-station maps.

# Vehicular Gender

I'm your vehicle, baby.
I'll take you anywhere you wanna go.
I'm your vehicle woman.
By now I'm sure you know.

—"Vehicle," performed by the Ides of March (1970)

The anthropologist Victor Turner claims that the journey—as event, personal experience, and cultural symbol—accumulates all kinds of communal meanings. Prominent in the repertoire of meanings identified with journeying in the West have been the meanings attached to itinerant masculinity. The historian Eric J. Leed acknowledges the constitutive masculinity of travel when he argues that, "from the time of Gilgamesh," journeying has served as "the medium of traditional male immortalities," enabling men to imagine escape from death by the "crossing" of space and the "record[ing]" of adventures "in bricks, books, and stories." He even labels this travel, which provides men the opportunity to achieve notable distinction through self-defining experience far from home, "spermatic" travel (286).[1]

Ever in the process of becoming "men," travelers affirm their masculinity through purposes, activities, behaviors, dispositions, perspectives, and bodily movements displayed on the road, and through the narratives of travel that they return home to the sending culture. Thus, travel functions as a defining arena of agency. We cannot imagine Odysseus without his travels, or Aeneas, or the knights of the Round Table, or Columbus, Captain Cook, Boswell, Byron, or Loti, or, closer to our own times, Jack Kerouac. Nor can we imagine them without their travel narratives. These narratives of travel can be read as journey myths "project[ing]," as Richard Slotkin suggests of myths generally, "models of good and heroic behavior that reinforce the values of ideology, and affirm as good the distribution of authority and power that ideology rationalizes" (507).

Leed contrasts the masculine logic of mobility with the logic of "sessility" (171). To be "sessile," in botanical terms, is to be permanently planted, tenaciously fixed, utterly immobile. It is, in a sense, to remain always "at home," which has been the traditional locale assigned to women. What Judith Butler describes as "the domain of socially instituted norms" (*Bodies* 182), through which gender identity and gendered relationships get reiterated in everyday occasions, secures the domestication of woman through protocols of proper femininity that tether her to home and thus to a requisite sessility. But she is not just resident in the home. As Karen R. Lawrence observes in *Penelope Voyages*, "She in effect is home itself, for the female body is traditionally associated with earth, shelter, enclosure" (1). Whatever particular women may be doing in their everyday lives, the idea of woman as "earth, shelter, enclosure," as "home," persists, anchoring femininity, weighing it down, fixing it as a compass point. Moreover, the "home" that is identified as feminine, feminized, and equated with woman becomes that which must be left behind in the pursuit of agency. This "stifling home," Meaghan Morris observes so tellingly, has been precisely "the place from which the voyage begins and to which, in the end, it returns" (12).

Yet, even though travel has generally been associated with men and masculine prerogatives, even though it has functioned as a domain of constitutive masculinity, women have always been and continue to be on the move. They climb aboard sailing vessels, or pull themselves onto horses, or grab a walking stick and set out along rutted paths, or rush to make a train. If traveling, being on the road, makes a man a man—and makes masculinity and its power visible—what does it make of a woman, who is at once a subject as home and a subject at home? What does it mean for a particular woman to gain access to this defining arena of agency in the West? These are the questions that nagged at me when I started this project some eight years ago.

Women's move to motion gained momentum in the late nineteenth and early twentieth centuries when increasing numbers of Western women participated in the cultural logic of the individualizing journey. Through this participation they could gain a modicum of enabling independence and a form of education outside official institutions closed to them, as well as exercise some measure of social and socializing influence and authority. Even as the protocols of the proper lady projected femininity as delicate, ignorant, cloistered, and disabling—sessile—the individualizing logic of mobility, as it translated traveling women into a masculine logic and domain, enabled some women to alter the terms of their "cultural construction in difference" (Mouffe 382), whether or not they identified with the new woman of the feminist first wave.

The expanding mobility of certain women in the middle to late nineteenth century came as an effect of modernity—democratization, literacy, education, increasing wealth, urbanization and industrialization, and the colonial and imperial expansion that produced wealth and the investment in "progress." In complex ways, that mobility functioned as a sign of modernity as well, since one register of "progress" in the West and one register of the success of first-wave feminism was precisely the increasing mobility of women. Indeed, the "progress" of Western civilization(s) could be gauged by the degree to which Western women had been "freed" from the cruel and "dehumanizing" practices of "backward" societies with their unequal social arrangements. Western women were women freed from the drudgery of daily survival and from ignorance, those conditions of everyday life that traveling women observed in their movements through colonized spaces (Kaplan 33-41). "By the latter part of the nineteenth century," notes Catherine Barnes Stevenson, "women travelers began to be singled out as exemplars of the new freedom and prowess of women" (3).

That newly gained freedom and prowess was made possible by the new technologies of motion that drove modernity. Large numbers of women began to leave home for the lure of the road as a result of the emergence of faster, safer, cleaner, and more comfortable machines of motion. It is precisely this aspect of travel, the "how" of travel, that has engaged more and more of my attention, forcing me to think about how the new machines transformed space, time, and the subjects of travel. For if a particular woman was discontented with the sessility "forced" by social relations at home—that "overdetermined . . . locus of female activity and identity" (Gilmore and Aldrich 44)—she had to choose a particular vehicle in which to head out on the road. That vehicle transported the traveler from familiar to unfamiliar terrain. Now, as Frances Bartkowski emphasizes in her exploration of travel and identity, "the demands placed upon the subject in situations of unfamiliarity and dislocation produce a scene in which the struggle for identity comes more clearly into view as both necessary and also mistaken" (xix). Bartkowski's linkage of the dislocation of travel and the unsettling of identities illuminates how vehicular motion becomes an altered way of seeing and of seeing oneself.

Nevertheless, I had to keep reminding myself, there is travel and then there is travel narrative, an activity related to but distinct from travel itself. I began to consider how these technologies of motion transform narratives of travel. If the mode of moving a body through space affects the traveler who moves through space as that body, then the mode of motion informs the meaning that the traveler sends back home in narration. Because travel narrative is commonly addressed to readers at home, it marks a return, even if it is not officially returned to the sending culture. And what is returned home is the meaning of a particular mode of motion as it affects the play of identity and its discontents.

Although Virginia Woolf was not necessarily preoccupied with new technologies of motion per se, in her modernist fiction she associated new technologies with new narratives and with the emergence of new kinds of identities for women. References to trains, planes, and automobiles, as well as references to more leisurely walking, abound in her fiction and her essays; and she makes these technologies of motion carry charged meaning in her modernist explorations of the change in social relations that occurred in the first decades of the twentieth century. In *The Voyage Out* (1915), her youthful protagonist, Rachel Vinrace, journeys via boat and foot into the South American jungle surrounding the coastal metropolis where she temporarily resides; and it is during this voyage that Rachel contracts the disease that will take her life. This novel was the young Virginia Woolf's "voyage out," a voyage through which she began to parse the compromised identities of young Englishwomen reaching beyond Edwardian manners. Woolf's manifesto of modernist aesthetics and politics, "Mr. Bennett and Mrs. Brown" (1924), takes off from a brief encounter the writer has with an older woman in a railway car. (I will say more about this manifesto in chapter 4.) The pervasive symbol of the dread and promise of a new era in social relations, and of the impossibility of interpreting cultural signs, becomes the airplane that zooms through the London scenes of *Mrs. Dalloway* (1925). In the concluding scene of *The Years* (1937), a young man and woman enter an automobile together. In this final orchestration of the mobility of the sexes, Woolf gestures toward the emergence of young men and women negotiating new social relations. Finally, in her posthumously published last novel, *Between the Acts* (1941), an ominous airplane drones inexorably, suggesting the imminence of violence and catastrophe. Woolf linked these modern technologies to narrative ends and means, suggesting throughout her writing career that modern technologies permeate the narratives of the twentieth century and the complex meanings of gendered mobility and mobile gender.

The powerful technologies of modernity have made new kinds of identities possible in the last century. Energizing new relationships to identity, they generate new narratives of mobility. As fascinated as I am with the history of transportation technologies and the gendering of the entire machine ensemble, I have chosen to focus in this study on how women travel and how those modes of mobility affect the stories women narrate about gender and bodies in motion in the twentieth century.

This study, then, is not about women travelers in the twentieth century—there are already many such studies. Nor is it about some hypothetical and universalized woman traveler. Women have always been in motion and for a variety of complex reasons; and their traveling has always been gendered and embodied traveling, situated within complex social, cultural, and historical forces. Given the increased access to and speed of mobility of all kinds—of choice and exile and expulsion and displacement and homelessness—and the proliferation of narratives of travel in the new global economy, no single study can do more than tease out some of these forces as they affect specific travelers or generations of travelers.

Nor is this study intended as a history of women's travel writing in the twentieth century or a developmental story of transformations in narrative modes and practices. There are already many cultures of travel around the globe, with their specific histories and their generic conventions. Others have engaged and will continue to engage these larger projects of historical scope or focus on nationally and regionally organized mappings of gendered travel. I have limited my scope to narratives written by women from Europe, North America, and Australia, for whom new technologies have been generally accessible and financially available, or for whom, despite the lack of familial means, effects of technological modernity have been at once defining and troubling.

To explore more precisely the relationship of modes of mobility and narrative practice, I have chosen, within that scope, to explore texts that clearly foreground a particular mode of motion. Some of them are well known. Some are rather quirky and probably little known, as it happens. And that is precisely the point. I wanted here to reach beyond commonly known narratives, to find tales of mobility in out-of-the-way places.

As I became immersed in this study, to my surprise, I discovered that all of the narratives I came to explore were by white women. Now, women of color have been writing narratives about their travels for the last century and a half, at least in the United States and the Caribbean, from Nancy Prince and Zilpha Elaw in the mid-nineteenth century, to Sarah Winnemucca Hopkins and Zitkala-Ša at the end and turn of the century, to Maya Angelou, Jamaica Kincaid, and Sara Suleri in the mid- to late twentieth century. In earlier work I explored literal, imaginative, and performative travel in the autobiographical narratives of some of these traveler-narrators, among them Zitkala-Ša, Zora Neale Hurston, Maya Angelou, Maxine Hong Kingston, Gloria Anzaldúa, Cherríe Moraga, Sally Morgan, and Michelle Cliff.[2] Although they may not figure themselves as inveterate travelers, as is the case with most of the women whose narratives are discussed in the following chapters, they do explore the meaning and effects of displacement and encounter. But these traveler-narrators do not foreground a particular technology of motion, and for that reason I chose to reach beyond narratives that might be obvious choices, to others that are now less well known. Unfortunately, Erika Lopez's *Flaming Iguanas: An Illustrated All-Girl Road Novel Thing* (1997) came to my attention too late for inclusion in this study. In this playful hybrid narrative, part comic-book illustration, part autobiographical reverie, part novelistic romp, Lopez takes a performative version of herself, whom she calls Tomato Rodriguez, on a motorcycle ride through the United States in order to interrogate stereotypes and to assert Latina agency.[3] This narrative and others like it offer prospects for further theorizing about cultures of travel, technologies of motion, and ethnic identity formation.

Moreover, a complicated set of intersecting constraints affects the Western woman of color when she travels, given the cultural politics of racial visibility and the vulnerability attending her transit in inhospitable spaces. Women of color often have themes to explore in addition to the empowerment and limitations of flight, automobility, locomotion, and foot travel. And for women displaced from postcolonial Asia, Africa, and the island nations of the Caribbean, many of whom have written of their travels to and in Europe and North America, issues of gendered citizenship, diaspora, and the (de)colonization of subjectivity, rather than technologies of motion, assume primacy. As bell hooks remarks, the figure of the journey rather than the figure of travel, tied as it is to the history of colonialism and imperialism, is a more appropriate means through which to understand the stakes of mobility for people of color, when that mobility is associated with such experiences as "immigration, enforced migration, relocation, enslavement, homelessness" (343). "To travel," writes hooks, "I must always move through fear, confront terror" (344).

The travelers whose narratives I explore here assume their ability to move through exotic and not-so-exotic spaces without the constraints of visibility politics as they elaborate a politics of technological mobility. In fact, for many of them, their relationship to the technologies of modernity is precisely the signifier of their privileged whiteness. And no matter what their class status—and they were/are by no means all middle class—they often figure themselves not as members of a collectivity or community of identity but as exceptional loners, sometimes even misfits. Their narratives often explore their status as outsiders, but that outsider status does not derive from the color of their skin or their ethnicity; nor does it necessarily motivate affiliation with a larger community of identity, though for some it does. Critically, the chosen technology of motion each narrator negotiates and the social context of its machine ensemble has materialized not only in gendered social relations but also in racialized and class-based social relations; and so issues of the race-class-gender nexus define the travelers' journeys and their narratives, as the following chapters will make clear.

Now to the plan for this study. In chapter 1, I situate this exploration of women's narrative relationship to modern technologies of motion, briefly reviewing how itinerant masculinity in the West has gotten reproduced and reinterpreted since the early centuries of Christianity, and how narratives of travel have been fundamental to the cultural production of these diverse versions of mobile masculinity. From assaying just what kind of men travel and travel narrating have made of travelers historically, I turn to explore, again briefly, the complex narrative negotiations required of women on the move up to the beginning of the twentieth century. I conclude this chapter with a consideration of the ways in which modern modes of motion affect the social relations of travel and travel narrating.

In subsequent chapters I offer readings of narratives about different kinds of motion—by foot, by flight, by locomotion, and by automobility. These readings engage the following questions: How does a woman have, get, or claim access to particular modes of motion? What does it mean for her to leave home and return home via the technologies of modernity? Why does she choose the mode she chooses? And where in the world does she want this technology of motion to take her? I'm pointing here not to the actual destination, although the destination is important, but to the traveler's designs on and uses of mobility, to the why of her particular choice. For it is through the choice of a particular mode of mobility that a woman becomes a certain kind of traveler who constitutes the meaning of travel in her own ways. What precisely does it mean for her to ride in machines of motorized modernity that have been identified as phallic—the train, for instance? or to assume command of those phallic machines of motorized modernity such as the airplane and the automobile?

To put some names and specific technologies with the narratives: What does Alexandra David-Neel make of disappearing into the disguise of the Tibetan peasant and making the journey across the Himalayas to Lhasa by foot, or Isabelle Eberhardt of donning the habit of a male nomad in North Africa, or Robyn Davidson of her camel journey across the hot outback of Australia? What do Amelia Earhart, Anne Morrow Lindbergh, and Beryl Markham, all aviators in the 1930s, make of climbing into the cockpit of an airplane? What does Mary Morris make of the failure of her train journey from Beijing to Berlin; or Linda Niemann, the boomer, of her frantic efforts to ride the brakes of the freight trains crisscrossing the western United States; or Daphne Marlatt and Betsy Warland of their lovers' journey from one side of Australia to the other? What does Beverly Donofrio make of the lack of an automobile once she's finished riding in cars with boys, or Irma Kurtz of riding the Greyhound into the bellies of American cities and towns? Journeys by foot across the hard or soft earth, journeys by air high above the huddling masses below, journeys along the rigid rails, haphazard journeys along highways and backstreets—women on the move have taken them all.

In their 1970s pop hit, the Ides of March intoned, "I'm your vehicle, baby. / I'll take you anywhere you wanna go." Self-confidently, the song conflated masculine subjectivity, the masculine logic of travel, and vehicular agency. *Moving Lives* complicates "baby's" relationship to the masculine logic of travel and to vehicular agency. Most importantly, by asking what meaning she makes of her vehicle when she writes about it, this study troubles the unexamined assertion of the Ides of March that "baby" can be taken anywhere she wants to go.

# CHAPTER 1

# The Logic of Travel
# and Technologies of Motion

In many societies being feminine has been defined as
sticking close to home. Masculinity, by contrast, has been the
passport for travel. Feminist geographers and ethnographers have
been amassing evidence revealing that a principal difference
between women and men in countless societies has been the
license to travel away from a place thought of as "home."

—Cynthia Enloe, *Bananas, Beaches, and Bases:*
*Making Feminist Sense of International Politics*

## The Masculine Logic of Travel

Between the fourth and the fifteenth centuries, three distinct kinds of
travelers traversed the vast and unfamiliar landscapes of Europe: the
scholar, the crusader, and the pilgrim. The itinerant scholar became a
common figure after the "barbarian" invasions of the fifth to ninth centuries destroyed central libraries and scattered classical texts, and with
them classical knowledge, across Europe and Asia. Crisscrossing Europe,
the Middle East, and the Far East searching for texts sacred and classical, scholars accumulated whole libraries of knowledge on their backs.
Through this journeying they helped bind Christendom, a vast conglom-
eration of disparate peoples and cultures, into an identifiable community.

But Christendom was bound together as well through the arduous
journeys of countless penitents in transit to sacred territory.[1] From the
fourth century onward, sacred texts asserted the centrality to Christian
consciousness of sacred sites, the most sacred of which was the Holy
Land. Pilgrimage to the site of the holy promised transformative arrivals,
most compellingly the arrival of eternal joy through penitence and purification (Leed 11). If the ceaseless movements of pilgrims created the

imagined community of Christians, then narrative accounts of those travels witnessed for folks at home about the meanings of "collective motion" to sites that were understood to be themselves "witnesses" of biblical figures and events (Campbell 19). In such narratives the penitent Christian attested to other Christians who could not undertake the difficult and lengthy journey the beneficial effects of identification with sacred sites and, through them, the sacred events of biblical history.

Medieval crusaders were religious pilgrims in militant dress, charged with gaining, recovering, and protecting the sites that ceaseless pilgrimages had sacralized. Brandishing sharp-edged swords and shouting their oaths of allegiance to a common god, the crusaders, like other pilgrims, joined together across cultures and languages (Leed 249). This rationalized militancy, suggests Leed, had profound social effects, "at once sanctif[ying] the soldierly profession and provid[ing] an appropriate destination for anomalous social elements" (148). Church fathers and feudal lords recognized that arming pilgrims and providing them with a heroic calling rid their communities of the restless, the unattached, the unruly, and the dangerous. It also formalized an appropriate rite of passage for the "apprentice knight" through which the critical transition from youth to adult soldier could be witnessed and legitimated (185). Crusader journeys channeled itinerant masculinity, whether that of common soldier or of knight, into its most socially useful shapes and curbed its destabilizing excesses.

Narratives of pilgrimage faded in importance as narratives of encounter and conquest proliferated on the bookshelves of the fifteenth, sixteenth, and seventeenth centuries. Adventurers, those sailors and soldiers who set out from European ports to traverse the globe, understood themselves as dauntless men unbound by insular tradition, men unwilling to be contained by the world as it was contemporaneously mapped, men willing to defy the superstitions and fixed itineraries of earlier travelers. Marco Polo, Christopher Columbus, Captain Cook—they sailed off, jumped onto unknown shores, named the land and its inhabitants, conquered and pacified those who resisted, pushed further into interiors, and crossed frontiers. These new European heroes materialized through new popular forms, particularly the survival tale, a story of dangerous navigation, overwhelming hardship and struggle, and encounters with the marvelous and the curious (Pratt, *Eyes* 20). The survivalist was a hero unlike the Christian pilgrims who traveled en masse to well-known sacred sites. A new aristocrat, he was an avatar of Odysseus, confronting the dangers of the unknown wilderness with independence and bravado.

These heroes mapped seas, traced coastal lands, and recorded the daily rhythms of their journeys. Through both technologies of knowledge production known to them—mapping and writing—they gathered the newly known world, transported that world back to Europe, and then reassembled it. Their accounts became cultural forms through which Europeans relocated themselves in an emerging natural history of the world. First through physical encounters with diverse indigenous peoples scattered across the globe, and then through the cultural work of describing those peoples and their cultures, early adventurers reimagined Europe as the most advanced civilization in the history of the world. In the differences they "discovered" between indigenous peoples and the peoples of Europe, adventurer-narrators and their reading publics projected what Mary Louise Pratt describes as "a European global or planetary subject," a "male, secular, and lettered" subject who looked upon the expanding world around him through a "planetary consciousness" (*Eyes* 9, 29–30).

As journeys of conquest and circumnavigation gradually gave way to journeys into the interior of continents, naturalists assigned to expeditions eagerly collected, described, named, and cataloged this vast natural world opened to Western travelers. Through Adamic acts of naming, these travelers transformed the profligate chaos of the entire globe into the orderly Latinate cosmos of Linnaean taxonomy, into a new "enlightened" knowledge.[2] This generation of traveler-narrators distinguished themselves from the earlier generation, whom they figured as reckless men prone to bring back misinformation about places and peoples. They, by contrast, were sons not only of Linneaus but also of Bacon, whose new inductive method affirmed the legitimacy of a particular form of observation "by which the eye, blighted by damnation, might recover its primal innocence, restoring that coherence between humankind and nature lost with the exile from the Garden" (Leed 181). For Bacon and his followers, the Adamic eye was recuperable through a proper skepticism about the ways in which the viewer's cultural embeddedness occluded clear vision. To see clearly required the stripping away of all sources of error, among them popular opinions, inherited traditions, taste, and even imagination (182).

The naturalists represented themselves as disinterested "scientists," men motivated by a benign curiosity and a refined sense of purpose, men pursuing objective knowledge, not corrupting power. In this too they contrasted with their predecessors, whom they figured as conqueror-adventurers, bloodthirsty and crude men who were excessively virile in their plunder of new lands and their slaughter of indigenous peoples. The naturalists, members of the newly educated bourgeois class as well as the older leisure class of gentlemen, worked with their brains, not their bodies. They kept their hands, and their pens, clean, so to speak.

Through their narratives, "enlightened" scientists reproduced an innocent vision of encounter, one purged, according to Pratt, of any brute "apparatus of domination" (*Eyes* 34).[3] This "conspicuous inno-cence" (57) signals a cultural shift in the European imaginary. The time of conquest, the brutal and direct appropriation of other people's lands through sheer force, had passed. The time of development had begun. Increasing the knowledge base of colonial and imperial frontiers also in-creased Europe's capacity to transform natural and human resources into commodities. Surveying all aspects of the frontier increased the sophisti-cation with which capitalist interests could transform local and makeshift organizations into a global system of extraction, transportation, produc-tion, exportation, and consumption. And so two masculine activities motivate such travels and narratives: the "impartial" pursuit of scientific knowledge and the aggressive pursuit of commercial opportunities. En-lightenment and imperial masculinities became mutually sustaining (36).

While naturalists, missionaries, bureaucrats, and commercial rep-resentatives spanned the globe accumulating information and organiz-ing settlement, other men set off by post chaise across Europe on a less arduous and less risky venture. What became known as the "grand tour" merged two earlier traditions of journeying—the initiatory rite of chivalric excursion and the educational itinerary of the *peregrinatio academica* (Leed 184–85). Through grand touring, young men of the aristocratic classes participated in a preparatory curriculum of travel. Eventually the grand tour provided a means whereby the young men of the emergent bourgeois classes could also participate in an aristocratic form of education (complete with the prescribed curriculum and set of exercises codified in guidebooks written by tutors). The effect of grand touring was at once democratizing—an egalitarian liberalism displaced aristocratic privilege—and differentiating—the grand tourist was distinguished as another avatar of the newly enlightened man. The grand tour thereby reproduced the bourgeois male subject and the network of patrilineal social relationships securing that subject. As Dennis Porter reminds us, the tour had the "character of a rite of passage following upon which one accept[ed] the responsibilities of the well-born male to family, class, and nation. One prepared for the time when one would assume one's father's place" (35). The grand tourist also confirmed prior observations, thus enforcing the tour as cultural norm.

Assuming one's father's place involved assuming the place of the enlightened European subject vis-à-vis the subjects of the world at large. Thus, grand touring and global travel were mutually informative. Scientists, capitalist entrepreneurs, and bureaucrats mapped, measured, and colonized the world beyond Europe and in so doing contributed to the ideology of European superiority. Men of the educated classes refined their knowledge of that superior civilization by traveling throughout the enlightened world comparing one European culture with another and assessing relative advantage.[4] That is why grand tourists seemed absorbed in ascertaining the ways in which different cultures organized political, religious, and sexual practices and relationships, three domains central to the promotion of human happiness as the fundamental goal of an "enlightened" civilization (Porter 28).

Assessment of the political and religious life of other cultures was primarily an observational activity. But the assessment of sexual practices and relationships invited grand tourists to immerse themselves experientially in the life of other cultures. In a striking way, the purposes of enlightenment and the pursuit of happiness played out on the traveling body, with the result that eroticism and travel became explicitly linked in the eighteenth century. Thus the grand threat of the grand tour. The grand tourist, that bourgeois gentleman whose identity required the submission of unruly passions to the control of the educated mind, had to be sent away from home to learn self-surveillance, the process whereby he internalized the control of mind over the unruly matter of body. Yet "exposure to temptation," Porter suggests, "risked subverting the institutional goals" (51). In other words, the grand tourist might never return to assume his father's place.

Other narrative modes accompanied bourgeois European men en route to the colonies and across frontiers in the late eighteenth and early nineteenth centuries. There were the narratives of missionaries, "uplifting" the dirty work of colonization (and perpetuating it) through the ideology of the "civilizing" mission. Such narratives reflected the cultural work of recreating the country, the social organization, and the peoples of "uncivilized" lands in the image of Europe and Euro-America. As missionary travelers spread across the globe in service to uplift, other travelers, motivated by technological and commercial interests, spread over the globe in service to development (Pratt, *Eyes* 146). For these traveler-narrators, the land was "underdeveloped" and its inhabitants backward, dirty, and lazy, in need of a secularized version of the civilizing mission. These travelers assembled in their narratives proto-ethnographic accounts that served mercantile interests, accumulating as they did much capital—descriptions of the landscape, peoples, and social organization—that prepared the way for further exploitation. Narratives of early settlers and representatives of chartered companies also accumulated the capital of information sent back as so much raw material to others considering immigration and settlement. Finally, there were the documents of the bureaucrats charged with integrating various networks of information central to binding together the colonies and administering them—legal records, census data, shipping information, and the like. In all these modes, the narrator positioned himself as the representative of a superior and civilized culture and an agent of beneficial change, and he was identified and rewarded as such (146–55).

In the midst of chronicling the work of civilizing and colonizing, some travel narrators chronicled as well a tale of cross-cultural love, inflected with the sentimentality that characterized the ideology of romance in the late eighteenth and early nineteenth centuries. Sentimental narratives such as John Stedman's *Narrative of a Five Years' Expedition against the Revolted Negroes of Surinam* (1796) unfolded through a biracial love plot that titillated the reader as it registered a cultural transformation from colonial relationships understood to rest upon concubinage, rape, and force to those predicated upon mutuality of respect and affection. Such love plots, argues Pratt, function as "imaginings in which European supremacy is guaranteed by affective and social bonding; in which sex replaces slavery as the way others are seen to belong to the white man; in which romantic love rather than filial servitude or force guarantee[s] the willful submission of the colonized" (*Eyes* 97).[5] Biracial love promised a new world order of reciprocity between the colonizer and the colonized, effectively mystifying the material realities of continuing exploitation and servitude. It also assured the male traveler, and his reader back home, of the benevolent force and effect of his superiority, a superiority secured now through racial and gender superiority. Native women loved European men, as they should. Affection was the inevitable and thus "natural" result of encounter. Colonization became in turn a form of benign domestication (97).

Alternatively, travel narrators chronicled experiences of sublime encounter with landscape, an encounter through which they celebrated the intensity of sensuality released from the bourgeois constraints forced upon the European body at home. Gazing upon sublime vistas, the romantic subject felt stimulated by "exquisitely beautiful sensations" (Porter 139) and filled to overflowing with a sense of euphoria. Because the sublime landscape upon which the traveler gazed was often perceived to be a pristine landscape, one not ruined by the artificial marks of civilization, the sight lifted the traveler out of historical time. Temporally displaced, he felt himself shed the debilitating consciousness that separated him from nature and from the pure sensations of his body and found himself absorbed by a primal sense of oneness with the landscape. In this way travel offered the traveler pleasure, and more pleasure, and more plea-sure. Exquisite sensations, charged engagements, and primal pleasures reawakened a virile masculinity from its sleep. In foreign terrain the Western traveler escaped the constraints of a "civilized" self and discov-ered a more "authentic" one.

At home in Europe and America in the nineteenth century, the educational agenda of the grand tour reconfigured as bildungsroman, the novel of education through which the dominant myth of bourgeois indi-vidualism was popularized. The itinerary of bildungsroman was individ-ualist; it tracked the evolutionary movement of the bourgeois individual into his, and increasingly her, place in society. But bildungsroman simul-taneously registered the increasingly constricted reach of individual will and desire that attended what Franco Moretti describes as the "industrial and political convulsions act[ing] ... over European culture, forcing it to redraw the territory of individual expectations, to define anew its 'sense of history,' and its attitude toward the values of modernity" (265). In the resolutions of its plot, bildungsroman reproduced the mechanisms for the compromise exacted of the individual and his no-longer-quite-so-great expectations in light of the emergence of mass society. "One's for-mation as an individual in and for oneself," Moretti continues, "coincides without rifts with one's social integration as a simple *part of the whole*" (16). The protagonists of bildungsroman go on the road, moving from one locale to another, gaining education on the way to compromise. The itinerary of this kind of travel exposes the transgressive effects of exces-sive passion and promotes the domestication of that desire.

As bildungsroman joined missionary, mercantile, and sentimen-tal narratives in reproducing the identity of the European and Euro-American at home and abroad, other narratives assessed the costs of that metropolitan identity to individual freedom and desire. At home, the romantic subject confronted the conformity necessary for a democratic consensus; the increasing dehumanization attending industrialization and urbanization; the marginalization of the artistic and literary life vis-à-vis the commercial life, forcing the dissociation of the writer-intellectual from a public masculinity; and the alienation of the human world from the natural world, intensified by the rapid pace of technological innovation and most vividly symbolized in the smoke, noise, and churning power of the steam locomotive. He also suffered the vigilant surveillance of bourgeois bodies and desires, surveillance designed to control what Darwin in his travels described as the "relic of instinctive passion" nestled deep within the "civilized" self (qtd. in Porter 155). In its post-Byronic mode, the journey south or east assumed "the form of flight from repressive authority with no intent of return" (Porter 132).

In flight from a pedestrian, repressive, emasculating culture, the traveler pursued "adventure" in exotic locales uncontaminated by the dehumanizing excesses of modernity (Bongie 12). As Peter Hulme reminds us, the word *adventure* originally unified two arenas of activity—economic acquisition and heroic action (183). But in the nineteenth century the close relationship of heroism and economics was sundered. Heroic action now took place outside the arena of economic ventures. This dissociation occurred at the precise historical moment when Europeans were busily wresting raw materials and cheaply produced goods out of pacified and bureaucratically organized colonies.[6] Paradoxically, the modern world that had been created out of the economic exploitation of lands and peoples was the very world the adventurer sought to escape; yet the penetration into exotic locales made possible the fantasies of exoticist adventure as a means of escape from modernity.

Narratives of exotic liaison chronicled the traveler's amorous involvement with the exotic woman and his introduction to alternative sexual practices and arrangements. In fashioning his account of an involvement that promised to return the repressed body to him, the travel narrator deployed various exoticist tropes that gained narrative currency in the late nineteenth and early twentieth centuries. One such trope was that of the sexually available stranger, a seductive woman whose body lay before him, lavishly and uninhibitedly accessible, whether in the "natural" state of the Micronesian islands or in the tightly controlled and secret sanctuaries of the "oriental" harem. To succumb to love with this exotic stranger involved a danger and a scandal, for such liaisons were always potentially alienating and devouring. If the traveler who resisted seduction registered the ability to exert manly control over his desires, he who succumbed registered the courage of his willingness to challenge the repressive systems of home and their domesticating injunctions by experimenting with forbidden desires. Encounters with exotic women promised the revelation of new kinds of knowledge and the satiety of desire too long repressed, as well as the adrenaline high of masculinity put at emotional and cultural risk. The imbroglio could end, as it did in Pierre Loti's *Aziyade* (1879), with death.

This all too brief survey of Western travel and travel narratives up to the end of the nineteenth century suggests how historically specific kinds of travel make for specific "models of good and heroic behavior that reinforce the values of ideology" (Slotkin 507): pilgrimage promotes the medieval supplicant; early modern exploration and encounter, the survivalist and conqueror; settlement, the new capitalist entrepreneur; scientific exploration, the enlightened observer; the grand tour of the eighteenth century, the aristocratic or bourgeois gentleman; missionary projects of the nineteenth century, the subject of progress; exotic flight at the end of the nineteenth century, the romantic rebel. These travelers returned with narratives that link mobilities to textual representations and in turn textual representations to identities. Of course, the narratives embody no universal expression of masculinity, because, as this elaboration suggests, versions of masculinity are plural, their expressions culturally and historically specific. Moreover, within specific locations—physical, cultural, and psychic—"disparate versions of masculinity," as Judy Wajcman cautions, "reflect class division, as well as ethnic and generational differences" (143). Yet, however various the subject of travel and his narratives, however plural the versions of masculinity that travel underwrites, "the traveler" has remained endurably "masculine"—one who stands in awe, supplicates, survives, conquers, claims, penetrates,

surveys, colonizes, studies, catalogs, organizes, civilizes, critiques, celebrates, absorbs, goes "native."

## Women in Motion in Premodernity

Yet women have always traveled; and some of them produced narratives
of their travels long before the twentieth century. In these narratives
women grapple with what it means to be undomesticated, if only temporarily. For, as Janet Wolff observes, "the ideological gendering of travel
(as male) both impedes female travel and renders problematic the self-
definition of (and response to) women who *do* travel" (234). As a result,
the meanings women make of travel are inflected with the protocols of
gender out of which, through which, and against which they negotiate
their movement from sessility to mobility.

Although medieval women became neither itinerant scholars nor
militant pilgrims, they did become scholars and pilgrims. In early and
medieval Christianity, organized pilgrimage became an occasion for ritual purification and cleansing at the site of the holy. As a result, women
as well as men narrated the journey of pilgrimage. In fact, Mary B. Campbell, in her history of pilgrimage narrative, identifies a woman's text,
Egeria's *Peregrinatio*, dating from the late fourth century, as the first pilgrimage narrative to differ markedly from what had been the more
common "logbook" available to pilgrims (20), at least to the extent that
Egeria puts herself in the narrative as a witness to the sacred sites. Some
one thousand years later, women continued to participate in pilgrimage,
though by then uncloistered women posed significant threats to the institutionalized church of the late medieval period, threats reflected in the
language the church leaders invoked in discussing uncloistered women
who claimed holy status. Women who traveled around making claims
ceaselessly in the name of the Lord were commonly condemned as heretics (as the Beguines were) and delegitimized as bearers of God's word
or interpreters of his purpose. But the drifting movements of women
claiming spiritual status were as much a threat to social as to spiritual stability (Leed 155). Vagrants moved fluidly from place to place and even

shifted identities, introducing social instabilities into the domains of the established church and the emerging states.[7]

Margery Kempe dictated *The Book of Margery Kempe* (1436) at this time of instability. Tireless in affirming the legitimacy of her culturally suspect claims to spiritual authority, Kempe took her excessive religiosity and verbosity on the road with her as she traveled the sanctioned routes of spirituality legitimized by the medieval church. She used travel and the narrative of travel to legitimate her authority as a religious person in her own right and to authorize the uncommon voice of her text. That voice was suspect because it issued from a body contaminated by what the medieval church condemned as excessive sexuality and worldliness. (She was, after all, a wife and mother of fourteen children.) Both the testimony within the narrative and the fate of the *Book*—it was "lost" until the early twentieth century—suggest just how suspect this mobile woman at the edges of sanctified spirituality appeared to be in the early fifteenth century. Paradoxically, mobility served as both the sign of her sanctioned spirituality and the sign of her errancy.

During the early modern period of exploration, conquest, and settlement, European women did not actively participate in discovering or in taking possession of other lands for European powers; they did not name new worlds or subdue indigenous inhabitants. But after the adventurers and discoverers, the soldiers of conquest, had done their work, the first waves of settlers crossed oceans and lands to establish new homes and communities. Then some women set out as wives and daughters of chartered families, colonists, or missionaries. And some set out as members of persecuted communities, such as the one that landed at Plymouth in 1620.

Other women traveled as well. Impoverished and dependent women became indentured servants, sent to the colonies to keep other people's homes tidy and their occupants comfortable. Incarcerated and condemned women were transported to penal colonies in places such as Australia, or they were transported to service the sexual needs of colonists and to help maintain the "purity" of European racial stock in the contact zone.[8] Thousands of African women were brutally transported to American, British, French, Spanish, and Portuguese colonies as slaves and were forced to serve others and to reproduce the slave population. And thousands of women from one colony were displaced to another colony as the wives and daughters of low-paid laborers and merchants. Bringing sex, affection, and domestic labor to frontiers and colonies, whether enthusiastically, stoically, unwillingly, or under forcible constraint, women from very different cultural locations were implicated in the reproduction of Euro-American cultural dominance. They played a role in transporting the culture of the settlers and colonial administrators, sustaining the authority of the metropolitan center, and "domesticating" the space of the frontier and the colony.

During settlement and colonization, survival was not always a struggle solely for male adventurers. It sometimes became a challenge for women as well, as it did for Mary White Rowlandson, who in 1682 wrote what was the first American captivity narrative. Following a Narraganset raid upon her Massachusetts community during King Philip's War, Rowlandson was kidnapped and forced to travel with the Indians until they traded her for ransom several months later. Restored to her community, she wrote an account of her captivity in which she sought to conform her experience of survival to the exemplary typology necessary for the edification of the Puritan elect. The Puritan authorities worked to keep Rowlandson's narrative house in order, carefully circumscribing the testimony of this mere woman. "Per Amicus" (probably Increase Mather) introduces, justifies, and sanctions the narrative, and, as originally published, her text is followed by one of her husband's sermons. Because they cannot be officially allowed to travel on their own, Rowlandson's words are forced between the initiating words of the communal patriarch and the concluding words of the familial patriarch.

A similar but even more direct bracketing occurs in the eighteenth-century tale of Isabela Godin des Odonais, a survival narrative chronicling the Spanish woman's trek through the interior of South America. In the reconstruction of this survivalist tale, Odonais herself does not speak. Rather, her story is recounted by her husband, whose narrative is in turn contained within the larger narrative of the French explorer La Condamine (see Pratt, *Eyes* 21–23). So, just as women survivors were forced into circumstances of mobility, they and their stories were often returned to readers under constraint of patriarchal interpretations. For the most part, a woman's narrative of travel could not be left unattended.

In the eighteenth and nineteenth centuries, a few women naturalists contributed to the great Linnaean project of cataloging all the species of the expanding world, although their participation in the new science of natural history was compromised by their qualified relationship to the rational life. Women naturalists, however, did not span the globe.[9] Rather, they tended to remain domesticated, assembling their collections from nature close to home; and so the reach of the realm upon which they exercised their observational acumen and descriptive powers remained circumscribed scientifically as well as communally.

But at least one woman did travel to places elsewhere to pursue scientific interests in botany and zoology. From the Netherlands, Maria Sibylla Merian set forth on a two-year journey to Dutch Suriname (1699–1701). During her sojourn she collected and raised insects, interviewed local people about the customary uses of plants, accumulated quantities of notes about insects, and assembled a portfolio of drawings for her 1705 *Metamorphosis of the Insects of Surinam*. Later she prepared exquisite engraved prints—delicately and precisely drawn, richly colored, and boldly designed—for inclusion in the 1719 edition of *A dissertation on Insect Generation and Metamorphoses in Surinam*.[10]

Nor, in the eighteenth century, were men the only grand tourists to send home versions of an enlightened education. When her husband was named British ambassador to the sultanate of Turkey, Lady Mary Wortley Montagu set out upon a grand tour of sorts. Over the course of the two years she spent in transit and in residence in the Turkish capital, she carefully composed and copied out a series of letters addressed to family and friends back in England. Turning keenly observant eyes upon the domestic arrangements of the cultures through which she travels, in these letters she provides her readers with detailed descriptions of the dress, behaviors, and activities through which women organized their lives. More particularly, she assembles a revisionary set of descriptions of life in the Turkish seraglio.

In these "embassy letters," published against her family's wishes and only posthumously, Montagu engages in a contestatory dialogue with the narrative accounts of previous travelers, challenging the descriptions of the seraglio sent back home through the "enlightened" eyes of male travelers (Lowe 31–32, 40–42). Without direct access to the seraglio, male travelers could only imagine the private sphere and in their imaginings misrepresented Turkish women, judging their lives to be a kind of enforced slavery. Montagu, by contrast, assumes the authoritative posture of the participant-observer with direct access to the seraglio and to Turkish women. From this authoritative position she "corrects" the accounts of others. Yet, like the male travel writers whom she rereads, Montagu frames the women of the seraglio as "a sign," not of "enslavement and barbarism" but "of liberty and freedom" (Lowe 45) beyond the constraining spectacles of femininity back in Europe.[11] Required to travel by marriage, Montagu found the knowledge of different spectacles of femininity gained through her tour of Europe and the Levant a knowledge that forever alienated her from her home and from the femininity required of her in that home. An educated traveling woman, Montagu discovered herself to be a woman out of time and place. Eventually, leaving her husband and adult children, she would live permanently and independently away from home, in Italy.

## Modernity and the "Lady" Traveler

Religious pilgrims like Margery Kempe traveled to witness God's spiritual presence. Mary White Rowlandson was forced through circumstance to travel with the Narraganset. Lady Mary Wortley Montagu traveled dutifully to Turkey as the wife of the English ambassador (even if she didn't return home the dutiful wife). But what of Mary Wollstonecraft, Flora Tristan, Frances Trollope, Harriet Martineau, Margaret Fuller, May French Seldon, Daisy Bates, Nancy Prince, Zilpha Elaw, Isabella Bird, Marianne North, Fanny Kemble—all nineteenth-century travelers? Their motivations for setting out en route were various: religious, familial, political, professional. But they were generally ambitious of adventure and knowledge and anxious about bourgeois constraints. If traveling men of the mid- and late nineteenth century sought to escape the unmanning of mass industrialization and repressive sexual arrangements, certain traveling women sought to circumvent dependent and infantilizing bourgeois femininity. To do so, they took their identities and their discontents on the road.

An ensemble of cultural influences identified with modernity led to the emergence by the mid-nineteenth century of this new kind of traveler, the woman of some independent means and some independence of mind who was just as eager as certain men of the time to expand her horizon of knowledge and her arena of agency through travel. By the mid-nineteenth century much of the world had been socially, economically, politically, and spatially reorganized and "domesticated" (or, as Annegret Pelz suggests, "interiorized" [46–67]) through colonial processes and relationships. The labors of Western women, who were understood as "experts" in interiors, were integral to those processes; and so were the consuming habits of women. At home in the metropolitan centers of Europe and the Americas, wealthy and newly bourgeois women benefited from the results of Western expansion and colonialism, becoming avid consumers of the commodities brought back from other worlds or produced with the raw materials extracted there and brought home. Increasing wealth brought with it, as well, interest in leisure activities. Thus, the consumption of travel experiences—of places, of peoples, of cultures—became an inevitable extension of bourgeois culture. Additionally, changes in the hereditary rights of women enabled some to retain family wealth and remain financially independent.[12]

The discourse of democratic individualism in the nineteenth century, despite its equation of the democratic subject with the white man of property, encouraged increasing numbers of middle-class women to understand mobility as a means to reimagine themselves as "citizens of the world," "free" to pursue their own itineraries, one of which was the satisfaction, in the words of Florence Nightingale, of the "active nature" of their minds (qtd. in Frawley 22). Further, the gradual articulation after the French Revolution of a purposeful and enlightened form of liberal feminism promoted the value of women's education and the social benefits of their access to professions (Stevenson 3; Foster 8). But with institutions of learning generally closed to women, those seeking satisfaction had to turn to travel for an empowerment that derived from the negotiation of cultural displacement. As travelers, women became active agents, learning for themselves about foreign cultures, languages, histories, social organizations, and natural environments, and exercising their independent observational powers.

Then too, the expansion of the domestic sphere to incorporate women's activities in certain sectors of social life, such as philanthropy, enabled women to maintain their claim to bourgeois femininity and to exert their proper influence through missionary and philanthropic work, work that might send them abroad (Riley 46–47).[13] Women could represent themselves as humanizing agents of "progress," extending the sphere of their influence beyond the narrow circuit of the home into the far reaches of an empire. Middle-class women became crusaders for a variety of social causes. As crusaders they traveled not only around their own countries—as Elizabeth Cady Stanton did in the United States—but also often overseas, as Florence Nightingale and Anna Leonowens did. From that elsewhere they sent home narratives in which they described efforts to "save" other women by working to improve their conditions, as well as efforts to "convert," to "educate," and to "civilize" other women and men (always their own cultural inferiors). Through their narratives they claimed cultural authority, testifying, as Caren Kaplan has argued, to their participation in the march of modern "progress" by promoting the social and moral enlightenment of other women (35–42).[14]

Yet, if bourgeois femininity could be packed up and taken on the road, a woman on the road still signaled femininity displaced from its founding attachment to domesticity and the requisite sessility. This was femininity trespassing upon the domain of the constitutively masculine. As Janet Wolff argues, "The ideological construction of 'woman's place' works to render invisible, problematic, and in some cases impossible, women 'out of place'" (234). So the constitutive masculinity of the traveler necessarily influenced the ways in which women traveled, the disposition of their bodies, and the relational dynamics of their interactions with others,[15] and it informed in profound ways the meanings these travelers made of travel in their narratives. Whether consciously or unconsciously, they understood themselves to be acting in unbecoming ways precisely because "their activities positioned them in important ways as at least problematic with regard to gender identification" (234).

Women's travel narratives reveal the complexities in their negotiations of such an unbecoming subject position. For instance, they had to employ certain rhetorical strategies in addressing their readers, whom they projected as enforcing "the domain of socially instituted norms" (Butler, *Bodies* 182). A bourgeois woman could not generously indulge herself in the autobiographical consciousness that was pervasive in men's writing during the nineteenth century and present herself as the hero of her own narrative. To do so would be improper; for the woman traveler, by virtue of her purposeful motion and purposeful publication, already threatened to become an ambiguously gendered subject (Foster 11). To avoid the impropriety of self-preoccupation and self-promotion that were so much a part of travel narratives, women often masked their curiosity and their agency by muting their narrative "I."[16] Some displaced any personal motivations for writing onto importunate friends and relatives who, the narrators hastened to tell their readers, pressed them to write (Foster 20). Others opened their chronicles with an apologia, gesturing to male travel narrators who had already covered the field, giving obeisance where it was dutifully due. Still others muted the pleasures of travel and independence and freedom from infantilization by assuming the identity of dutiful wife or daughter. Certain motivations for travel were admissible to women—the search for improved health, for instance, or the devotion to a self-sacrificing mission—whereas others remained inadmissible (Foster 8–10). The admissible were those that reinforced the traveler's identity as a proper lady.

The woman travel narrator also had to negotiate the propriety of topics she explored when she wrote home about her travels. Her attention could most properly be trained upon social arrangements, domestic relations, and the activities and lives of women. As a result, women travelers contributed cultural information in what became a popular narrative form, the narrative of customs and manners, what Mary Louise Pratt calls "ethnography's antecedent" ("Scratches" 139). Reporting on manners and customs, women travelers exercised their eye for fine and practical details, a mental habit identified as proper to femininity. Such reportage signaled as well the traveler's attentiveness to the social space of domesticity, the space to which bourgeois women were assigned. In this way women travelers-narrators maintained their properly feminine interests as they crossed seas and contact zones.[17]

If women had to attend carefully to narrative address, justification, and topical preoccupation, they also had to attend to the implications of narrative itinerary. The travel narrator could not, for instance, indulge herself in exoticist narrative tropes, because a proper woman could neither confess to sexual desires nor describe sexually explicit behaviors if she wanted to maintain her social respectability. Perhaps more to the point, the bourgeois traveler sought the release of travel to escape the matrimonial expectation. Unlike the romantic male traveler who looked for the affirmation of a revivified masculinity in liaisons with "exotic" women, the bourgeois woman often set in motion to avoid what she perceived to be a degraded femininity. Thus, women travel narrators eschewed romantic plots, because such plots either exposed improper behavior or maintained the centrality of heterosexual romance, which was founded upon a degraded form of femininity.

Despite these constraints on their narrative possibilities, Western women understood travel to be a means to an enhanced authority of experience; and it was this authority of experience that women translated into travel narratives. As Maria H. Frawley emphasizes, traveling and writing were often intimately joined actions in the world (15).[18] Travel provided women an acceptable occasion to record, describe, catalog, analyze, reflect on, and report what they had seen, what they had learned, and what they had had to do in order to see and to learn. It provided, as well, stretches of time conducive to writing, so that someone like Barbara Leigh Smith Bodichon could undertake to "write as much as I can without blinding myself" (122). Through their travel writing, women affirmed for the public their intellectual curiosity and depth, their physical prowess, their daring enterprise. Further, in turning travel experiences into travel narratives, women positioned themselves as credible, authoritative, and competent "professionals" (Frawley 24).[19] In critical ways, they used their narratives to reimagine themselves away from the spectacles of femininity constraining them at home.

## New Technologies and Traveling Women

> There is a wonderful difference between sitting calmly by while another is driving and actually handling a car herself. There is a feeling of power, of exhilaration, and fascination that nothing else gives in equal measure. When the ponderous car begins to move and the motor seems a living, breathing thing responding to your slightest touch, easy to control and simple to manipulate, then comes the realization of "motoring" in its truest sense.
>
> —Mrs. A. Sherman Hitchcock,
> "A Woman's Viewpoint of Motoring" (1904)

Of course, the distinguishing logic of itinerant masculinity has always had to do with the relationship of men to their animals or their machines of motion. Think, for instance, of Odysseus's vessels filled with communities of men bound together in an ethos of camaraderie; or of the sometimes too intimate enclosed carriage of the grand tourist; or of the man on horseback crossing vast expanses of land; or of the slow and often exhausting trek by foot across deserts, mountains, ice, or tundra; or of the automobiles of Jack Kerouac. Each of these modes of motion is identified with masculine competencies. Sailing calls for brute strength, sophisticated knowledge of navigation, courage before the mast, and resilience. Travel by foot calls for endurance, the capacity to defend oneself from possible attack, and a lack of concern for the niceties of the bath. Horsemanship requires stamina and fine knowledge of brute animals, and it mandates, to accommodate speed and rugged terrain, a straddling posture. Travel by car involves speed and the danger that comes with sheer mechanical force, the power of not one but four hundred horses.

The mechanics of motion before the nineteenth century—foot, horse, coach, sailing ship—were relatively slow, elemental, and often undependable means of travel. As the narrator of Marguerite Duras's *The Lover* (1986) recalls wistfully, "People were used to those slow human speeds on both land and sea, to those delays, those waitings on the wind or fair weather, to those expectations of shipwreck, sun and death" (115). Medieval pilgrims, among them Margery Kempe, made the long, arduous journeys to sacred sites by ship and foot. Mary Rowlandson endured her forced removal with the Narraganset on horseback and foot. Lady Mary Wortley Montagu traversed eastern Europe by carriage. But in the mid-nineteenth century the experience of travel changed forever with the technological advances of the Industrial Revolution.

In the 1840s the steam engine harnessed tremendous forces formerly unimaginable. With its billowy signature, the steam engine accelerated the pace of modernization and forged a new compact with nature and a new standard for what it meant to be "civilized." The locomotive moved large numbers of people and goods across difficult terrain on a dependable schedule at relatively moderate expense. The luxury steamship and the steam locomotive also provided the physical safety of protected enclosure and relatively comfortable passage at increased speeds. Within a half century a succession of new forms of transportation—the bicycle, the airplane, and the automobile—further increased the safety, the comfort, the reach, the speed, and the availability of transportation. With these new technologies came a reorientation to time and to space, dramatic cultural shifts that gained momentum between the 1880s and the First World War.

The powerful engines that propelled vehicles through space at heretofore unimaginable speeds became increasingly pervasive symbols of that modernity, audible from far distances. The grinding sound of locomotive engines, the drone of airplane wings, and the humming of unruly automobiles became the background noise of what Virginia Scharff calls "motorized modernity" (167), announcing at every interval of the day the remarkable achievements of powerful economic forces and imperial ventures. Products of increasingly sophisticated science and engineering, they were engines of dramatic change, extending the capabilities of human beings, taking them faster, farther, and with more protection (and sometimes more danger) across the consecutive social spaces of cities, nations, continents, and the globe itself. Western women embraced the mobility these technologies offered. They bought timetables and climbed into railway cars. They found flying schools and suited up for the cockpit. They took the wheel and sped along miles of roads. They headed off.

If, as Kristin Ross reminds us, "modern social relations are ... always mediated by objects" (5), then the social relations of travel and travel narrating in the twentieth century are mediated by these technologies of motion. Foot, animal, ship, train, plane, automobile—these technologies of motion are never neutral means of moving a body from one location to another. As Alan Tractenberg notes in his introduction to Wolfgang Schivelbusch's *The Railway Journey*, new modes of travel introduce "*new system[s] of behavior*: not only of travel and communication but of thought, of feeling, of expectation" (xiii). Vehicles of motion are vehicles of perception and meaning, precisely because they affect the temporal, spatial, and interrelational dynamics of travel.

Noting how time has been transformed by these technologies of modernity, Schivelbusch writes that "transport technology is the material base of potentiality, and equally the material base of the traveler's space-time perception" (36). The extended reach of the locomotive and the inevitable need to coordinate its movements across space (and to coordinate the instant communications across telegraph wires) led to the imposition of World Standard Time, the organization of time sense that ceaselessly marks off the segments of days in cultures across the globe. This is time segmented and bureaucratized—and time universal. Yet the speed with which the locomotive, automobile, and airplane ply space encourages in travelers an imaginative and private sense of time through the complex blurring of notions of past, present, and future.[20] Thus, the mechanics of motion generates dynamic tensions affecting the way the traveler experiences the private, as opposed to the public, movement of time. Stephen Kern elaborates certain implications of this transformed experience of time when he notes that the new technology "speeded up the tempo of current existence and transformed the memory of years past, the stuff of everybody's identity, into something slow" (129). This is irregular personal time, a sense of time in conflict with the pace of modernity.

Then too, throughout the twentieth century, complex transformations of spatial relationships have followed upon the introduction of new technologies of motion. Because vehicles of motion hold bodies in and to precise alignments with the ground, they fix and unfix distances—perceptual, temporal, and social—between the traveler and the landscape through which she moves. Propelled through space, the traveler becomes conscious of constantly shifting sensual data and impressions—sounds, sights, and smells. In this way the speed at which new impressions press upon the traveler's consciousness, the spatial distance that separates her from the source of those impressions, and her perception of potential intimacy and disconnectedness can expand and contract, contract and expand, depending upon the mode of transport. More broadly, modes of motion organize the entire sensorium differently and thus affect the conditions, the focalizing range, and the position of the perceiving subject, differentially connecting and disconnecting her to and from the terrain of travel, differentially organizing her ways of negotiating unfamiliar territory, and differentially affecting systems of behavior. The locomotive, for instance, wrenched the intimate connection between traveler and ground of earlier forms of travel, such as foot and coach, sundering the traveler within the locomotive car from the land through which she moved. The airplane further severed the sense of intimacy with ground, transforming ground into background pattern, abstracted far below.

New technologies of motion have also created new social relations over the last century. Consequently, they have affected the conditions, the rhythms, even the presentational styles of contact between the traveler and other travelers, between the traveler and strangers. They determine the specific dynamics of social encounters—their duration, their form, their potential effects, and their modes of communication. Train passengers meet for several hours or days, establishing fleeting friendships that dissipate in stations. Travelers in automobiles, unlike those in trains, can seek out-of-the-way places and peoples on the obscure back roads. As they regulate the possible directions of movement through unfamiliar terrain, vehicles determine the traveler's itinerary through social spaces, down to the specific avenues of entry into and departure from destinations. Trains take travelers to city central, airplanes to a city's outskirts. Finally, they affect who can travel and how, for various travelers have differential access to vehicles of motion and to specific sections within those vehicles, depending upon their cultural location. In the early twentieth century, "hoboes," among them "sisters of the road," hopped on and off boxcars while proper ladies stayed in passenger cars. Nowadays, people of constrained means cross the United States in Greyhound buses while others jet expeditiously overhead.

The social spaces through which vehicles and their passengers journey are themselves organized by and around these very technologies. In the late nineteenth and early twentieth centuries, railroad tracks, for instance, came to transect landscape and cityscape, becoming the de facto dividing line separating wealthier from more impoverished communities, separating communities by race as well as class, separating the "right" from the "wrong" side of the tracks. Those tracks also served the plans of colonial administrators to consolidate bureaucratic control of vast empires, linking interior sites of natural-resource extraction with coastal sites of shipping. In the mid- to late twentieth century, the increasing accessibility of the automobile led to the suburbanization of life in Europe and America with all the attendant social consequences of a radical reorganization of urban and rural economies.

However vast the scope of change in behaviors and social organization, however, these objects, the industries that have produced them, and the social spaces that surround them remain entangled in the technologies of gender that differentiate a sedentary femininity from a mobile masculinity. Throughout this long century and a half of motorized modernity, as Virginia Scharff reminds us, "the critical cultural categories of masculinity and femininity penetrated, applied to, and organized" (165) the world of emergent technologies of motion. For instance, the invention, design, and production of machines have been coded as masculine endeavors. The thrusting power identified with machines such as the steam engine has been represented as decidedly phallic power. Originally these objects—the car and airplane especially—were celebrated because they promised to put individualizing and defining adventure back into travel, thereby rejuvenating an exhausted masculinity in a time of mass tourism. As industries grew out of the early experiments in mobility, women gradually became potential consumers of motion; and so successive stages of design made the machines and their traveling environment increasingly more comfortable, producing the sleeping car, the automatic transmission, and the jetliner. Even as they were embraced by male travelers, these "improvements" were presented as feminizing designs, changes catering to the disabling characteristics of a dependent femininity.

Throughout the reorganization of time, space, sensual perception, consciousness, and identity attendant upon the emergence of modern technologies of motion, "the domain of socially instituted norms" (Butler, *Bodies* 182) has persisted—at home and in transit. In myriad large and small ways, the technologies, the social world transformed by them, and the logic of travel itself remain saturated with defining protocols of masculinity and femininity.

## Women, Mobility, Technology, and Narrative

If identity functions as a perceptual point of transition, neither fixed nor entirely unfixed, through which the provisional meaning of travel materializes and fractures, then the specific vehicle of motion, with its power to organize space, time, passage, perception, and encounter, affects the identifications and disidentifications of travel. The mode of motion, whether locomotion, flight, automobility, or foot, itself defines the logic of mobility. Thus, technologies of motion contribute in fundamental ways to what George Robertson and the other editors of *Travellers' Tales* describe as the "corrosiveness" of travel (5). They become the literal and figurative vehicles through which the traveler uses mobility to alter the terms of identity, whether or not she considers travel an enabling force in her struggle with women's cultural construction in subordination (Mouffe 382).

The technology of motion that the traveler chooses to carry her away from home affects the repertoire of identities available to her. Sometimes it offers her new identities; sometimes it forces her to new identities. Moreover, it affects the pace at which identities drift, the context and location of drift, and the meaning the traveler makes of that drift. And because the mode of mobility affects how the traveler leaves home and how she returns, as well as the sense of progression through the journey out and the journey back, it affects the plotting of that drift of identity.

Affecting the traveler's experience of temporality and spatiality, of departures from home, transits, and arrivals home (beginnings, middles, and ends), of progression and pace, of perspective and self-location, technologies of motion determine the point of departure, the itinerary, the destinations, the duress, the rhythm and degree of encounter, and the achievement of travel. They organize where consciousness comes to rest and where it wanes. Now, these are also features of narrative itself (though not all its features); for narrative is about time and spatial mappings, about progression and pace, about the positioning of the narrating subject, about the concentration and the waning of consciousness. If vehicles of motion drive the plotting of mobility, then they inevitably drive the engine of plotting, the narrative itinerary, and the logic of travel that such plotting enacts.

But it is not only itinerary that vehicles of motion organize. They also affect narrative intentions. Various modes of mobility generate specific narrative intentions. These intentions determine strategies through which the narrator embarks, sojourns, and returns, through which the "I" narrates what she comes to know on the road, how she comes to know it, and how she returns home. Intentions might be descriptive or ethnographic or religious. They might be dramatic or heroic or educational. They might be economic or political. Intentions take historically specific forms; forms materialize intentions. There are journals kept while traveling and narratives written after return. There are meditations, romances, personal essays, poem cycles. There are accounts that read like first-person novels, foregrounding the autodiegetic nature of travel narrative.

There are those that read like anthropological or sociological treatises, minimizing the autodiegetic aspect of the narrative. Within any one narrative there may be oscillating movements across kinds of writing, shuttlings back and forth from the plotless to the plotted (Porter 88); from the descriptive/informative to the narrative/suspenseful; from the practical/political to the poetic/visionary. This play of intentions drives the narrator's taking up, adjusting, and putting away of identities in transit and her degree of investment in or resistance to the masculinist logic of travel.

Intentions are conveyed through narrative conventions. The powerful technologies of modernity have made possible new kinds of mobile identities, identities through which the masculinist logic of travel has to be renegotiated: the air pilot, the ace, the boomer (railroad brakeman), the hobo, the hot-rodder, the low rider, and the Greyhound bus rider, to name but a few. These technologies, as they generate possible identities, energize new narratives of mobility with their defining conventions: aviator narratives, "buddies on the road" narratives, great-train-ride narratives, narratives of peripatetic touring, and "exotic" narratives of crossdressing, again to name a few. Through such narrative conventions the travel narrator locates the world, the space, and the time through which she has moved or is moving. As she situates land, landscape, language, and people, she also locates herself as a subject in motion through that world. Thus, the narrator is always engaged in the process of self-locating, and self-locating becomes an occasion for self-scrutiny, more or less consciously undertaken.

*Moving* by foot, plane, locomotive, or automobile, the woman traveler assumes a place in the history of that technology of motion, even if she remains oblivious to it. That history encompasses the emergence, development, and transformation of a particular transport technology, its uses and design features, its rise and fall. Moreover, it is inseparable from the history of modernity, with all the implications modernity has for the mapping of modern social relations. *Narrating* travel by foot, plane, locomotive, or automobile, the travel narrator negotiates the dynamics of and contradictions in the drift of identity, and reveals the ways in which modes of mobility—engines of temporality, spatiality, progression, and destination—are (un)defining. But she may also define the meaning of a particular mode of motion in new and different ways and, in doing so, disentangle travel from its masculine logic. For even as the traveler-narrator finds herself negotiating the cultural construction of femininity as sedentary, degrading, and constraining, she may discover elasticities of and in motion. Indeed, she may reimagine her relationship to technology and rethink its history, even as it remakes her.

# CHAPTER 2

# On Foot:
# Gender at Ground Level

What one cannot do in one's own Western environment—where
to try to live out the grand dream of a successful quest is only to
keep coming up against one's own mediocrity and the world's
corruption and degradation—one can do abroad. Isn't it possible in
India to do everything? be anything? go anywhere with impunity?

—Edward Said, "Kim, the Pleasures of Imperialism"

Until the middle of the nineteenth century, sailing ships, carriages,
horses, or sturdy feet moved bodies through space, so travel had been a
rather slow affair. Captain, crew, and passengers of sailing vessels suffered
delays in ports, waited for winds, worried through storms, and watched
the seemingly interminable cresting of waves. Passengers in carriages and
stagecoaches rumbled over rutted roadways, drawn onward by two or
four horses of power. Equestrian travelers and those on foot moved ardu-
ously forward. The duration of travel stretched across days and weeks
and months. But the introduction of the steam engine changed all that.
Locomotives pulled legions of travelers over miles of iron track. Steam-
ships chugged out of port on schedule, progressing despite unfavorable
wind conditions. Eventually airplanes condensed time and space so that
any point on the globe could be reached in mere hours. Motorized
modernity altered forever the terms of mobility.

As trains, and later planes and automobiles, delivered increasing
numbers of travelers to their destinations efficiently, the forces of modernity began to foreclose the possibilities for individualizing travel sustained by mythic models of heroic action. Travelers could no longer be
assured of earning any real distinction in mobility, especially as they too
easily melded with tourists, those hordes of people seeking prepackaged

destinations in comfort. In the contemporary age of tourism, the possibilities for arduous travel have been almost entirely eliminated for
Western travelers.

Various phenomena contributed to this foreclosure. The demise of
colonialism, which came to an end in sometimes violent and sometimes
peaceful transitions of exploited colonies into self-determining nationstates, accelerated the pace of modernization (if differentially) across the
globe. The processes of modernization intensified global realignments
following two world wars and affected the West's horizon of exotic
otherness, so long identified with "the Orient" and with other "outposts"
of progress. Gradually that horizon disappeared into more complex sets
of economic and political relationships that opened spaces formerly inaccessible to the common traveler. The rise of consumer culture stimulated
desire in the masses to accumulate "experiences" through exposure to
the increasing number of formerly inaccessible sites around the world
that were, as a result, turned into tourist "attractions"—the bane of the
true traveler. And now the increasingly fragmented quality of contemporary life makes any attempt to unify consciousness around a singular
point of identification and a singular model of heroic action increasingly
difficult. As a result, identities, values, and relationships become trivialized by a mass culture that projects a mishmash of desirable lifestyles,
scripts, and destinations. The modern tourist is out to "get a life" in all
the right places.

Travel experiences have become mere commodities, "manufactured
and sold," as Dean MacCannell argues, like any other commodity (21).
With all the danger and inconvenience virtually eliminated, they no longer
produce mythic models of heroic action. An Odysseus in leisure clothes,
standing before a manicured tourist site or snapping photographs of
friends he's made on the tour bus or the cruise ship, cannot be Odysseus.

Yet not all twentieth- and twenty-first-century travelers have embraced motorized modernity or the diminished terms of mobility that
modernity has furnished. For some, the evacuation of heroic action from
the world of motorized modernity and the cultural exhaustion attributed
to industrialization and urbanization have resulted in the fierce desire to

find a more "authentic" world, a protected or "primitive" way of life not yet infected with modernity. Because the spread of mass transportation technologies has contributed to this evacuation and this exhaustion, the pursuit of such desire requires journeying by means of a simpler mode of travel. In the midst of modernity's rapacious extension—the "gaping sore which admits infection," as Maurice Vlaminck so plaintively described the railway (qtd. in Freeman 134)—that simpler mode of mobility promises to take the true traveler where she can differentiate herself from the mere tourist. It takes her to destinations not easily accessible to the literal engines of progress.

In this context, journeys by foot or by animal take on new meanings. Travel close to the ground signals the desire to reach "the outer edges of modernization's scope" (Ross 13), edges that are spatial (the edges of wilderness, desert, and mountains) and temporal (the edges of the past). Thus, the cultural meanings made of this kind of travel are often effects of the history of colonization and decolonization (7), for what better edges of modernity's spread can be found than the edges assigned to the constitutive outside of modernity, the edges of colonies not yet entirely ensnared in modernity's contaminating progress? The Maghreb, the mountains of Tibet, the Red Centre of Australia, the ice fields of the Arctic—these are vast "premodern" spaces, uninhabited by urbanized peoples. They are spaces far distant from overcrowded metropolitan centers, spaces as yet unmarked by the rampant and rampaging signs of progress, by the tracks of locomotives, the pavement of superhighways. They are spaces not yet oversaturated with consumer products and comforts. Journeys close to the ground, into the desert, or across seemingly insurmountable mountains in the midst of blinding heat or cold are journeys into belatedness, a belatedness projected by and only imaginable from within an alienated, routinized world.

In the twentieth and twenty-first-centuries, the desire to pursue defining mobility at modernity's edges renders the terms of mobility every bit as critical to the project as the destination. Travel by foot or by animal attaches the traveler bodily to the ground. An intimate of the ground, she imagines herself an intimate of the people of the land. She may even dress as one of the local inhabitants. Identifying in this way with "premodern" subjects, she travels "as if." If only temporarily, she assumes, literally and figuratively, another identity, that of a premodern subject "left behind" by the processes of modernization, a subject to the side of, if not outside, modernity: the nomad of the Maghreb desert, for instance, or the mountain peasant of Tibet, or the Pitjantjara of the Red Centre of Australia.

In becoming another kind of subject, in grounding herself in an other's identity, the traveler imagines herself un-becoming Western. Shedding conventional identities and behaviors, stripping away the residue of modernity, she becomes other to her ordinary, unheroic, "feminized" self. That transformation is registered in the body, because the traveler feels the weight of mobility that her narrative later registers as an index of the edges reached. Subject to the elements, the pedestrian or mounted traveler meets the defining test of the travail of real travel. The terrain of the test puts normative femininity under duress. Endurance, vigor, willpower, fearlessness, ingenuity, all qualities necessary for the negotiation of life at the edges, become so many defining indexes of heroic action.

The same thing happens to the perception of the traveler's groundedness in locale. There is no material surround, no metallic carapace, sheltering the traveler. She cannot look out upon landscape, towns, and people in sedentary passivity. Nor is there dramatic speed. Without the encapsulating carapace, without the speed of railway or automobile travel, the traveler cannot easily detach herself from the space of travel. Evanescent reality—that detached sense of reality that technologies of speed introduce through modernity, that reality rushing past train and automobile windows or disappearing into vapor from the altitude of airplanes—has been left behind for another kind of reality, a more immediate and situated reality recovered through a visceral mobility. "Scenes" are not merely two-dimensional effects of distance and speed, viewed panoramically from within protected and protective enclosures. The three-dimensionality of space is restored, as is the long duration of time. This mode of travel secures the traveler's connection to proximate space. In the midst of and in spite of modernity's embrace of speed and iron and steam, the traveler finds a means to recover premodern locatedness, to find a reality more desirable than the reality of modernity.

The three travelers whose narratives I take up in this chapter enter and traverse spaces historied with colonialism. The Maghreb that Isabelle Eberhardt traverses in the first years of the twentieth century has been claimed and administered as a French colony. The Tibet that Alexandra David-Neel surreptitiously enters in 1924 is not quite colonized by a specific Western power but is under the pressure of at least three colonial powers; it is a space wedged precariously between lands claimed by England, Russia, and China, empires anxious for dominance in the region. And the Red Centre of the Australian desert through which Robyn Davidson journeys in 1977 remains an indigenously postcolonial space overwritten by two hundred years of white-Aboriginal conflict.

As each woman moves through an exotic locale, she journeys close to the ground, engaging in intimate ways with a radical otherness through which she imagines and enacts more enabling models of heroic action. On foot, on horse, or on camel, this traveler, becoming other to her "civilized" self, un-becomes the enervated woman. And yet, as modernity and "the primitive" are mutually constitutive (the "primitive" can be imagined only from within modernity, as Marianna Torgovnick notes in *Gone Primitive* [17]), she can never realize her desire to escape modernity's scope. Hers is a belated un-becoming.

## The Passionate Nomad: Isabelle Eberhardt and the Aesthetics of Intimate Encounter

> I shall start another diary. What shall I record there, and
> where shall I be, the day in the distant future when I shall
> be closing it, the way I am closing this one today?
>
> —Isabelle Eberhardt, diary entry, January 31, 1903

In journals recovered after her death in the Maghreb desert in 1904 and republished as *The Passionate Nomad* in 1988, Isabelle Eberhardt describes the North African desert to and through which she traveled as "a refuge where my tormented soul can go for relief from the triviality of modern life" (41).[1] Seeking to escape what Chris Bongie terms "the constitutive mediocrity of the modern subject" (21), Eberhardt has fled a European subjectivity that modernity has rendered a degradation and a danger to the soul, characterized as it is by grinding monotony, enervating self-satisfaction, and bourgeois repressions. As she records her nomadic travels away from Europe and across the Maghreb, then, Eberhardt figures travel as a return to what she imagines as a true home from which she has been estranged. Further, identifying the "oriental" Russia (the home of her parents, who were exiles in Geneva) with the "oriental" Maghreb, she also figures travel as a return to the homeland from which she has always been exiled.[2]

The nomadic peoples traversing the expansive spaces of the Maghreb provide Eberhardt a metaphor for the kind of life she desires. Apparently unrooted, autonomous, and free, nomads represent that otherness Eberhardt identifies deep within herself: "A nomad I was even when I was very small and would stare at the road.... A nomad I will remain for life, in love with distant and uncharted places" (96). This figural trope of nomadic sensibility was, according to Laura Rice, a potent fin de siècle metaphor: "The constant displacement of nomadic peoples symbolized freedom—the escape into a timeless otherness—for late nineteenth-century Europe. The very distance between this mirage of an eternally changing pattern of otherness rooted in a dimly biblical past and the codified everyday life of modern European cities fascinated the European subject" (151–52). With other romantic intellectuals, Eberhardt ascribes to the nomads an essential difference she taps for an image of her "true self," transforming the nomadic subject within her imagination into a superiority of soul.

The ceaseless mobility of the nomad serves Eberhardt as a metaphor for her own ceaseless pursuit of a more authentic, truer self that can be discovered only through the intimate immersion in an other's culture. And so, traveling away from Europe, Eberhardt heads home to the otherness in herself through the identification with the otherness of the nomad. She embraces the everyday accoutrements or signifiers of difference—the language, dress, and religious affiliation of the nomads—all of which secure her an incommensurable difference from "those idiotic Europeans" (99) with their vitiated, mechanized culture. She dresses as a North African holy man, speaks the language, studies the religion, and travels as the nomads travel. She takes an Arabic name, Mahmoud Saadi. Her journals continually register this identity in otherness. Throughout, she intersperses Arabic phrases with French ones. A convert to Islam, she often meditates upon its promises, its practitioners, and its authority and incorporates Islamic tenets and sayings into the journal.

The heroic nomad of Eberhardt's narrative functions as the self-consolidating other to the questing European subject. The mystery, inscrutability, and exoticism of the sublime dreamscape she projects onto Africa answer her desire for a commensurate otherness of mystery, inscrutability, and exoticism within. She takes these "properties" of the nomadic landscape and the nomadic subject as her own, and it is through these properties that she defines her difference from Europeans, whom she describes as "idiotic." In other words, this European woman "goes primitive," to invoke Marianna Torgovnick's phrase. "Going primitive," writes Torgovnick, "is trying to 'go home' to a place that feels comfortable and balanced, where full acceptance comes freely and easily" (185). "Going primitive" mandates a certain relationship to the terms of mobility. To "go primitive" is to go slowly, to go intimately, to go as one would if one were "native," a "nomad." And so Eberhardt moves by horse or by camel—that is, by modes other than the modes of modernity. Her movement is movement outside technology and progress, movement that is nomadic, prehistorical, timeless, romantic. It is defining and defiant movement "by other means," that is, by the other's means.

If it is the prerogative of the romantic traveler escaping the ravages of modernity to go primitive, that going primitive offers only the illusion of becoming other. Central to Eberhardt's performative nomadism is her very Western commitment to abstract individualism. Regenia Gagnier describes abstract individualism as "the belief that essential human characteristics are properties of individuals independent of their material conditions and social environment" (100). It is precisely this Western belief that Eberhardt carries with her into the desert. "I am utterly alone on earth," she announces in inaugurating her journal (1); and throughout, she identifies herself as a "lunatic," a "pariah" (2), and a "tramp" (77), as well as a "nomad." These are resolutely solitary figures, and that solitariness differentiates them from the figures of actual nomads. Eberhardt's is romantic solitude, a solitude through which she believes herself to be autonomous and free. "Far from society, far from civilization," she writes, "I am by myself, on Muslim soil, out in the desert, free and in the best of circumstances. The outcome of my undertaking is therefore up to me" (24). The "undertaking" to which she refers is her romantic quest for a true self, "an 'Ideal,' something mystical and eminently desirable that fires [the] soul" (9).

In taking this history of abstract individualism into the desert with her, Eberhardt assumes the heroic subject to be male (Busia 97). Consequently, in certain journal entries she positions herself explicitly as a man, as when she writes that "life in the Desert ... will complete my education as a man of action, the Spartan education I need" (10). Or she positions herself through the masculine referent, as when she professes her desire to "write a novel, tell the unique story of a man—rather like myself—who is a Muslim and tries to sow the seeds of virtue everywhere he goes" (102). She imagines her heroic quest through a masculine code in which she acts the "hero" who has "faith, repentance, the desire for moral perfection, the longing for a reputation based on noble merit, and a thirst for great and magnificent deeds" (8).[3] And she stakes her legitimate claim to a place in the "brotherhood" of revered travel writers by incorporating passages from the journals of fellow travelers who have gone primitive, among them Pierre Loti and the Goncourt brothers. Through these rhetorical moves and through the intertextuality of her journal, Eberhardt frames her romantic "self" and her "experience" through the textual forms of a daring and experimental masculinity.

Eberhardt's masquerade as a peripatetic nomad involves a doubled crossing, then, from Europe to North Africa and from a female to a male identity, signified by the male name she takes in the desert.[4] With this masculine identification comes the disavowal of women and the female body in the pages of the journal. The unsympathetic treatment of her impoverished sister-in-law and the conventional colonialist figuration of Arab women register Eberhardt's sustained critique of women and femininity. She allies Arab women with animals when she describes how "the expression in their large languorous and melancholy jet black eyes is resigned and sad like that of wary animals" (3). Elsewhere she assigns them anonymity and denies their individuality by consigning them to an undifferentiated mass: "The problem with Tenes is its herd of neurotic, orgiastic, mean and futile females" (98). Herdlike and voiceless, North African women remain, to use Abena Busia's phrase, "simply not real" (94) for Eberhardt (except for one religious mentor).[5] Not only, then, does Eberhardt disidentify with European subjects, both male and female, she also disidentifies with the mass of women, both European and North African. For Eberhardt, the female can have no "character," because the two traits she allies with character—an "unflinching and invincible will" and "integrity"—are, she claims, "so hard to find in women" (4), who lead sedentary, trivial lives, uninformed by the quest for a truer self.[6]

The disavowal of the female body within the pages of the journal is far more complex than the disavowal of women alone. Central to Eberhardt's quest for a truer self becomes her quest for sexual knowledge. Even as she critiques the feminine and female embodiment throughout her journals, then, Eberhardt fills it with confessions of a desiring subject. Her attraction to the Maghreb as a home in which she can find her true self is an attraction to a landscape saturated with erotic possibilities. In this place, new landscapes of desire, new forms and practices of sexuality, promise ecstasies beyond the conforming pleasures of the "modern" European body, disciplined and repressed. In this expectation of pleasure, Eberhardt participates in the orientalist fabrication of the "East" as "a coffer of erotic delights and unlimited freedoms" (Kabbani v). The freedom to develop a more authentic character implies the freedom to discover a body unconstrained by bourgeois repression. Her journals record the calls to and discoveries of such ecstasies. "Day after tomorrow," she writes with anticipation, "I can give in to these physical cravings and spend whole nights in wild sensuality" (41).

Yet Eberhardt seems to acknowledge, albeit indirectly, that her pursuit of sexual freedom and experimentation tests the cultural borderline separating the culturally sanctioned from the promiscuous sexual activity of women. Even speaking of sexual desire and the pleasures of the body tests the limits set between the culturally speakable and the unspeakable. Eberhardt attends to this risk by carefully differentiating herself from the "herd" of women whose bodies are part of the traffic in the bodies of prostitutes, the nomadic traffic of women's bodies from one man to another. "I have now reached the depths of poverty, and may well be going hungry soon. Yet I can honestly say that I have never, not even for a moment, entertained the notion of doing what so many hundreds of thousands of women do," she writes. *"That is out of the question*, period" (71). The emphasis Eberhardt adds to the declaration reveals a fundamental discomfort. The bodies of prostitutes come too close to Eberhardt for comfort. They represent a menace, what Georges Van Den Abbeele describes as "the disruptive liminality women are represented as occupying" in narratives of travel (xxvi). These women and their bodies are seductive of the subject of travel. Critically, the seduction in Eberhardt's journal derives not from the otherness of the prostitute's body but from the sameness of that body. This threat of sameness incites Eberhardt's hostility and the gestures of critique in the journal. She refuses to be positioned as the debased female.

Further, she incorporates her pursuit of culturally errant sexuality into the mythic plot of the artist-traveler in search of knowledge. "Sexual matters will continue to hold my attention, of course, from the intellectual point of view," she explains, "and I would not give up my research in that domain for anything in the world" (79). By turning sexuality into an arena of research, Eberhardt opens a distance between herself as romantic subject of the quest and her body as object of experimentation. In this way, the female body is objectified and neutralized as a threat to her project. (This neutralization is also signified by the male clothing she adopts and the anorexic body that those male "habits" envelop.)

Cross-dressing as an Arab male and speaking as a male subject of travel, Eberhardt finds a way to speak her body but to do so with some kind of residual legitimacy, because she speaks through the voice of the ceaselessly questing artist. The body becomes a source of the heightened aesthetic experiences for the artist who pushes courageously against the mediocrities of "his" culture in pursuit of new knowledge and a "better self." In this way, the body remains the feminized object of intellectual contemplation, and the traveler retains his status as masculine knower, the subject who turns his gaze upon the object of study.

Eventually, in this ceaseless quest for (sexual) knowledge at the premodern edges, Eberhardt, as Pierre Loti had done before her, becomes an actor in what Bongie calls the "quintessentially romantic plot: one of forbidden love between a giaour and his native paramour" (88). Not only does Eberhardt take the language, the habits (in both senses of the word), and the profound faith of the other into herself, but she also goes further, marrying her "native" lover and, despite her sexual infidelities, faithfully devoting pages of her journal to him. "Simply holding him in my arms as I did yesterday and looking into his eyes brings me back to life" (41), she writes. Her lover's eyes bring her to life as an exotic subject, essentially different from and more alive than those idiotic Europeans.

Literally and symbolically marrying difference, Eberhardt espouses an aesthetically compelling and culturally transgressive love and exposes the unsatisfactory nature of love in Europe. She figures her union with her husband, Slimene, as an ideal relationship, one that contrasts with the conventional European marriage with its repressed and repressive sexuality (for women). The elaboration of the details of sexual experimentation in her journal function, therefore, as a gesture of cultural critique of modern Western marriages in which young girls experience unsatisfactory sexuality at the hands of their clumsy European husbands (80).

Enacting this romantic script, whose plot becomes the imaginary means through which the European subject makes intimate contact with the other, Eberhardt affirms in one more way her rightful place in the brotherhood of male travel writers at the turn of the twentieth century. But the exoticist plot of the love between the female giaour and her exotic other differs from the normative male plot. The traditional exoticist narrative joins European man with exotic woman, mutually reinforcing the hierarchy of racial differences through the hierarchy of gender differences. The other culture (signified by the other woman) remains in the inferior position. Here, however, the relationship is reversed, and the effects of that reversal are contradictory and complex.

The language of romantic love through which Eberhardt represents her exotic relationship with Slimene positions her as the enthralled dependent. She would, she writes, subdue her desire for authority and power and adopt a posture of "obedience" toward her "master": "I must learn the very thing that is hardest for someone of my temperament, namely obedience (which of course has its limits and must on no account turn into servility)" (48). This European woman seeks the position of obedience in relation to the North African man, thereby becoming the subservient other of the colonized other, because she desires the knowledge associated with his otherness and with his culture. As a result, Eberhardt's representation of the liaison, while seeming to reproduce a normative script of female subordination, confuses the scripting of the power relations between colonizer and colonized. This confusion of established relationships of power in the colonies leads Annette Kobak to suggest that Eberhardt "threaten[s] the precarious fiction of European dominance and Arab submissiveness upon which the colonial venture in Algeria was built" (130).

Yet even as Eberhardt represents herself as subdued before the "Arab" lover-other, she reveals her desire to "subdue" Slimene. Throughout the fourth journal, she describes her efforts to "educate" him up out of his ignorance. To educate Slimene is to prepare him to identify with, as well as to be identified with, European culture and values. It is to prove his educability, his equality, his potential for modernization. It is therefore an act whereby Eberhardt would translate him out of his premodern otherness and difference. As Rice suggests, "To the extent that the local people became Europeanized ... they denied their essence as the exotic other" (153). Thus, even as she transgresses the tenets of colonial relationships, the narrator enacts the "civilizing mission" used to justify the colonial project. Furthermore, Eberhardt's exotic plot translates herself and Slimene into "the couple" as a unit of cultural meaning, which as Malek Alloula points out, is an imported and modern structure of relationship (39).[7] Love for Slimene involves Eberhardt in the domestication of the other. Figuratively, Eberhardt takes Slimene home to Europe with her by making him over into her own image of a lover.

Eberhardt's mode of representation keeps her anchored in the cultural practices of Europe, no matter how far her "primitive" mode of mobility has taken her from its metropolitan centers. Thus, it is important to consider in more detail how the journal serves as the appropriate writing vehicle for the romantic subject who "need[s] to keep searching, come what may, for new events, and flee inertia and stagnation" (36); the subject who wants to calibrate the increments of change in that endless quest; the subject who wants to become "other" to herself by engaging the other; the subject whose progress toward a true self requires exacting self-scrutiny. The "apparent egocentricity to be found on every page of this diary" signals not "megalomania," according to the narrator, but rather the "need to compile a record that will give me, later on, a true image of my soul as it is today. That is the only way I shall be able to judge my present life and to see whether my character has progressed or not" (13). Because the journal luxuriates in the quotidian, the incidental, the intimate, and the individualistic, it is a form correlative with the fragmented subject, a form in which nothing is put together finally, in which everything remains vague, unfinished, provisional.

Through journal entries, Eberhardt tracks the fractures menacing the questing subject. At times the subject splits along the public-private axis: "I seem to wear a mask that bespeaks someone cynical, dissipated.... No one so far has ever managed to see through it and catch a glimpse of the sensitive soul which lives behind it" (1). Other times the subject splits along the adventure-contemplation axis, as when she delineates the competing attractions of two lives, "one that is full of adventure and belongs to the Desert, and one, calm and restful, devoted to thought and far from all that might interfere with it" (11). Yet another split falls along the body-intellect axis: "I feel more and more disgusted with my second self, that no-good oaf who rears his head from time to time, usually, if not always, under the influence of physical factors. Better health, in other words, would clearly result in an improvement in the intellectual and spiritual side of my life" (11). Elsewhere she writes, "The human body is nothing, the human soul is all" (45). Finally, there is the split along the heart-head axis: "I feel a tranquil heart is mine at last; the same cannot be said for any peace of mind, alas!" (29). There is always a split to be sutured—if not here, then there.

The journal places the traveler constantly anew on the page, caught in the exigencies of the moment in a nomadic context of restlessness. Through many entries, Eberhardt tracks her movement from threshold to threshold. "Period[s] of incubation" are followed by periods of "new understanding of people and of things" (51) through which she anticipates achieving her better self. Six months after a murder attempt on her life in January 1901, she writes: "Periods of restlessness, discontent and uncertainty have always been followed by the emergence of a better version of myself. A subject to be analyzed, and described perhaps in a short story or a novel" (69). The journal promotes an aesthetics of renewable self-consciousness: "Everything is radically different now, myself included" (107). Everything is in motion.

But as the venue of nomadic restlessness, the journal ultimately reveals that the quest has always already failed, that the "better self" can never be realized, that "home" is nowhere. In this way, Eberhardt's journalistic practice participates in the fin de siècle exoticist project. "The exotic necessarily becomes, for those who persist in search of it," writes Bongie, "the sign of an aporia—of a constitutional absence at the heart of what had been projected as a possible alternative to modernity." Like the texts of other exoticist writers, Eberhardt's journal "register[s] the exotic as a space of absence, a dream already given over to the past" (22).

The narrator's self-preoccupation drives the journal's continuous present tense of incident, impression, feeling, and reflection, and thereby sustains an unerring focus on the experiencing subject, that is, a kind of psychological timelessness. The preoccupation with the sublime landscape and the exotic love plot promotes another kind of timelessness, that of the prehistoric, unchanging, unspoiled realm of experience outside history. Eberhardt washes everything with a patina of vagueness, inscrutability, and mystery. The time of desire becomes the more authentic, more primitive past. Immersed at once in the timelessness of the psychological present and the timelessness of the primitive past, the writing subject seems to evade any totalizing history with a capital *H*, that history of modernity she desires to leave behind.

From a certain perspective, Eberhardt does seem to evade some of the big-*H* history of colonialism. The adoption of a nomadic identity and mode of mobility enable her to take certain positions toward the culture of the desert space that distinguish her from other participants in the French colonial regime in North Africa. These positions derive from what Rice calls Eberhardt's "reverse assimilation" (162). The desire to assume the identity of the nomad leads Eberhardt to develop a critical perspective on the impact of colonization upon North Africa rather than to assume, with other participants in the regime, the inferiority and inequality of the colonized subjects. Thus, she countervalorizes nomadic society. "Whatever their unenlightened way of life," she pronounces, "the lowliest of Bedouins are far superior to those idiotic Europeans making such a nuisance of themselves" (99). And she bemoans the cost to the indigenous peoples of prolonged exposure to Europeans and their culture, especially in "border" cities, those seaside towns that were ports of entry for everything European, including soldiers and colonial bureaucrats. They are, she writes, "unhinged and vitiated ... by ... contact with a foreign world" (32).

But of course the journal fills with the history of modernity and colonialism it seeks to escape; for, as Bongie notes of Loti's narrative, "the journal and the subject who is writing it are constantly being rewritten within the terms of that which they would remain outside, or to the side, of" (87). The frontier of difference Eberhardt traverses is a frontier created through the very colonial project she critiques, because "the imperialist vision shapes public opinion, offering it the possibility of boundless horizons as compensation for the dismal prospects of industrial society" (Bongie 21). There can be no exotic adventure without those very border cities Eberhardt maligns, nor without the imperialist penetration she bemoans. Thus, the "home" of Europe has always already domesticated the exoticist voyage toward a more legitimate home, because, as home, it serves as "the transcendental point of reference" (Van Den Abbeele xviii). Modernity with a capital *M* organizes the exoticist project as a project outside history.

Even as she traverses the sublime landscape dressed as an Algerian marabout, even as she masquerades in the dress of communal male identification, and even as she enacts a poetics of reverse assimilation with the "other," Eberhardt reveals the distance of essential difference and the proximity of European sameness. Eberhardt exploits the North African backdrop for her own cult of the individual. She can go about her business of cross-dressing and violate all kinds of indigenous Algerian codes, codes that Algerian women could not have violated, precisely because she carries her European identification with her into the desert. The cross-cultural-dressing situates her as an eccentric whose very eccentricity protects her. Eberhardt cannot go incognito, for her very subjectivity, even her life, depends upon the visibility of her masquerade. She even acknowledges that the indigenous people are more afraid of a European eccentric than they are of the poverty-stricken "countryman" and that she is, for this reason, safer in the masquerade. Moreover, her eccentricity as a "destitute beggar" enables her to survive upon the generosity and benevolence of the indigenous population.[8] There is thus a disturbing irony underwriting parts of the journal of this romantic artist who traveled close to the ground. The European woman, having appropriated the identity of the colonized nomad to find a truer self, lives off the very people she mimes. She depends upon them for her very survival—both literally and figuratively.

## The (Un)Belonging Lama: Alexandra David-Neel and the Grounds of Intimate Mimicry

> I delightedly forgot Western lands, that I belonged to them,
> and that they would probably take me again in the clutches of
> their sorrowful civilization.
>
> —Alexandra David-Neel, *My Journey to Lhasa* (1927)

Like Isabelle Eberhardt, Alexandra David-Neel fled the exacting constraints and the prosaic secularism of bourgeois civilization. Like Eberhardt, she was drawn imaginatively, intellectually, and spiritually to a particular locale, in her case Tibet.[9] Like Eberhardt, she devoted years to the study of her adopted culture, absorbing all she could about Buddhism and Sanskrit and Tibetan languages, literatures, and religions in the silent spaces of the Musée Guimet in Paris and under the auspices of the Theosophical Society. She spoke Tibetan fluently, studied the ancient Tibetan texts, and immersed herself in the culture of East Asia, studying with Tibetan lamas and philosophers. She traveled extensively in India, Sikkim, and China and spent considerable time at the Lachen hermitage and the monastery at Kumbum. Like Eberhardt, she took the natives' religion as her own, becoming a Buddhist and eventually a lama, a title acknowledged by her coreligionists. Like Eberhardt, David-Neel sought a cultural and geographical space distant from the reach of motorized modernity. And again like Eberhardt, though after the fact, she narrated her journeying close to the ground, publishing *My Journey to Lhasa* in 1927.

Yet if Eberhardt's journeying is nomadic, restless, and romantic, David-Neel's journeying is purposeful and "scientific." And it requires disguise. For, unlike Eberhardt, David-Neel had to go incognito into Tibet when she sought to reach the capital city of Lhasa in 1924. In the 1920s, Tibetan authorities, seeking to minimize the penetration of external influence and to hold the line against the imperial designs of the British and the Russian Empires, doggedly policed Tibet's borders, forbidding entry to all "philings" (foreigners), excepting British officials. Further complicating matters, the British Raj had closed the borders into Tibet from India because it feared the loss of influence to representatives of the Russian Empire. David-Neel had already been refused entrance into the country and, more dramatically, expelled from the province of Sikkim (Foster and Foster 71). These early failures only increased her resolve to journey to the interior of this "forbidden" country: "What decided me to go to Lhasa was, above all, the absurd prohibition which closes Thibet. A prohibition—one would hardly think it possible—that extends over a gradually increasing area is now placed on foreigners who wish to cross territories over which they could travel at will a few years ago" (David-Neel, *Journey* xx).[10]

To succeed in "show[ing] what a woman can do" (9) by reaching the forbidden city of Lhasa, David-Neel and her "adopted son" Yongden (a Tibetan lama with whom she traveled) must "'disappear,' as we used to say, and assume other personalities" (8). They must, that is, become unobtrusive ciphers in the landscape. "Our best plan," she explains to her reader, "was to merge at once in their number, like inconspicuous, common *arjopas*" (16).[11] If Eberhardt assumes the habits of the heroic male nomad, David-Neel assumes the habits of the inconspicuous peasant, cross-culturally dressing as the other woman, the very woman so efficiently suppressed in Eberhardt's narrative.[12] Surreptitiously entering and traversing this forbidden territory, the Western woman and her companion trudge inconspicuously over rugged terrain, in constant touch with the ground and with the grounds of everyday life in the mountains of Tibet. Traveling by foot becomes the imperative mode of mobility for this impersonator.

But this is to suggest the motivations of her cross-dressed mobility and its consequences in terms of the journey. How precisely does the grounded cross-dressing function within the context of that prototravel which is the travel narrative itself? Obviously David-Neel does not go incognito in her narrative. Nor does she position herself textually as the inconsequential peasant mother. She speaks not as the subaltern but as the Western subject who has successfully mimed inconspicuous peasantry. How, then, does she figure herself as a traveler on foot?

David-Neel emphasizes that her travels by foot as a common *arjopa* sustain the distinguishing logic of travel, enabling her to reach a destination not accessible by means of the literal engines of progress. Thus her preoccupation throughout *My Journey to Lhasa* with her privileged status vis-à-vis earlier travelers. She notes that her performance of common peasantry distinguishes her from Western adventurers such as Sven Hedin, Annie Taylor, Mrs. St. George Littledale, and Suzie Rijnhart who tried but failed to trek through the impenetrable "land of snows."[13] She differentiates herself from travelers who succeeded in reaching Lhasa but who gained access only to Tibet's religious leaders: "To the knowledge I had already acquired about the religious people of the country I would add another and quite intimate one, concerning its humblest sons and daughters" (76). She has not misrecognized the country for its elites but has negotiated the everyday life of the peasants, which, she proposes, is the "real" Tibet.

David-Neel thus claims membership in an "elite" club of legendary travelers—one that includes Richard Burton and William Lane, both of whom traveled incognito through potentially hostile territory. Her ability to ally herself with Burton and Lane derives not only from the rigors of her itinerary but also from the knowledge of the culture and the peoples of Tibet that she brings with her on the road. Like these male travelers, she is so knowledgeable about the culture and the language that she can "pass" for an authentic Tibetan peasant. She can put on Tibetan "drag," so to speak. Sara Mills, in analyzing the narrative uses of the trope of the "westerner in disguise," describes this figure as one "of great textual power since [disguise] demonstrates great knowledge to a western audience, and at the same time it asserts even greater power over the people of the colonized country since they are represented as being fooled by the disguise" (140). The narrative of disguise functions as a ground of textual and cultural authority as *My Journey to Lhasa* joins two rhetorical modes: scholarly observation and suspenseful narrative drama.

David-Neel's challenge to borders derives from her identification as scholar and intellectual. The scholar's journey David-Neel presents as the objective search for knowledge unaffected by political expediencies. Even though she criticizes the British government for its policies affecting Tibet, she is no political partisan, no revolutionary woman breaching borders in order to challenge imperialism. She makes her position quite plain in the introduction: "As for myself, I profoundly despise everything which is connected with politics, and carefully avoid mixing in such matters" (xxi–xxii). To "mix" is to become contaminated. It is precisely her distance from the sullied and interested realm of the political that guarantees the scholar's authority, her claim to an unadulterated, "objective" knowledge. If politicians create borders, the scholar must defy borders in pursuit of knowledge.

Throughout her narrative, David-Neel incorporates an encyclopedia of knowledge about the language, religious practices, literature, and culture required for successful duplicity. To this knowledge she adds her observations of the geography, the culture, and the family life of the mountain peoples of Tibet. The cumulative data she incorporates in the narrative becomes a body of knowledge she produces about Tibet. Concomitantly, the production of that knowledge affirms her identity as a serious scholar who is lifting "the veil that hides the real Tibet" (198), a space of belatedness far distant from the reach of modernity, the reach of automobile and airplane.

The status of David-Neel's knowledge is authenticated through a rhetoric of scholarly inquiry. The narrative voice is, as Mills notes, straightforward, attentive to detail, voracious in its scope of interest, and descriptive. This is, Mills writes, "a style which does not draw too much attention to itself as language, and which attempts to appear 'transparent' through its lack of foregrounded elements. The language items which are chosen are simple, common-core items, with all technical terms of foreign words being footnoted" (136). The footnotes that periodically interrupt David-Neel's narrative remind the reader of the status of the narrator as one who knows and the status of the knowledge as "verified" and "verifiable" through "research." The specificity of description testifies to the depth of her penetration into the interior of the unknown and the forbidden, and her pointed discussion of psychic phenomena situates her as a scholar who shares research interests with other orientalist scholars (112). Attending to contemporary debates about Tibetan cultural practices, David-Neel inserts herself into ongoing scholarly inquiries taking place in Europe. Throughout the narrative, then, we find the voice of the Western scholar—objective, distanced, and authoritatively reportorial.

This is the voice of the Enlightenment subject, confident in "his" demesne of knowledge. Contributing to this confidence is David-Neel's access to orientalist tropes, for the more David-Neel sees and the further she penetrates, the more she has been prepared to see through the structures of a history already produced in the West as part of its Enlightenment inheritance. Her several motivations for assuming the identity of the other, which are evident in her introduction to the travel narrative, are the motivations of a Western subject complicit with as well as critical of imperial practices. She asserts that she has no desire to "conquer" and "subjugate" the country, the "natives," or the culture. She even tries, as in the following passage, to honor the complexity of Tibetan life: "The views of these lonely ascetics and the teachings they impart to those whom they take as disciples are interesting in many respects, and may be a revelation to those who consider Thibet a land of benighted savages" (180). She does, however, desire to "penetrate" Tibet's interior, and presents herself in that act of penetration as "one who kn[ows] the 'Land of Snows' and its religious folk" (25) from firsthand experience, not just from books.[14] It is this displacement of conquering with knowing that Mary Louise Pratt so effectively traces in her discussion of "imperial eyes" (*Eyes* 136). David-Neel speaks as a Western subject educated in Western archives (as well as Eastern monasteries) and, as such, participates in certain orientalist tropes in her travel narrative, tropes that, as Mills emphasizes, form part of the authenticating discourse of travel narratives.[15]

For instance, although David-Neel often uses the term *savages* ironically, as a way of challenging her reader to rethink the status of Tibetans and their culture, she also uses the term as a more literal referent (xxii). She homogenizes Tibetans by melding them into an undifferentiated mass: "Asiatics do not feel, as we do, the need of privacy and silence in sleep" (208). She foregrounds the exotic and mysterious nature of the people and the land. She sometimes infantilizes the Tibetans by identifying them as children, which may account for her recurrent attribution to them of "overflowing gaiety" (61). And she produces Tibet as a pastoralized space outside modernity and its history, a space inhabited by subjects of belatedness. Paradoxically, then, it is through the orientalist tropes reproduced in books, and specifically in travel books, that she authenticates her firsthand experience.

In incorporating certain tropes even as she resists others, David-Neel asserts her word as what Don Bialostosky terms "the authoritative word": "The authoritative word can be received and repeated but is not to be responded to, modified, or questioned. It is the voice ... of given rules and conventions that must be observed but that do not have to account for themselves." In the "distanced zone" of the authoritative word, all seems objective and impersonal. Yet the basis of the authoritative word in this text is what Bialostosky calls "the internally persuasive word" (15), the persuasive word of the woman who has narrated the story of suspense and endurance in pursuit of the knowledge transported back home by the authoritative word.

The suspenseful drama of David-Neel's narrative derives from her reconstruction of the behaviors necessary for the maintenance of the disguise of "an oriental woman and beggar" (44) and the manifold difficulties of sustaining that disguise. Will she be betrayed? Will she inadvertently expose herself as an impostor? Recalling one moment in which a traveler whom she and her companion meet almost "penetrates" her disguise, she notes that she had to "perform all the menial work, leaving the lama seated on the carpet that had been spread for him near the fire in an entrance room, for we were not invited to enter the family kitchen" (201). The narrator must maintain the sense of danger by drawing out the moments of possible exposure, even though she knows and we know that she has succeeded in her journey. "The morrow," she writes, "was to be the first of a series of eventful days, well qualified to prostrate with nervous breakdown one less strong than myself" (54). Offering her reader a series of near misses, David-Neel heightens the sense of her journey's adventure and its stakes, and enhances her status as heroic adventurer— someone with the rigorous self-control, the daring, the resilience, the wariness, and the improvisational ingenuity to perpetrate duplicitous disguise.

The narrative of suspenseful disguise is also the source of the humor and playfulness of the text. David-Neel recalls how, temporarily forgetting that her face is darkened with soot, she washes and then notices in time the dirt that comes off on the cloth. Describing how she escapes brigands by playing the "initiated and ordained wife of a black *nag spa*" who calls upon the "most dreaded ones, uttering their most terrible names and titles," she notes: "I am a tiny woman with nothing dramatic in my appearance; but at that moment I felt myself rising to the height of a powerful tragedienne" (222). She narrates with humor the scene in which she slips and slides down a mountainside (155). She confesses to epicurean delight: "After the nights spent in the *sa phug*, the warmth that spread into the closed room thrilled voluptuously in me the epicure which is always lurking in the corner of the most ascetic hearts" (165). Even survivalist behaviors become the source of narrative humor. "At the risk of appearing a character devoid of all poetry," she tells her reader, "I confess that I ate a large quantity of barley-meal butter" (60).

The length of the journey, the ruggedness of the terrain, the dangers confronted and vanquished, and the vulnerability to exposure of various kinds all combine to register the impersonator's bodily endurance. The living conditions she describes are rough, the food minimal, the accommodations dirty, the weather rugged, the manners makeshift. There are no bourgeois comforts or commodities, no tents, no phonographs. Her very body is under duress, wracked with fatigue, hunger, thirst, and numbing sensations.[16] It is also a body in disarray, unclean, unmannered, and ungainly. The narrator takes obvious pleasure in her self-presentation as common, coarse, and gluttonous, in her enactment of anything but the clean and proper bourgeois woman.

*My Journey to Lhasa* braids the chronological narrative of personal travail in disguise (romance) with precise descriptions of landscape, mountain peoples and their customs, living conditions, and social organization, and the way of life of the itinerant lama. The effect is to produce not only the heroic pilgrim in the travail of her feat (on her feet) but also the scholar in pursuit of knowledge. The two modes, narrative and descriptive, are mutually attesting.[17] The traveler suffers to gain and reproduce knowledge for the reader back home. Conversely, the discourse of the objective scholar-ethnographer, organized through tropes that secure the position of the scholarly travel narrator, further enhances as it makes instrumental the heroism of the personal narrative.

The two modes as well enable David-Neel to contest normative spectacles of femininity back home in Europe. In self-portraits such as the ones aforementioned, David-Neel figures herself in a variety of postures, some of which seem designed to affirm her continuing allegiance to normative repertoires of femininity—those, for instance, which seem self-diminishing in a woman who threatens to exceed the bounds of proper womanhood (Mills 125–52). But such portraits also disrupt prescriptive repertoires of femininity by calling attention to two apparently mutually exclusive identities: that of the rather prosaic, conventional, middle-class matron; and that of the coarse *arjopa*. David-Neel's crossdressing puts her into a different and degraded femininity vis-à-vis the middle-class femininity she left behind in early-twentieth-century Europe. She dresses as a peasant woman out of her class, out of her race, and out of her culture. In this sense her cross-dressing functions as an undressing through which she becomes an unclean and improper woman.

David-Neel's self-representational levity thus effects a disconnect between the repertoire of behaviors identified with bourgeois femininity and the makeshift manners and inelegant physical contortions of the impersonated *arjopa*. The narrator thereby unsettles the cultural pressure for social structures "to channel recognitions toward uniform and unchanging identities" and reveals how the very "pressure to be one thing ... creates a counterpressure to be many and to escape the confinements of a fixed and unitary self" (Leed 279). The epicurean undoes the ascetic; the common *arjopa* undoes the bourgeois matron. This woman in transit is out of place precisely because she has become the (excluded) otherness within. To be out of place in this sense is to act out of line, to access materially an otherness within that empowers her to resist normative scripts of femininity.[18]

David-Neel returns to the West, through her narrative celebration of physical hardship and endurance, another possibility for "woman," one that displaces the identity contents of matronly femininity under Western eyes. She emphasizes her ability to withstand the kind of life that her performance of subalternity entails. This impersonation of another kind of woman, a woman constituted through radically different spectacles of femininity, marks David-Neel's disidentification with bourgeois constructions of femininity in Europe and relativizes the Western bourgeois idealization of the white woman as fragile, sessile, and cautious.[19] David-Neel does not, as Eberhardt does, want to escape the identity of woman. In fact, she expresses admiration for Tibetan women, specifically for their independence and their physical and emotional stamina in the midst of harsh environmental pressures (Foster and Foster 270). Tibetan women are presented as agents rather than as exotic objects of desire. Physically hardy and autonomous, they manifest an alternative femininity to Western norms.

In effect, what David-Neel's disguise and her on-the-ground mobility seem to facilitate is temporary freedom from the Western metropolis and its construction of woman. It is the freedom to be, if only temporarily, another kind of woman in another cultural context of femininity.[20] The remarkable success of the project, as well as the high risk of discovery that haunts the narrative, means that David-Neel can use her narrative to redefine the identity contents of woman by figuring herself not as some feminized traveler but as a constitutively masculine scholar and hero of quest like Burton and Lane before her. "No traveller other than one who was really believed by them to belong to the same peasant stock," she asserts, "could have gathered the same treasure of observations that I collected" (95). To the degree she was able to perform the peasant successfully, she retrieved more detailed, and more scientific, information about the country and its inhabitants than other travelers had done. Thus, her remarkable and successful performance of subalternity draws David-Neel out of the normative spectacles of femininity that would preclude her from being a recognized scholar in Europe.

But there is more to read in David-Neel's grounded impersonation of the subject of belatedness. Peter Bishop explores how twentieth-century Western travelers to Tibet, sensing themselves to be out of place, had to find alternative modes of being "in place" in their ungainly difference, the difference registered in the vast distance between the metropolitan centers of western Europe and modernity's remote edges. If "the surest solution was somehow to *belong* to Tibet," he suggests, then "the first half of the twentieth century witnessed an unprecedented number of travel accounts claiming to have been written from *inside* Tibetan life" (228). What better way to claim insider status than to narrate a story of successful impersonation of a peasant Tibetan, a "real" Tibetan?

But David-Neel is not just any Tibetan. She embeds within her narrative of the impersonation of a common *arjopa* another narrative of identity, in which she represents her most authentic identity as that of the Tibetan lama.

Toward the end of her narrative, David-Neel records an oneiric vision in which a lama comes to her. "Jetsunma," he says to her "this dress of a poor laywoman, and the role of old mother which you have adopted, do not suit you at all. You have taken on the mentality proper to the part. You were braver when you wore your *zen* and your *ten-treng*. You must put them on again later, when you have been to Lhasa" (244). Even though she has chosen to assume temporarily the identity of the subaltern, David-Neel asserts that her identity as the lowly *arjopa* masks her "true" identity as an honored and worshiped Tibetan lama. This identity-trace of the lama keeps disrupting the masquerade of the subaltern, as in the following passage, in which she describes how she and Yongden come upon a man dying by the roadside. While he begs Yongden to pray for his life, David-Neel begins to describe the pleasures of the afterlife to him. He listens intently to her, touching her dress as he does so. "Maybe," she proposes, "he believed that *khandoma* or a goddess had seen his distress and assumed the shape of a pilgrim to console him" (42). In the midst of expressions of sensitivity to human suffering, David-Neel reveals her sense of superiority to the people she encounters and her desire for elevation to her "true" identity as a holy person, the incarnation of *khandoma*, or the mother goddess. She even expresses her desire to be a god capable of bringing happiness to the Tibetans she encounters: "How heart-rending was the sorrow of these humble folk! It is on such occasions that one would like to be a God and to have at one's command an inexhaustible treasure of welfare and happiness to pour out to all alike" (122).

This identity of lama provides David-Neel a sense of cultural belonging, but on her own terms. Through that identity she assumes her incorporation into the place of Tibet, an incorporation psychological as well as physical.[20] She claims a home for herself, a home in which she can claim authority as a religious practitioner, a Buddhist lama, in contrast to the position of inferiority she would be assigned as a devotee

"Looking out": the slow journeying of carriage travel in the early nineteenth century. Courtesy of the Transportation History Collection Print Collection, Special Collections Library, University of Michigan.

The locomotive, the station, the mingling of men and women on the move, circa 1850. Courtesy of the Transportation History Collection Print Collection, Special Collections Library, University of Michigan.

The transition from sails to steam—visible in one vessel, the *Servia*, circa 1880. Courtesy of the Transportation History Collection Print Collection, Special Collections Library, University of Michigan.

## QUI M'AIME ME SUIVE.

Bicycling femininity. From *Velocipedes* (circa 1890), a set of sixteen colored plates, mounted as a folding plate. Courtesy of the Transportation History Collection Print Collection, Special Collections Library, University of Michigan.

Ballooning femininity as imagined in the mid-nineteenth century. *Aéonefs-Omnibus de la compagnie générale.* Courtesy of the Transportation History Collection Print Collection, Special Collections Library, University of Michigan.

"On the road" by herself at the turn of the twentieth century. Courtesy of the Transportation History Collection Print Collection, Special Collections Library, University of Michigan.

# FLY

## THE NATIONAL AERONAUTIC MONTHLY

Photo, Boston Photo News
Hamel giving Final Instructions to Miss Quimby before starting to Fly the English Channel

Ten Cents
a Copy

JUNE 1912
VOL. IV.  NO. 8

One Dollar
a Year

Harriet Quimby preparing for her flight across the English Channel. Cover of *Fly* magazine, June 1912. Courtesy of the Clements Library, University of Michigan.

The pleasure of a bus ride just after the turn of the twentieth century. Courtesy of the Transportation History Collection Print Collection, Special Collections Library, University of Michigan.

Women on the move. An advertisement in *Automotive Industries,* July 1930, for "the powerful motor car and the huge passenger airplane." Courtesy of the Transportation History Collection Print Collection, Special Collections Library, University of Michigan.

The young Isabelle Eberhardt dressed as sailor. Photographed by Louis David in Geneva in 1895. Reproduced in Kobak.

of Christianity in that alienating place of Europe, a place, for her, of unbelonging. David-Neel suggests that this cosmic misplacement has been recognized and acknowledged by the Tibetans themselves. They identify her as a holy lama whose holiness can hardly be veiled by the disguise of the subaltern.

The effect of her identity as lama is that she can imagine herself away from the constraining embodiment of Western femininity. Take, for instance, her description of how she survives freezing temperatures by heating her body through an act of will. Such body heating, she informs her reader, is one of the psychic feats identified with Tibetan Lamaism, along with levitation and telepathy. For David-Neel, such practices are not spiritual but scientific. As she wills her body into obedience, David-Neel exerts the power of mind over body, a power she attributes to her preparation as a devotee of Tibetan Lamaism. Bishop notes that in the early twentieth century, as opposed to the nineteenth century, travelers in Tibet became preoccupied not with the awesome landscape but with "an *expectation* of occult mysteries and power" (233). David-Neel herself wrote that "the fame which Tibet enjoys in foreign countries is largely due to the belief that prodigies happen there as plentifully as wild flow-ers grow in the fields" (*Magic* 288–300). Her knowledge of Tibetan psy-chic practices enables her to resist the frailties and the vulnerabilities of material embodiment. In this way she gains scientific and mental control over the very materiality that attaches her to a diminished humanity in the West. She wills herself, and writes herself, out of embodiment.

Perhaps this identification as one of the spiritual elite is where the trope of romance rejoins the transcultural politics of David-Neel's text. This goddess would pour out upon the Tibetans her goodwill; the orien-talist scholar would "deliver" Tibet to the West in all its mystical essence. She would be the nurturing goddess, the maternal benefactor to Tibetan culture itself. In Tibet, David-Neel can imagine herself as nurturing god-dess, lama, and maternal benefactor. She can imagine herself elsewhere than in her cultural construction in difference in Europe.

Paradoxically, then, David-Neel assumes the identity of the peasant-beggar, the "common," indigenous subject, as a means of elevating her difference from others, both Western and Tibetan. She is the Western woman who is a learned lama; she is a learned lama who is a Western woman. She throws both identities into disarray, destabilizes the securing power of each one, and secures the terms of her own legendary uniqueness before the reader.[21] But her desire for uniqueness is ultimately a romance of the Western subject, a subject who assumes she is "free" to quest after a "true" identity, to travel where she may: "I am one of the Genghis Khan race who, by mistake and perhaps for her sins, was born in the occident. So I was once told by a lama" (*Journey* 61).

## Tracking Spectacle: Robyn Davidson's Muscular Myth

> I grew muscles on my shit.
>
> —Robyn Davidson, *Tracks* (1980)

At the turn of the twentieth century, Isabelle Eberhardt journeyed close to the ground as romantic artist. In the mid-1920s, Alexandra David-Neel journeyed close to the ground as scholar. For both, the terrain at the edge of modernity's scope was a space conducive to self-constitution. In the late 1970s, Robyn Davidson journeyed close to the ground as Australian feminist, taking, like her foremothers, the measure of her self-transformation in the challenge of the journey. Through her arduous mode of travel by foot and camel across the Red Centre in the interior of the Australian continent, Davidson would escape the motorized postmodernity at the urban edges of Australia's coastal region and with it the constitutive constraints of disabling femininity in metropolitan centers. Negotiating the edges of (post)modernization's scope, Davidson renegotiates her identity as feminized woman. Her dream of transformation thus takes her toward contact with Australia's indigenous people on their traditional lands and culminates in the publication of her narrative of that contact as *Tracks* (1980).

As Davidson makes clear in *Tracks*, by the time she completes her camel trip across the Australia desert, the woman traveling by foot (and camel) through the outback becomes a tourist attraction, "the camel lady." Traversing the desert by foot and camel as a way of taking control of her life by shifting identities, Davidson discovers that she cannot maintain control, precisely because she cannot control public representations of her journey. Through the Western drive to turn the arduous trek into an exotic spectacle of the individualizing journey, her dream is compromised.

During the year she prepares for her trip in Alice Springs, Davidson writes that she is assigned the identity of "camel lady," an "image which I should have nipped in the bud right there" (43). In Alice Springs she comes to understand how the idea of her journey functions as a screen upon which other people project their own fears, desires, and politics. Some discourage her from making the trip, fearing that her success might effectively undermine the constitutive masculinity of life in the Red Centre and the bush. Others see her project as an attempt to commit suicide, or as "penance for my mother's death," or as a gesture "to prove a woman could cross a desert," or as a sign of her craving for publicity (101), all diagnostic scripts that flatten out, through pat psychologizing, the complexities of her motivations for journeying and that code such flamboyant journeying as excessively personal.

A Marxist activist whom Davidson meets in, of all places, Utopia, condemns her as a bourgeois individualist. From his point of view, her plan to walk across the desert with camels unmasks the self-absorption with the inner life that a true revolutionary understands as retrograde. In recalling her response to the charge, Davidson begins to define for herself and her reader what the project might originally have meant to her. For one thing, she asserts that the project had to do with "tak[ing] control of my own life" (99). In that sense, she would indeed be an "individualist"; but she undermines the label of "bourgeois" by critiquing the way in which the Marxist "saw any entry into the morbid internal landscape as traditionally at least, the realm of the female" and therefore as "counterproductive" (100). Davidson recognizes that the Marxist understood her project as personal, unfocused, and indulgent, the solipsistic preoccupation with interiority commonly coded "feminine." Thus she makes her counterclaim, that the charge of bourgeois individualism masks the

Marxist's masculine fear of any unruly otherness within, an otherness she willingly embraces through her journeying.

The complex projections of Davidson's identity as camel lady become even more disruptive when she agrees to accept underwriting by the National Geographic Society. This acceptance "meant that an international magazine would be interfering—no, not overtly, but would have a vested interest in, would therefore be a subtle, controlling factor in, what had begun as a personal and private gesture" (102). As she heads out of Alice Springs, Davidson gives herself over to Rick Smolan, the *National Geographic* photographer assigned to "track" her journey. He meets her at prearranged locations, snaps photos for the magazine, and leaves (and, by the way, becomes her temporary lover). Her "progress" is thereby charted and authenticated through the evidence provided by the camera. "Click, observer. Click, observed," she writes (112). With ironic discontent the narrator acknowledges how heroic journeys become commodified as exotica. Beholden to *National Geographic*, she cannot be sure whose journey she's taking. Nor can she control public representations of her journey.

Smolan's camera is not the only camera snapping pictures of her as she traverses the desert. As news of her journey spreads, increasing numbers of tourists and journalists begin to "track" her progress relentlessly. Davidson presents these tourists as invaders from the world of motorized postmodernity, which she identifies with boredom, ennui, purposelessness, and degraded femininity. Comfortable in their outback vehicles, they come to record the work of real traveling. Even as her close-to-the-ground trek serves as an individualizing journey through which she differentiates herself from these prosaic tourists and opportunistic journalists, these same tourists and journalists aim their cameras at the camel lady and thus reproduce images of the "exotic" white woman crossing the terrain of the "black" outback. In this way, they turn her into an instant celebrity, a spectacle of mythic womanhood whose story, as she recognizes, joins four salient ingredients: "woman, desert, camels, aloneness" (237). An uncanny traveler in the desert, the camel lady becomes a tourist attraction, a marked site of individualist journeying.

At the conclusion of her narrative, which focuses on her return to "civilization" after her arrival at Hamlin Pool on "the far side" of Australia, Davidson explores how she comes out from the desert into the limelight of the media spectacle that celebrates her as a phantasmic camel lady:

> I was now public property. I was now a feminist symbol. I was now an object of ridicule for small-minded sexists, and I was a crazy, irresponsible adventurer. . . . But worse than all that, I was now a mythical being who had done something courageous and outside the possibilities that ordinary people could hope for. And that was the antithesis of what I wanted to share. That anyone could do anything. If I could bumble my way across a desert, then anyone could do anything. And that was true especially for women, who have used cowardice for so long to protect themselves that it has become a habit. (237–38)

This late-twentieth-century traveler-narrator comes to understand that, in the age of global communications, stories of eccentric travelers circulate as the fact occurs, not after the fact; and that, in the age of global tourism, the old kind of traveler-adventurer can easily be remade as a sacralized site of touristic fascination. Paradoxically, "the camel lady" herself becomes a material site of premodernity at postmodernity's edge. The effect of this mythification of the premodern, the woman-adventurer who is visibly liminal, is that the achievement of her journeying is disconnected from the everyday life of ordinary people.

The reduction of Davidson's journeying to the scenario of exceptionalist individualism is an effect of the publicity surrounding her journey. Through the photographic gaze of *National Geographic* photographer, tourists, and journalists, her project is stripped of its historical, social, political, and personally transformative dimensions. But *Tracks*, the narrative of that journey by foot, becomes another matter altogether. As much a metanarrative about journeying in an age of tourism as it is a narrative of "going primitive" in the Australian bush, *Tracks* becomes the means through which Davidson can rescue her memory from the media myth by insisting on the everydayness of journeying rather than its exceptionalism, by attending to the transformation of her identity from cowardly woman to un-becoming woman, and by putting the historical narrative of black-white contact back into the story by means of the gaze of Aboriginal Australians. If the tourist's camera and the lens of the *National Geographic* photographer have made her into a spectacle, Davidson uses her narrative of the journey to take back her identity from the representations of the camel lady as exceptional woman and to frame her journey on her own terms.

To demystify herself as exceptional adventurer, Davidson dedicates the first half of *Tracks* to the wholly unspectacular drudgery of preparation for her journey and to the dynamic struggles to master the skills she needs to succeed and to summon the courage requisite to setting off. She describes how she adjusts to the hostile environment of Alice Springs, finds mentors to teach her how to muster camels, and gains the requisite physical conditioning for the long trek across the desert. Refusing to erase from her narrative the labor involved in journeying, Davidson foregrounds the often tedious preparation of the body for endurance, stamina, and resilience, and the mind for the technological mastery of camels, preparations that would make her journey possible. Critically, she foregrounds the labor of becoming another kind of woman, one who can negotiate "this no-woman's-land of tools, machinery and so on" (94).

Davidson finds herself negotiating the gendered politics of journeying long before she heads off across the Red Centre. In the crucible of Alice Springs, "where men are men and women are an afterthought" (20), Davidson learns to fight against the forces that would make a woman give up and give in, including psychological weaknesses deeply internalized. "I hated myself for my infernal cowardice in dealing with people," she recalls as she describes her relationship with the often violent Kurt, on whose ranch she works gratis in exchange for his (undelivered) promise of camels. "It is such a female syndrome, so much the weakness of animals who have always been prey" (30). To become "a changed woman," she develops strategies for responding to "brute force and domination" (73): "I was also aggressively ready to pounce on anyone who looked like they might be going to give me a hard time" (48).

To survive as a "woman of the bush," Davidson develops a "range war mentality" and forges the "bad girl" identity of the rugged individualist evacuated of normative femininity. No longer "sweet, pliable, forgiving, compassionate and door-mattish" (48), Davidson represents herself as ready for her journey. Through hard labor and physical stamina, the urban woman escapes the constitutive mediocrity of the feminized subject, to paraphrase Bongie's phrase, a subject the narrator identifies with vulnerable animals.

Crucially, Davidson entwines discourses of masculinist Australian national identity, including the discourse of mateship and the rugged individualism of the Aussie battler, with the discourse of feminist transformation. As she considers the nature and effect of her "badness," she offers this analysis of bush mateship:

> I was surrounded by people who for some reason found my very presence a threat. And had I not been able to stand up to them on their terms, I would be somewhere back on the east coast, my tail between my legs. But it was more than that. For many outback people, the effect of almost total isolation coupled with that all-encompassing battle with the earth is so great that, when the prizes are won, they feel the need to build a psychological fortress around the knowledge and possessions they have broken their backs to obtain. That fiercely independent individualism was something akin to what I was feeling now—the stiffness, the inability to incorporate new people who hadn't shared the same experience. I understood a facet of Alice Springs, and softened towards it, at that moment. (80–81)

Having arrived in tough Alice Springs from urban Australia, Davidson learns to develop a "bush mentality" and to acknowledge the mateship that emerges among those who have struggled against the intractable Red Centre, even as she critiques the sexism and racism that are so central a part of that ethos (48). She adapts for her own purposes the masculinist logic of the bush and thereby un-becomes feminized woman.

In the second half of *Tracks*, Davidson describes the initiatory phase of desert traveling, which she calls "shedding burdens," and then the long journey through the desert. For Davidson, the structure of her journey-ing—preparation, shedding burdens, long journeying, arrival—captures the psychological structure that is characteristic of any attempt to go forward through radical change. As she sets out, she describes herself as leaving behind "the last burning bridge back to my old self" (115), which she associates with feminine passivity, boredom, weakness, and insecurity. She presents her journeying, then, as a voyage toward a new concept of self as much as it is a journey into and through the bush of Australia. Critically, this story of transformative journeying is the narrative of black-white contact, as Davidson seeks some kind of at-oneness with the indigenous people of Australia and some kind of atonement for the bru-tal history of conquest, colonialism, and persistent racism.

On one level, Davidson's is an ur-story of the westerner who treks across inhospitable land, dependent upon her own resourcefulness for survival and eventual success. In this sense, Davidson becomes a con-ventional adventurer-hero who meets the defining test of endurance, the travail of travel in its premodern sense. Yet even as she adopts the con-ventions of heroic travel, Davidson adapts the conventions to her partic-ular purpose. As she claims a place for women in the misogynist and inhospitable bush of Australia, her literal and narrative feat is to present the adventurer-traveler with a difference. "He" is a woman, but a woman who has become what she is not naturally understood to be. As she treks through the desert, her body is redefined away from urbanized white femininity to hard, durable, unfeminine muscle: "I felt like a cast-iron amazon" (123). She describes with relish how she walks naked through the outback, hair matted, menstrual blood oozing irregularly down her legs. She thereby represents herself in the outback as "wild" woman, the woman of muscle, unclothed, unconstrained, undomesticated. This is the distinguishing difference between woman as adventurer-traveler and man as adventurer-traveler. He becomes even more what he is naturally understood to be. She un-becomes the feminized woman trapped in her reliance upon the rituals, spectacles, and degraded embodiment of nor-mative femininity. She becomes other to herself.

Within the larger narrative frame of the adventure story, Davidson incorporates the romantic trope of descent into psychological isolation, chaos, and dissolution followed by transformation, reintegration, and arrival at a new sense of self. During the first weeks, she writes, "I was exactly the same person that I was when I began" (136). Yet she gradually recognizes that the trip "was changing me in a way that I had not in the least expected. It was shaking me up and I had not even noticed" (141). For one thing, she discovers the otherness, or what she calls the "Kurtishness" (after her violent mentor), within: "I had been out of control when I beat [one of the camels] and began to recognize a certain Kurtishness in my behaviors. This weakness, my inability to be terrified with any dignity, came to the forefront often during the trip, and my animals took the brunt of it" (132). Moreover, the early stage of her journey brings immersion in the desperate isolation that trekking with camels enforces—the total concentration on survival and the practical details of daily routine (loading camels, following maps and tracks, unloading, gathering wood, cooking, sleeping, and attending throughout the night to the safety of the camels). Eventually she experiences what she describes, after the fact, as a "mental collapse, though I would not have described it in such a way then" (149).

This mental collapse Davidson associates with the recognition of her positioning in the gaze of Aboriginal people whom she meets. Leaving the town of Docker, some Aboriginal people ask her for money, thus registering her position as a "whitefella tourist on the outside looking in" (153). In their gaze Davidson recognizes the futility of her original goal of making contact with Australia's indigenous people (150). Then too, she finds herself killing wild camels, the very animals through which she seeks to make contact with the Aboriginal people. Camels, she writes, were to her "a key in relating to Pitjantjara people" (129), because the Pitjantjara had used camels for transport across the desert until cars replaced them in the 1960s. Thus, "the journey had lost all meaning, lost all its magical inspiriting quality, was an empty and foolish gesture" (154). Meaningful contact, outside the context of touristic contact, seems impossible. In the tropes of Western journeying, this moment of total chaos is her "dark night of the soul": "I woke into limbo and could not find myself. There were no reference points, nothing to keep the world con-trolled and bound together. There was nothing but chaos and the voices" (158). The multiple voices emanating from within—one strong and hate-ful, one calm, one screaming—signal the chaos attendant upon the disso-lution of any stable identity.

Davidson describes how, in the midst of this chaos of her dark night, she emerges from the endless dunes (a geographic space of erasure) and comes upon a herd of passive camels. At the same moment she hears the sound of a car, which is driven by Aboriginal people. One of them, Eddie, chooses to go "walkabout" with her. With contact established, the next stage of her journey commences. If the dark night of the soul followed her positioning as tourist in the gaze of Aboriginal people, her epiphanic transformation comes with her positioning in kinship with Eddie and with the Pitjantjara people, inhabitants of traditional Aborig-inal lands.

Obviously, then, Davidson's narrative of her journey across the desert is a narrative of exchanges in the contact zone. The white Aus-tralian woman projects Aboriginal people, terrain, and consciousness as the "premodern" difference and belatedness resident within the nation-state. Far distant from metropolitan centers teeming with people of modernity, and not yet fully marked by the rampant and rampaging signs of progress, "black" Australia beckons with its promise of transforma-tive redemption from the life of degraded modernity and degraded fem-ininity. Thus, her sojourn with Eddie she represents as a coming to knowledge about the desert itself, about Aboriginal people, and about Aboriginal history. Traversing the land for two weeks with Eddie as her Aboriginal guide, Davidson learns how to see differently, to see as if she is looking through Eddie's eyes: "I don't think I have ever felt so good in my entire life. He made me notice things I had not noticed before—noises, tracks. And I began to see how it all fitted together. The land was not wild but tame, bountiful, benign, giving, as long as you knew how to see it, how to be part of it" (178–79).

The new consciousness Davidson describes achieving in her walk-about with Eddie shifts her relationship to time, space, and self. In her memory, this time of traveling remains a "blur," time "undifferentiated" rather than time linear, time Aboriginal rather than time Western. For she no longer measures the day to register the progress of her journey. Gesturing toward this alternative notion of time, she chucks her clock. Just as her linear itinerary dissipates, so too does her adversarial relationship to space. Davidson learns to reject the representation of the desert as hostile, inhospitable space and to reframe it as sustaining domestic space. The environment becomes "an animate being" encircling her, a premodern space outside the grip of motorized modernity: "It will not be long ... before the land is conquered, fenced up and beaten into submission. But here, here it was free, unspoilt and seemingly indestructible" (194).

In this time and space of freedom, the boundaries of individual selfhood dissolve: "I too became lost in the net and the boundaries of myself stretched out for ever" (195). With this new reality (196), the self "becomes limitless" (197), no longer "an entity living somewhere inside the skull" (196) that is bolstered by habit. Thus, Davidson understands the new consciousness she achieves in the desert as the triumph of the fluid over the solid, a letting go of the encrustations of the mind, "a giant cleansing of all the garbage and muck that had accumulated in my brain, a gentle catharsis" (190). When she catalogs what knowledge she has gained in the desert, she foregrounds the unlearning of the habitual, that is, the comfortable, secure, contained routines of everyday life that, even as they keep chaos at bay, intensify the daily fragmentation of life in the modern metropolis. She thus comes to understand the habitual as the antithesis of freedom.

Like Eberhardt and David-Neel earlier in the century, then, Davidson "goes primitive," both in the sense that she traverses the terrain of the Red Centre of Australia as an indigenous person living a traditional lifestyle might and in the sense that she seeks access to an "Aboriginal" way of life. She learns to read the signs of nature, pursues an ethics of care for animals that attachment to the land instills, rejects the straitjacket of Western social conventions, responds to a new notion of time, and hardens her body through endurance. With her "native" guide as companion, (a common trope of narratives of exotic escape and one we noted in

David-Neel's narrative of impersonation), this white woman experiences herself as other to her everyday Australian self. Traveling close to the ground, Davidson escapes the constitutive constraints of normative femininity by un-becoming white woman and becoming like an indigenous Australian.

Davidson participates in certain historical practices through which white westerners have constituted "Aboriginality" as radical difference, a radical difference whose curative powers can deliver an enervated westerner to a "truer," more satisfying experience of self. Granted, she does not reiterate the discourses of degraded humanity through which white Australians represent the indigenous people with whom they come into contact.[22] On the contrary, her representation of "Aboriginality" harkens back to certain anthropological discourses that romanticized Aboriginal people as "primitive," outside and therefore less corrupted by the processes of modernization. Represented as more directly related to the land, animals and plants, and the spirit world, they were imagined as conducting a more "authentic" way of life that promised curative powers for the westerner enervated by the comforts, habits, and vacuities of modern life. Yet this romantic discourse, like the discourse of degraded Aboriginality, fixes indigenous Australians in a premodern state of essentialized, ahistorical difference. And it reproduces a notion of Aboriginality that serves the personal, social, and political purposes of white Australians.

Despite the ways in which her narrative tropes reproduce certain of the essentializing discourses of Aboriginality, however, Davidson does present a cultural narrative that has social as well as personal salience; for she seeks to do important cultural work through her narrative, the cultural work of reconciliation. She refuses to erase the history of the land she traverses to create a national narrative of heroic Aussie endurance. Thus, throughout the narrative, she interweaves the history of white-Aboriginal relationships during 160 years of colonial occupation, including the contemporary manifestations and legacies of racism and of discrimination and internalized self-denigration (58–61) and the history of Aboriginal reserves (127). In the third section of the book, she incorporates an extended discussion of her understanding of Aboriginal

Dreaming, history, traditions, and, by implication, consciousness (170), acknowledging in the midst of her attempt at "translation" that "apart from the fact that I am no authority on the subject, trying to describe Aboriginal cosmology briefly is like trying to explain quantum mechanics in five seconds" (172). She is duly self-reflexive about her position as a white Australian eager to incorporate in her narrative the history of white Australian colonization of black Australia. In fact, it is this self-reflexiveness about the impossibilities of a white woman's "going primitive" in the Australian bush in the late twentieth century that distinguishes Davidson's invocation of conventional tropes of exotic journeying and her reiteration of white Australia's romantic discourse of Aboriginality.

It is this ironic self-scrutiny, and what Patrick Holland and Graham Huggan note as "her uneasiness with the genre" of travel writing (123), with which Davidson closes her narrative. In the final pages, the narrator draws back from identification with the subject of her narration, the Robyn Davidson of the journey, and casts her gaze upon herself. In hindsight she becomes a "poor fool" who "really believed all that crap" about feeling as free at the edge of the sea as in the desert. She presents herself as having become a figure of her own media myth even as she recalls with ironic distance her discomfort with "the new adventuress's identity kit" (253). In this hardheaded finale to the narrative, Davidson recapitulates the ironic distance she evinces elsewhere in the narrative, for instance, when she admits her complicity in the commodification of her journey: "I did not perceive at that time that I was allowing myself to get more involved with an article about the trip than the trip itself. It did not dawn on me that already I was beginning to see it as a story for other people, with a beginning and an ending" (144–45). Through an antinostalgic rhetoric, Davidson refuses the individualizing logic of the heroic journey: "I knew even then that, instead of remembering the truth of it, I would lapse into a useless nostalgia" (254). She redefines any challenge to comfortable habit as a "camel trip." In the end, "camel trips, as I suspected all along, and as I was about to have confirmed, do not begin or end, they merely change form" (254). And the next form of the camel trip is the difficulty of remembering the trip itself outside the poetics of nostalgia.

## Conclusion: Getting Away from It All

These three white women seek through their traveling close to the ground a respite from the constitutive constraints of a degraded femininity. Released into the vast exteriority of a different landscape, they seek a new interiority of agency forged through the arduous process of cross-cultural identification. Requisite to this interiorization of agency is the identification with subjects of radical difference—Algerian nomads, Tibetan peasants, indigenous Australians—subjects assigned an intimate connection with space rather than time (history), subjects imagined as living out more "pure" or "true" or "heroic" or "meaningful" lives than the masses of people ensnared in an enervated modernity.

Theirs is intimate journeying, close to the ground, close to the culture. Eberhardt, David-Neel, and Davidson all assume the habits and dress of the peoples indigenous to the space of radical difference. Comingling with the valorized other, they comingle in themselves qualities and attributes and beliefs and physical capacities that they find noble in the other and enabling in themselves. They also become embodied in new ways. Embracing the travail of travel and leaving the comforts of "civilization" far behind, these travelers find new ways of being in their bodies. David-Neel finds a resilient, durable body. As Davidson's body shapes itself into durable bone and sinew, she grows muscles on her shit. Eberhardt finds in North Africa an eroticized body, one released from the bourgeois constraints of vapid heterosexual relations. Through these embodiments all three enact plots of profound transformation.

These narratives of journeys close to the ground chronicle what their narrators take to be the ethics of transformation. Eberhardt chronicles the endless quest for a truer self; David-Neel chronicles the clever manipulation of disguise, the magnitude of the feat, and the sheer competence of her scholarship; Davidson chronicles training, breakdown, and recovery. Through these narratives, all register what they take to be the benefit of impersonation: that in becoming like the other they become other to the everyday version of femininity at home.

Yet all three of these travelers are belated travelers. They cannot become other, because becoming other is paradoxically becoming more like the subject of modernity. Think, for instance, of Eberhardt in the North African desert. However fierce her desire to separate herself from the bourgeois modernity of Europe, Eberhardt carried its ideology of romantic selfhood with her into the desert. It rode her as fast as she rode her horse across the sands. It grounded her even as she sought to ground herself intimately in the everyday life of the Maghreb through her language, dress, habits, and religious practices. In leaving Europe for the North African desert, Eberhardt participated in a defining Western practice. Thus, her journal celebrates not the way she assimilates into the populace but the way in which she stands out from the populace in her radical individualism. Nor does it celebrate the way her subjectivity becomes another kind of subjectivity through what Françoise Lionnet has called transculturation. It reveals, rather, the degree to which cross-cultural mobility sets her apart. She presents herself in her profound particularity, a profound particularity that, she argues, is recognized by those very "natives" among whom she travels and with whom she converses. In promoting an aesthetics of renewable self-consciousness, Eberhardt's journal fashions an "artist"—a "male" artist—in exile and thus promotes what Lillian Robinson argues is "a fundamental precept of bourgeois aesthetics": "Good art ... is art that celebrates what is unique and even eccentric in human experience or human personality. Individual achievement and subjective isolation are the norm, whether the achievement and the isolation be that of the artist or the character" (226).

Eberhardt is forever seeking and never finding the authentic experience or the authentic self promised her in the dream of fin de siècle exoticism. She can find no place of comfort, no community of kindred souls, no alternative cultural affiliation, for she can never get to any home with "nomads" who have escaped the history of European colonialism. And she can never get to any "other" in herself that is not permeated by the European identity she seeks to shed. There is no place of origin outside the history of European relationships with North Africa, colonial relationships in which Eberhardt herself plays her part. There is no going home precisely because there is no going primitive possible at the beginning of the twentieth century. There is only writing about what has already been written and written over.

Or think of David-Neel writing of her arduous journey across the Himalayan mountains to the sacred city of Lhasa some twenty years later. For her, as for Eberhardt, the space of transformation is an exotic, dangerous, mysterious, pastoralized space of primeval legend. Her journey by foot to the capital of Tibet is thus a journey back into an imagined past uncontaminated by modernization. Her narrative reveals how getting to know the Tibetans at such close range is generative, for her, of an empowered female identity far from the metropolitan center of an exhausted and spiritually bankrupt modernity. At the edges, this traveler finds the grounds of distinction as a scholar.

But the narrative also registers the grounds of that empowerment as the subjectivity made possible by the very modernity David-Neel would escape. In resisting her own positioning in debilitating spectacles of femininity in the West, the woman scholar depends upon orientalist knowledge and privileges the universal subject who produces that knowledge. Invoking the Bible, David-Neel establishes her claim to inalienable rights of passage across the entire globe (xxv), rights that supersede the authority of any nation or empire to establish impenetrable borders. But, of course, her claim is the claim of a specific subject—a Western subject who assumes that "he" should have access to any land. David-Neel presents herself as a universal subject of travel, challenging through her journey the closure of borders to any subject and celebrating the "freedom" of the "individual" to travel the earth in quest of knowledge.[23] Tacitly acknowledging the constitutive masculinity (objectivity) of the scholar-traveler, this woman assumes the universal subject position as her own, emboldened to do so by the very scholarly credentials that authorize her to construct Tibet in all its belatedness. In turn, through her production of the "real" Tibet in the travel narrative, David-Neel attempts to secure her cultural authority as a respected orientalist scholar in Europe.

At the end of the twentieth century, Davidson, a foot traveler who seeks freedom from the constitutive constraints of postmodernity, comes to critique the myth of freedom on the road. If she remembers moments of feeling free of the constraints of gender, class, and social practices, figuratively stripped down to the muscle of self just as she is literally stripped down to the bare flesh during her trek, she also emphasizes how, even in the desert, constraints surrounded her—the constraints of her involvement with *National Geographic*, of her sexual involvement with Smolan, and of her frustrating encounters with tourists and journalists. She goes to the desert only to encounter agents of postmodernity: tourists, photographers, and journalists. Turned into a tourist attraction, she knows only too well how the journey can be remade by others for their own purposes.

Davidson reflexively provides a strategic reading of such pseudo journeying by challenging the visual evidence of the trip that was produced in such places as *National Geographic*. At a point during her trek, Smolan photographed Eddie, Davidson's Aboriginal guide. The photo, which she includes in her book, appears to show "a woman smiling at an old Aboriginal man, whose hand was raised in a cheery salute." But Davidson reinterprets Eddie's gesture in light of her knowledge of his resistance to being photographed. The gesture of raising his hand, she counters, is a gesture warning Smolan off from taking his picture. "So much for the discerning eye of the camera," Davidson cautions. "That one slide speaks volumes. Or rather lies volumes. Whenever I look at it now, it sums up all the images of the journey. Brilliant images, exciting, excellent, but little to do with reality. While I love the photos Rick [Smolan] took, they are essentially of his trip, not my own" (190). In this plaintive resistance to the fixing of the journey close to the ground, Davidson registers the lesson learned on foot, that she cannot escape the touristic recuperation of the experience of "premodern" travel. She's had her contact, but she leaves her reader with the demystifying redefinition of the camel trip as merely metaphor.

There is a postnarrative turn of events to the publication of *Tracks* that reminds us how journeys by foot to the edges of modernization's scope can be reproduced endlessly in this postmodern age and how the narratives that we use to insist on our own meanings to our journeys can be overwritten by media representations of those journeys. With

Davidson, Rick Smolan, the *National Geographic* photographer, turned Davidson's journey into a CD-ROM entitled *From Alice to Ocean*. Available on-line, it is described in various write-ups as "one of the most stunning and creative multimedia publishing achievements ever." Ironically, through the advances of postmodern technologies, this late-twentieth-century journey into premodernity has gone digital. Now your fingers can do all the walking, taking travel to the digits. Virtual journeying substitutes digitized images for the real work of travel. In the end, there's no necessary relationship at all between the woman traveling, the space traversed, and the identity earned.

# CHAPTER 3

# In the Air: Aerial Gender
# and the Familiarity of Flight

This new sport is comparable to no other. It is, in my opinion, one
of the most intoxicating forms of sport, and will, I am sure, become
one of the most popular. Many of us will perish before then, but
that prospect will not dismay the braver spirits. In devoting
themselves to the new cause, those who have the true aviator's soul
will find in their struggle with the atmosphere a rich compensation
for the risks they run. It is so delicious to fly like a bird.

—Marie Marvingt, "The Intoxication of Flight,"
*Colliers*, September 30, 1911

By the close of the nineteenth century, the secular myth of evolutionary
progress had displaced the sacred myth of Christian teleology as the
popular narrative of humankind's destiny. Powerful technologies became
the engines of transformation, transcendence, and perfection: the steam
engines, the gigantic turbines, and the dynamos Henry Adams eloquently,
if ironically, heralds in his *Education of Henry Adams*. Driven by electric-
ity or by steam, these engines of progress whirred away, their pistons
thrusting up and down, their capacity for the production of energy seemingly inexhaustible. Across the landscape, that remarkable progress was
registered graphically by the locomotive, which chugged tenaciously and
dependably along its miles of steel rails, sounding the rhythms of inex-
orable industrialization and national and imperial spread.

Yet at the end of the nineteenth century, technologies of motion—
the locomotive, the automobile, and the bicycle—remained earthbound,
terrestrial technologies. With its inelegance and routine obedience, the
locomotive had become a somewhat prosaic, autochthonous beast. Certainly there was still the excitement of acceleration, the brute power

of persistent motion, the promise of speed, and the terror of accident; but there was no takeoff, no ascent. Technologies of motion remained earthbound.

All that changed with Kitty Hawk. At Kitty Hawk the Wright brothers lifted their heavier-than-air flying machine off the ground and held it suspended in air for a few fleet seconds. In trial flights and subsequent demonstration events in Paris, the airplane and its pilot seemed to lift every spectator into another register of being. Dreams of flight that had preoccupied human beings for centuries, informing their myths, their imaginations, their science of observation, and their mechanical inventions, materialized in midair. Spectators, reporters, and pilots themselves proclaimed the end of the old order and the dawn of the new, one in which humans would defy the laws of gravity to conquer even the skies.

"As a semimagical instrument of ascent," suggests Lawrence Goldstein, "the flying machine offered to its apostles a form of *transport* in both familiar senses of that word. It provided a mobile and beatific vision of a new heaven and a new earth" (5–6). The radical disruption of gravitational pull evidenced in the ascent of the new machine signaled a radical rupture with the degenerate and constraining ground of the past and the inauguration of a new dispensation. Human beings were no longer earthbound; they were now heaven bound. The modern century had taken off in a vehicle assembled out of nuts, bolts, cloth, sheet metal, and rubber tires.

Kitty Hawk and successive flights in the early decades of the twentieth century captured the imaginations of people on both sides of the Atlantic Ocean. Hundreds of thousands of people flocked to air races, where they accorded the new aviators overnight celebrity, lavishing them with money and homage for their daring aerial exploits. Wright and Wright, Blériot, Santos-Dumont, Farman, Latham, Lefevre, Chávez, Conneau; and the aces, Garros, Boelcke, Immelmann, Richthofen, Guynemer, Baracca—these were celebrity names in the early decades of aviation. Later, of course, there would be Lindbergh. Flight delivered the pilot from the clutches of chthonic groundedness, a groundedness that was historical and cultural as well as material. Thus, the aviator became a new type of hero—thoroughly modern and modernist man.

In the early reports of Orville Wright's 1909 exhibition flight in Paris, the typology of the air pilot with Wright as progenitor was fixed through such defining characteristics as self-reliance, loneliness, stoic spirituality, dedication, and indifference to the masses on the ground (Wohl 27). This myth of exceptionalist individuality stretched the distance between the hero and the common grounded mortal caught in the net of bourgeois respectability or industrial dehumanization. Flight secured the metaphorical elevation of the new hero over the masses, whose aspirations to escape the earth he carried with him into the heavens. His was mythical transport.

The aviator's escape was represented as a gendered trajectory in which the new hero shed his complacent attachment to the enervating past and rose toward a revolutionary future (Wohl 268). Modernist poets and intellectuals, such as the futurist poet F. T. Marinetti, fervently embraced this renewed masculinization of the skies through aerial ascent from Mother Earth. Dedicating his 1909 play, *Poupées électriques* (Electric puppets) to Orville Wright, Marinetti described the aviator as a man "who knew how to raise our migrating hearts higher than the captivating mouths of women" (36). Groundedness Marinetti identified with the moist, warm, malleable, seductive, devouring, and emasculating orifices of women. Mother Earth and her female minions kept men too attached to the ground, to the baser realm of instinct and desire. Wright would take them up and away from such terrestrial snares, delivering them to a purified, lighter-than-air masculinity. Soaring heavenward, the aviator evaded the groundedness identified with umbilical cords and an intolerable sessility. Then too, soaring heavenward, he transcended the sexual anarchy on the ground, a product of the crisis in gender identity that was so pervasive in the first decades of the twentieth century (Pykett 19). The aviator-hero was one potent answer to the crisis of masculinity below.

Aviator and machine were at one, soaring high above those on the ground in a dazzling display of aerial virility. Defying the laws of gravity and embracing the risk of the modern, the early aviators and air aces flirted with death with every ascent, a flirtation that became the value added to the adventure of flight, the risky cost of escape from enervating sessility. Celebrating the élan and ethos of the aviator, the poet Gabriele D'Annunzio announced that "danger seemed the axis of the sublime life" (68). This same D'Annunzio climbed into the cockpit during an air race in Italy in order to experience flight firsthand, thereby aligning himself with the "celestial helmsman" who triumphed over nature, space, and time. D'Annunzio's was a fervidly masculinist ethos. But his futurist ethos was a product of the general ethos of the time. In Vienna, Sigmund Freud pondered the symbolic identification of flying machines with the penis, noting "the remarkable characteristic of the male organ which enables it to rise up in defiance of the laws of gravity" (qtd. in Beer 265).

The new hero achieved his transcendence as he mastered "the cold, inhuman machines that the nineteenth century had bequeathed" and "transform[ed] them into resplendent art and myth" (Wohl 29). Unlike the machines that displaced man, controlled him, and dwarfed him, airplanes enhanced the reach of his mastery. A prosthetic extension of the male form, the airplane functioned as a symbolic object through which masculinity could be restored. Here was technological, rational, thoroughly modern masculinity for an age awed by new technologies yet concerned about the ways in which those technologies contributed to the disciplining of individuals and the emasculation of men through systems of mass production. Magnified by mechanical form rather than diminished by it, men could be men rather than the "cautious, timid, and obedient workers" Michael S. Kimmel describes as the efficient products of those systems (16). During the First World War, the aces "exemplified more purely than any other figure of their time what it meant to be a man" (Wohl 282). Alone in the sky, fighting to the death, in control of the new machine, meeting his adversary man to man, and dependent upon his own ingenuity in maneuvering his machine, the ace epitomized motorized heroic masculinity. Below him, the masses of common soldiers huddled impotently in trenches, suffering the emasculating effects of fatigue, nerves, hysteria, and shell shock during the long, intolerable wait at the lines.

In other global locations, the stunned members of the "backward" races, awestruck before the magic of new technology, gazed heavenward in fear and trembling, recognizing their own impotence before the remarkable power of aerial masculinity. Or so cartoons and posters serving the emergent airline companies implied in their representations of colonial relations (Wohl 81). The invention and increasing sophistication of the airplane in the early twentieth century, just like the invention and spread of the railway system in the nineteenth century, reaffirmed for the West the superiority of its heroes and cultural achievements. Hard-pressed to make the case for the utility of flight in the everyday lives of citizens, at least in the early decades of the century, the proponents of aviation directed attention to the promise of aviation for national and imperial spread and thus for dreams of "conquest" fulfilled in and through the air.

With its promise and delivery of a regenerative masculinity, flight rejuvenated an only-apparently-spent modernity. But aerial masculinity went further, linking technological and perceptual logics and transforming the aviator into what artists and intellectuals of the early twentieth century described as a "poet of the air." Aerial subjectivity introduced a radically new way of perceiving the world (Wohl 272). Early enthusiasts such as Marinetti celebrated "the changing perspectives of flight," which, he announced, "constitute an absolutely new reality, one that has nothing in common with the traditional reality of terrestrial perspective" ("Aeropainting" 295).

In flight, as earlier in railway travel, the aviator discovered speed without rootedness. Buoyant with speed, the airborne subject experienced the rush of lifting into (an illusory) immateriality. With ascent, the scope of space and distance that the eye could take in expanded exponentially. Incarcerated in a flying eye socket, severed from connections to things earthly, the aviator became a focalizing point of panoramic vision, producing for himself an order that took in vast space, an order from above rather than an order from eye level. No longer a sojourner in proximate space, he produced for himself as well a perception independent of local roots and cultural contingency. Details of changing vistas melted away, because distance made the ground and objects on the ground less individuated. Figures on the ground shrank until they vanished into insignificance. Whole villages and single buildings, mountains and fields all diminished in size until they compressed into two-dimensionality. Far below, the world appeared as a vast project of still fixedness. Increased distance between the aerial subject and the ground flattened out the world outside. A panoramic, abstracted, impersonal reality became the new reality of flight.[1]

Embracing a durable, if temporary, isolation, an individualism *à l'air*, the aerial subject could imagine himself an omniscient subject, mastering space from above and rescuing distance from time and time from distance. The early aviators embraced flight for the kind of subjectivity it delivered to them. Enveloped in their cockpits, (an interiority nested inside a mechanical interiority), they looked down and pondered the dynamic relationship of ground to flight. They maneuvered through this space between ground and "I" by means of the mechanical prosthesis that was the plane itself, an extension of the body but not the body. The aviator thus became an early avatar of what Donna Haraway calls the cyborg subject, part human, part machine—a new kind of perceiving subject.

**Aviator Narratives**

To reproduce the myth-history of the aviator as new man, there had to be narratives by the aviators, as well as poems, paintings, newspaper accounts, and promotional materials produced by the emergent aviation industry. Aviators themselves recognized the profitability—in both monetary and celebrity terms—of writing about their experiences as air pilots. And so, by 1920 a new genre of aviation narrative had taken shape with its own conventions: dramatic stories of life-threatening incidents, commentaries on the land and people passed over, autobiographical information in the context of the flight, a record of emotional responses in flight, and a description of the reception upon landing (Wohl 271). As the aviators produced narratives through which they could secure their celebrity and could profit from their status as new men, the narratives themselves produced the aviator as a certain kind of myth-hero.

Aviator narratives immediately became popular in the emerging film industry. In fact, the technologies of aviation and of the motion picture were contemporaneous developments, and they soon became mutually informing technologies. The history of aviation films begins in 1912 with Elvira Notari's Italian movie *The Heroism of an Aviator in Tripoli*. Soon after came the French film *Marriage by Aeroplane* in January 1914; *An Aerial Revenge* (1915); *Dizzy Heights and Daring Hearts* (1915); and *The Great Air Robbery* (1919) (Pendo 2). In many of these early films the thrill and suspense of the filmic narrative centered on the dangers faced by the aviators, which was the central focus of the written aviator narratives themselves. Yet joined to this plot of danger was a romance plot, integral to the narrative of homecoming. The returning aviator was rewarded for his heroism with a very grounded and grateful woman (Wohl 278). The romance plot of the early aviator films positioned women visually where they were understood to be—firmly on the ground, in sessile repose and anticipation. If they were involved in any kind of ascent, it was the ascending arc of their heads as they directed their gaze toward the sky. Raising their eyes heavenward, they watched passively with awe and anxiety the fate of the intrepid man in his prosthetic machine.

The conventions of normative femininity grounded woman, for she was identified with a femininity tethered to embodiment. The aviator Jean Conneau articulated the relationship of woman to aerial flight when he claimed that "aviation is for adults, alert, vigorous, of robust health, and capable of resisting fatigue. Such organic qualities are rarely found in women, and it's really a pity" (135–36). Women might be identified as "birds"—recall Torvald's appellation of ideal wife Nora in Ibsen's *A Doll's House*—but they were not expected to fly like a bird, at least not of their own volition, their own technical skill, their own daring. The sky was male territory and its conquest a male prerogative. To enter the cockpit of the airplane required the aviator to be technically skilled, quick to understand and to identify with and through the machine, courageous, death-defying, and dogged.

Aviator narratives and films and popular discourses of aviation projected the sky as an imaginary domain uninhabited by women and thus far removed from the crises in gender identity roiling down below. On the ground, female sexuality had been released as a threat, as had the possibility of female enfranchisement. In the release into risk that accompanied ascent, the aviator seemed to rend the umbilical cord tying him to sexual disorder and degenerate masculinity (Kimmel 16). He promised a return to an earlier period before the crisis in masculinity when, according to Kimmel, manly virility was synonymous with the character projected from deep within the rugged and isolated individual (15). His was the virile integrity of danger and distance from the masses swarming as so many ants far below. Yet he was indisputably and reassuringly modern, as his was sure mastery of the powerful engines of modernity.

## Women of the Air

Like all such imaginary territories of identity, the sky proved to be about as unstable a domain of modernist masculinity as the ground below, for the gendered terms of social relations on the ground were contradictory and fiercely contested. Thus, although women may have been unwanted as compatriots in the "conquest of the air" and although they may have found it difficult to find men willing to give them flying lessons or to work with them on fashioning their machines, they became aviators. The increasing influence of motorized modernity created desires in women for speed and distance. In a time of purposeful, if cacophonous and competing, feminisms, women quickly realized the value of technical expertise. They forged their own relationships to the new technology. They imagined themselves as well leaving the earth below. "It is so delicious to fly like a bird," enthuses Marie Marvingt in 1911, just months after Orville Wright stunned the other developers of flying machines in Paris. Women claimed the exhilarations of flight that male aviators claimed: the sense of freedom, the mastery of the machine, the escape from sessility, the danger, and the pleasures of a new vision accessible to the chosen few (Wohl 256–57). They too became agents of aerial modernity.

Raymonde de Laroche, Marie Marvingt, Harriet Quimby, Eugenie Shakovskaya, and later Mathilde Moisant, Ruth Law, Bessie Coleman, Katherine Stinson, Marjorie Stinson, Amelia Earhart, and Anne Morrow Lindbergh—women found ways to get lessons, even if they had to disguise themselves as men to do so.[2] Raymonde de Laroche, in 1910 in France, was the first woman to earn a license. Harriet Quimby earned the distinction of being the first American woman to earn her pilot's license, on August 1, 1911 (Holden 56). Even the African American Bessie Coleman found a way to get the training she needed to do stunt flying, although she had to go to France because no schools were open to African Americans in the States. Despite these obstacles, in 1921 Coleman became the first woman to earn an international pilot's license. Although commercial aviation was closed to women, women in the years 1910–1929 found jobs as stunt pilots. They found ways to buy their own machines. They found records to break, such as the new long-distance record Ruth Law set in 1916. They found sponsors for their attempts to break records. And they found ways to distinguish their new identities through dress. In the air, these women became avatars of the modern woman, comfortable with powerful and dangerous machinery.[3] Whatever their expressed political views, theirs was a tacit motorized feminism.

Thus, the age of aviation introduced a new spectacle of femininity. Mastery of this radical mode of mobility shifted the defining logic of identity. Flight transported the modern woman to a new imaginary domain. Here she could negotiate the constitutive constraints of normative femininity and its discontents through familiarity with modern technology, and with that familiarity she could escape, if only temporarily, from sessile femininity.

## Cultural Iconography and the Aviatrix

With the new woman of the air came cultural narratives through which the "aviatrix" was made visible as a particular type of modern woman and through which cultural anxieties about gender identity and sexual anarchy in the skies were played out. Before turning to a discussion of three aviator narratives, I want to consider briefly the narrative of the aviatrix reproduced through the popular media. She was decidedly athletic, as hers was an aerodynamic, almost weightless body, one that appeared to have severed the relationship of femininity and sessility. Free of fleshly excess, hers was a taut body designed functionally for mobility. Mannish, even boyish, the slim and active feminine body of the aviatrix signified, according to Barbara Green, "a pared-down modernism and machine-age aesthetic" (23). Hers was a glamour combining streamlined body, speed, and mechanical precision, a glamour characteristic of the late 1920s and 1930s. Thus, the aviatrix presented young girls and women with a way of imagining themselves as thoroughly modern—active, independent, competent agents proficient with technology. Her body was also, as Susan Ware emphasizes, a normatively white body, and her mien aristocratic (19). The thoroughly modern, gender-blended young woman was a woman of a certain race and class.

The conjunction of female body, machine-age aesthetic, aristocratic heroism, and cultural anxiety that inflected the popular iconography of the aviatrix is especially salient in two films of the 1930s: *Dishonored*, directed by Josef von Sternberg and starring Marlene Dietrich; and *Christopher Strong*, directed by Dorothy Arzner. It is the latter film that interests me here. Based on a novel by Gilbert Frankau, *Christopher Strong* tells the love story of the aviator Lady Cynthia Darrington and Christopher Strong, a respected and married member of Parliament. Because aviators like Lindbergh were such popular icons by the early 1930s and because women aviators in their exceptionality had achieved remarkable celebrity status, the film version of the narrative shifted the arena of Lady Darrington's exploits from car racing to aviation, thereby enhancing the film's commercial appeal. Two aviators in particular would have come to the viewer's mind: Amy Johnson in England and Amelia Earhart in the United States.

Playing Lady Cynthia Darrington was Katharine Hepburn, in her first star billing. The features of the Darrington character would become signature features of Hepburn's screen persona. A very modern young woman, Darrington is forthright, independent, athletic, resourceful, courageous, and self-controlled—all aspects of celebrity femininity in the 1920s and 1930s, when the female athlete as well as the aviator became a cultural model (think, for instance, of Babe Didrikson). From her first appearance in the film, where she races her motorcar against a motorcyclist and wins, Darrington is identified with the most advanced technologies of speed and with dangerous competition. Moreover, she is positioned as woman unattached. Preoccupied with the transcendence of flight (she has as her immediate goal breaking the high-altitude record), this modern woman seems to have escaped the shackles of what Judith Mayne, in her study of Dorothy Arzner, calls "lethal" heterosexuality (145), that coupling and consequent motherhood that would tether her to the ground of embodied femininity. The irreconcilability of her "daring" mastery of technology and her surrender to romance becomes the tension that drives the filmic narrative.

Darrington and Strong, played by Colin Clive, meet at a party to which each has been brought as the object of a treasure hunt. She is a young woman who, though over twenty-one, has never had a lover; he is a married man who has never been unfaithful to his wife. The party scene is particularly fascinating for how it visualizes Darrington's place as an aviatrix within heteronormative society. Amid the party goers Darrington appears out of place in the sense that she presents a hybrid identity, neither male nor female, among the throng of people dressed in indisputably feminine and masculine fashion. Her distinctive couture, what Kaja Silverman refers to as a "vestimentary code" (149), announces her liminality. Dressed to fly, she wears jodhpurs, a beanie, and a tailored jacket—a style, Mayne suggests, that "borrows from both masculine and feminine attire" (116). Strong exudes normative masculinity and the power attached to it—he is, after all, a member of Parliament.

As Darrington and Strong fall in love and negotiate their illicit relationship, the shift in Darrington's vestments signals the stakes in heteronormative identity. Their first intimate meeting occurs when Strong seeks Darrington out at her home to get her advice about his daughter's involvement with a married man. Dressed for a costume ball, Darrington rivets the camera's attention as object of the filmic gaze. Here we see what Laura Mulvey describes as classic cinema's projection of femininity as "to-be-looked-at-ness" (19, 25). A tight-fitting headdress closes around her head, much like the aviator's helmet. But it is no helmet. Two long and looped antennae spring delicately from the cap. A full-length gown, luscious in silk and elegantly shiny, clings to her slender, taut body. A cape surrounds her, like wings. Darrington is sleekly and shimmeringly feminine to Strong's "strong" masculinity. Her previous identification as aviator seems occluded by the way this stunning costume identifies her ironically with a fragile insect—the moth. The visual imagery and the style of her body capture proleptically the imminent identity transformation of Darrington from butch aviator to feminine and feminized paramour. The shift in vestimentary codes signals the shifting grounds of femininity of this subject of aviation. The gaze of the camera effectively contains the errant excessiveness of the speed-obsessed aviator by turning her into a spectacle for celluloid consumption.

Yet at this site of filmic modernism (even the most conventionally narrative film, as Miriam Hansen notes, announced itself in a modernist mode) a certain reflexiveness enters. The costume is obviously exaggerated (Mayne 120). The campiness of Darrington's identification as insect seems to parody the conventional narrative logic that scripts femininity as fragile and masculinity as durable. A tension emerges between narrative logic and the visual pleasure of the costume, with the effect that the excessive costume interrupts the seemingly transparent march of linear narrative. Moreover, I like to think that the film nods, via the costume, to the plane that was a very well-known small craft in the 1920s and 1930s and the one Amy Johnson flew from England to Australia in May 1930—the Moth. This extrafilmic allusion disrupts the transparency of the narrative by linking the imaginary aviator with actual aviators, thereby exceeding the control of the filmic frame and the narrative frame-up.

Strong is drawn to Darrington because of her dynamic exceptionalism and thus her exoticism as a woman of flight. She exudes sexual energy identified with and through the engine of modernity. But in securing his exotic object of desire, Strong makes Darrington over into a "safe," redomesticated woman. Meeting her in New York as she finishes an around-the-world flight, Strong rewards her with a gold bracelet, which we see him place on her wrist. As Mayne observes, this is the only moment in the film when we hear her voice but cannot see her body; we can see only her arm (117–18). "Now I'm shackled," she tells him. Having submitted, Darrington has been reduced to a naked arm upon which the shackling of normative heterosexuality takes place. Triumphant in his shackling, Strong asks her to give up the altitude challenge, a request to which she accedes. The aerial figure is drawn back down to earth through illicit love—as if a licit relationship could not keep her grounded. In being drawn downward from the air, Darrington shifts from the agency of acting to the passivity of merely appearing, that is, of being pleasingly there for Strong. But here, as in the moth scene, the reflexive dimension in the film resists the transparency of the narrative: the director undermines the romance of true love by explicitly identifying Darrington as a commodified woman (Mayne 118).

Darrington cannot survive the dangers of illicit heterosexuality. Nor can she survive the cultural panic about women's uncontained sexuality. A year passes in grounded time; she discovers she's pregnant. Instead of precipitating a rupture in Strong's proper marriage, she chooses suicide, thus becoming, as Mayne notes, the mediator who restores Lady Strong's husband to her and thereby restores official forms of heterosexuality (122). To accomplish her suicide, Darrington returns to flying to break the altitude record. Rising above sixteen thousand feet, she puts on her oxygen mask, a necessary lifeline. Then she tears off the oxygen mask, collapses, and plunges to her death. The final image is a Darrington who rips off the unfeminine (ugly) accoutrement of aerial agency and restores a beautiful (composed and sacrificial) face to the viewer.

According to Mayne, the Hepburn character "exists quite literally in two different worlds" (121), signified by two quite different costumes: the costume of butch flight, identified with competence, intelligence, and independence; and the costume of heterosexual femininity, identified with constraint and sessility. Unable to escape the radical alterity of two spheres of identity—hybrid woman and feminized woman—Darrington dies. In the logic of the narrative, the woman aviator functions as an emblem of impossible desires. There is either flight outside normative femininity or normative femininity without flight. The commercial conservatism of the plot ensures that the very modern woman is effectively eliminated as a threat to both heteronormative social relations and the masculinization of the skies. Here the airplane functions as a deus ex machina that keeps the skies safe from feminization and the ground safe for coupling.

This Hollywood film capitalizes on and reproduces the female aviator as a popular icon, exploiting her celebrity exceptionalism and containing its agency through the logic of the romance plot. The aviatrix is at once an active agent of aerial modernity and the commodified carrier of a more conservative script of domesticated femininity. And yet, through the figure of Darrington, Dorothy Arzner insinuates a complex critique of the very logic the film appears to enact. In this way the film, even as it glamorizes the aviatrix for Hollywood effect (Jay 84), participates in the reflexiveness that is so central a component of modernism by encompassing without fully resolving the anxieties of modern social relations provoked by the airplane.

In their narratives of flight, the famous women aviators of the 1930s negotiated, in distinct ways, the iconography and the cultural anxieties that attended the female aviator's exceptional feats. Through their narratives, Amelia Earhart, Anne Morrow Lindbergh, and Beryl Markham presented themselves as agents of aerial modernity, women comfortable with technology and the dangerous zone of flight.[4] Unlike the Cynthia Darrington figure in Hollywood's version of exceptionalist femininity, they were not defined through the logic of the romance plot. Yet each of these modern women attended to the ways in which the zone of dangerous flight was associated with masculine mobility. It is to their narratives that I now turn.

## For the Fun of It: America's Girl and the Commodification of Flight

> Woman's place is in the home, but failing that the airodome.
>
> Lady Mary Heath

Amelia Earhart wrote two narratives of flight: *Twenty Hrs. Forty Mins.: Our Flight in the "Friendship": The American Girl, First across the Atlantic by Air, Tells Her Story* (1928); and *The Fun of It* (1932). *Twenty Hrs.* capitalizes on her celebrity status after the record-breaking flight of the *Friendship* on June 18, 1928. The book's production and publication was, from our point of view, startlingly swift. Earhart finished writing the narrative on August 25, barely two months after the flight. The book hit the bookstores two weeks later, on September 10 (Ware 108). The speed with which her narrative reached the mass public testifies to the utility of narrative in the marketing of celebrity. Her publisher, Putnam, recognized what a salable commodity Earhart had become. If the flight of the *Friendship* made Earhart's name a household word in Europe and the United States, then her narrative of that flight could play a critical role in catalyzing the public's romance with Amelia. Soon there would be other commercial venues of celebrity: a line of clothes and a line of airline luggage, speaking tours, and advertisements for products such as Lucky Strike cigarettes. But first there had to be narrative.

Earhart's complex relationship to celebrity femininity is captured in the reflexive passage with which she concludes her narrative. Here she invokes the metaphor of the text as plane:

> Finally the little book is done, such as it is. Tomorrow I am free to fly.
>
> Now, I have checked over, from first to last, this manuscript of mine. Frankly, I'm far from confident of its air-worthiness, and don't know how to rate its literary horse-power or estimate its cruising radius and climbing ability. Confidentially, it may never even make the take-off.
>
> If a crash comes, at least there'll be no fatalities. No one can see more

comedy in the disaster than the author herself. Especially because even the writing of the book, like so much else of the flight and its aftermath, has had its humor—some of it publishable!" (280–81)

The tone here is one of tongue-in-cheek apologetics. In pointing to her vulnerability as a writer and her competence as an aviator, Earhart re-affirms her knowledge of planes, the locus of her credibility as author; but she also reveals how critical the book is to her achievement of celebrity, in a way second only to flight itself.

Earhart's book becomes a metaphorical plane, a form of transport technology carrying flight into the everyday life of her readers and trans-porting "Amelia Earhart" throughout the world as a popular icon. To maintain her public identity as aviator, she must fly; to fly, she must raise money; and to raise money, she must remain a public icon. Thus, her return home through narrative must be a return to publicity. The female aviator must become and remain a public spectacle in order to maintain her celebrity. Having lifted off the ground, Earhart can remain aloft only through the imperative of visibility politics.

The photographs, title, and opening testimonial that Putnam edi-tors attached to *Twenty Hrs.* function as framing devices that "package" Earhart as a particular kind of celebrity. Scholars of the Hollywood "star" system have argued that the celebrity figure "gives a form of embodiment to the mass subject" (Hansen), fleshing out for the consuming masses imaginary selves and imaginary lives. For such embodiment, visibility is essential; thus the obligatory photographs incorporated into the text. Identifying Earhart with the engine of modernity (the airplane) and with a monumental event (the flight across the Atlantic), the photos collec-tively present the spectacle of the exceptionalist individual—with a partic-ular style of flesh. In these photos, "Amelia" is made visible and proximate through a visual iconography associated with athletic femininity. Slim, boyish, open-faced, hers is a gender-blended embodiment of heroic mod-ernism. This emblem of modernity offers the public, especially young girls, a way of imagining themselves as thoroughly modern young women without having to mark themselves as too visibly masculinized.

The book's title and testimonial familiarize the exceptional young woman as well. The epithet the long title attaches to this thoroughly modern subject of flight is "the American girl." "American" designates Earhart's role as emblem of the national modern, a sign of America's advanced status in the community of modern nations. Thus, Earhart's achievement can be understood not as transgressive but as part and parcel of the national agenda of "progress." The more familiar appellation "girl" defuses cultural anxieties about female exceptionalism by containing the aviatrix within normative repertoires of "girl" femininity. This exceptional aviatrix is really the wholesome girl next door. Unlike the Darrington figure in *Christopher Strong*, she does not exude a sexual energy that has the potential to disrupt protocols of normative heterosexuality. Earhart is the girl next door who has dedicated herself to serving others, not pursuing her own self-interest. This is the message offered in the book's introductory testimony of Marion Perkins (11–17), head worker at Denison House, Boston's second oldest settlement house. According to Perkins, the daring young woman who has penetrated the domain of aerial masculinity is really a social worker and educator, a familiar of the traditionally feminine sphere of work and traditionally feminine values.

Supplements to Earhart's narrative, the framing devices of photos, title, and testimony render the exceptional aviator simultaneously a modern and a traditional young woman. To the degree that the technical feats of the modern young woman in the flying machine are celebrated and mediated by traditional norms of femininity, she becomes a figure at once remote and familiar. Such remoteness in familiarity and familiarity in remoteness is critical to the making of the celebrity status of the female aviator.

The narrative that Earhart offers her reader does similar kinds of work, but with far more complex effects. On one level, *Twenty Hrs.* unfolds according to the formulaic logic of aerial adventure. The aviator opens with a brief autobiographical sketch of her childhood and young adulthood; she describes her training as a pilot; she describes how she was chosen to make the trip; she chronicles the long, torturous delay in Trepassey, Newfoundland, including the indolence from the wait, the abortive attempts at takeoff, and the isolation; she gives a detailed account of the flight itself and, of course, the arrival and reception in Great Britain. This is the standard fare of aviation narratives, designed to foreground the character traits of the indomitable hero, "his" mastery of the new technology, and the exceptional (because dangerous) feat of adventurous flight. In effect, this is the story that must be told, the defining fable of aerial mobility. It provides the aviator with a characterological portrait and an action script of agency. But there's a woman rather than a man in the cockpit of the narrative, a young woman negotiating the strange celebrity that attends her fortuitous adventure in the domain of aerial masculinity. To that negotiation she brings familiar moves. That is, through discursive strategies coded as appropriately feminine, Earhart represents herself as less than truly heroic.

For one thing, she reframes her achievements as modest rather than risky. In the foreword of *Twenty Hrs.*, she is diffident, self-denigrating. Admitting her inability to write "a work," she expresses hope that the book catches the "fun" of flying and "that some of the charm and romance of old ships may be seen to cling similarly to the ships of the air" (9). Suddenly catapulted into fame, "the American girl" presents herself as flying for the fun of it rather than for more serious purposes as men do. And she signals that, as a woman of somewhat comfortable means, she does not have to fly to make a living. Thus, she offers indirect assurance to her reader that she is not seriously competing with men for mastery of the skies nor challenging the identification of the aviator as new man.

"The American girl" also anchors her professional identity in the sphere of social and educational work rather than the sphere of adventure. She describes her early interest in nursing and in settlement work, as well as her job at Denison House. Later, in recalling her activities in London after the flight, she tells of her tour of Toynbee Hall, the London settlement house that served as a model for such houses in the United States. In this way, Earhart implies that her values have not changed with her entry into the world of aviation, that she remains a young woman dedicated to serving others.

The logic of serving comes through, as well, in her detailed report of the flight across the Atlantic. Here she enacts her role as educator when she uses the logbook as a teaching tool. Incorporating passages copied directly from the logbook as the narrative spine of the journey, Earhart interprets, for the uninitiated reader, the nitty-gritty details of flight: how the plane was organized, where the gas tanks were located, how she spent her time, what the crew ate. "The gastronomic adventures of trans-oceanic flying really deserve a record of their own," she writes facetiously. "Ham sandwiches seemed to predominate en route" (141). These are the domestic details of flight. She uses the occasion to inform her reader about the technicalities of flight as well. "People are so likely to think of planes as frail craft that I draw attention to this entry," she writes: "*Friendship* weighs 6000 pounds empty, and on the flight she carried about her own weight again" (176). She explains how, against common sense, the higher one flies the safer one is. In this attention to the quotidian, Earhart familiarizes her reader with the world of aviation, making the world of flight more common rather than uncommon.

Rather than concluding the narrative of her historic flight with a self-aggrandizing description of the hero's welcome she received in London, Earhart diverts attention away from herself as heroic protagonist in two ways. First, as a missionary for aviation, she addresses larger issues having to do with the state of aviation (especially with women as passengers and aviators). In the chapter entitled "Aviation Invites," Earhart prognosticates that aviation can and will become part of everyday life and proclaims the experience of flight to be "matter-of-fact" (216). When she translates the technology of flight through the technology of automobility, using the experience of driving to capture for her female reader the experience of flight (220), she brings airborne subjectivity back down to earth. She also dismisses her reader's fear by poking fun at those who express fear of flying: "I know a woman who was determined to die of heart failure if she made a flight. She isn't logical, for she rolls lazily through life encased in 100 lbs of extra avoirdupois, which surely adds a greater strain on her heart—besides not giving it any fun, at all" (218). Ultimately, Earhart makes the airplane over into an everyday item of consumption. "It is the modern note in transportation," she declares, "comparable to the electric refrigerator, vacuum devices and all the other leisure-making appliances of the household. Aviation is another time-saver ready to be utilized" (237–38). Likened to a vacuum cleaner, the plane becomes just another household commodity. By implication, the aviator becomes a kind of aerial housewife going about routine domestic duties.

Second, in her final chapter Earhart assesses her notoriety as a "public character" (281) but with a lightness and humor that undermine any lionizing self-promotion. She catalogs the mail she receives, including several examples of strange and humorous correspondence, offers of marriage, letters condemning her sponsorship of Lucky Strike cigarettes, silly photos, and poetry (289). An editorial diminishing her contribution to the flight is sent her by someone who underlines certain passages in it, such as "her presence added no more to the achievement than if the passenger had been a sheep." To this Earhart responds whimsically with a parenthetical comment: "This is the zoological last straw! After two weeks of mutton at Trepassey I'm sure the boys would not have endured the proximity of a sheep as cargo on the *Friendship*" (292). She notes an editorial that asserts she had little to do on the flight and that her notoriety came only from the fact that she was a woman. She reproduces the long joke she receives about her being a stereotypical "back seat driver" (295–301). In a text designed to ensure her celebrity status, Earhart simultaneously establishes her celebrity credentials and pokes fun at herself as a celebrity.

The antiheroic rhetoric of domesticity, the logic of service, the missionary purpose, the self-deflating humor—these are discursive features through which Earhart positions herself as a traditional American girl through an ethics of domestication.[5] They are presentational features through which she neutralizes the identification of the female aviator as threateningly masculine, as out of place. But in representing herself as less than truly heroic, she also effects a transformation of the imaginary domain of flight itself. As it joins traditional repertoires of femininity to the modern spectacle of aviation, Earhart's narrative undoes, even as it reproduces, certain defining features of aviator narratives. With the invocation of the word *fun* in reference to aviation, and its recurrence in the title of her 1932 sequel, *The Fun of It*, Earhart shifts the associative register for imagining aviation from "danger" to "fun." Emptying the sky of much of its "danger," this female aviator severs the identification of flight with a masculinity of risk. The "intrepid birdman" of an earlier era of flight has become the proper girl next door.

Then, instead of romanticizing the journey and distancing herself from her grounded readers, she educates them, sharing her knowledge in a voice of intimate engagement. In educating the mass public, and specifically women, about the quotidian details of this spectacular "event," Earhart encourages a familiarity with flight that is potentially empowering for women. She also reimagines flight as a domestic drama in which the uncommon aviator is brought back down to earth. Familiarizing flight and deflating the heroic difference of the aviator, Earhart redefines the relationship of women to this engine of modernity. As she does so, she demystifies flight as a domain of aerial masculinity and the aviator as a remote and uncommon subject.

Critically, this demystification of the domain of aerial masculinity through the figure of the ladylike young woman (remember that Earhart was dubbed "Lady Lindy") was part of a larger cultural transformation. With her historic flight across the Atlantic in 1928, Amelia Earhart was drawn into the selling of aviation. In order to domesticate aviation and to facilitate the development of commercial aviation—to make the skies a safe and comfortable space for consumers of air transport—the earlier representation of flight as daring, dangerous, remote, and romantic had to be displaced by another kind of representation. Flight had to be remade as practical rather than exotic so that masses of people, formerly so many dots on the ground, could rise up into the air. The "intrepid birdman" image had to be displaced, and women were enlisted by the airline industry to do the work of transformation. As Joseph J. Corn acknowledges, it was the cultural stereotype of women aviators as "frail, timid, unathletic, and unmechanical" that opened opportunities for women aviators in the late 1920s and 1930s: "Who better could supplant the masculine, athletic image of fearless, superhuman aviators and allay people's anxieties about flight?" (559). From 1927 to 1940, women were hired to demonstrate planes and to sell them. They were funded to enter races and undertake promotional flights. Their celebrity was sustained by the industry that needed them to launch the new age of aviation. (Of course, once the transformation had been effected, women had little access to jobs as pilots in the airline companies. The figure of the lady air pilot was then displaced by the figure of the stewardess [Corn 570–71].)

An agent for the airline industry and for the cause of flight more generally, Earhart appeals to conventional gender stereotypes when she talks of women as customers. "As [women] become an important factor in passenger revenue," she predicts in the chapter entitled "Women in Aviation," "their requirements will be increasingly studied and met" (238). She assures her readers that the airline industry will make over the spaces of aviation (airplane and airport) as attractive and suitable places for women. They will become comfortable, safe, clean, "feminized" sites. Yet when Earhart discusses women as pilots, she discards the discourses of gendered differences and assigned spheres. She recognizes the difficulty women have in getting the requisite training because they do not have access to the armed services, where many men learn to fly (240). Nor do they have easy access to other training opportunities. Having nodded to their disadvantages in gaining access to aviation, she proceeds to describe for her readers how women excel in the kinds of skills required of the aviator, as well as the risks encountered and the safety factors. In the course of her discussion, she casually dismisses arguments against women's participation in aviation based on some essential incapacity for technical challenge and constitutional aversion to danger. Individual women can make their way and can claim a legitimate place in aviation on their own individual merits. Promoting women as aviators in this way, Earhart claims a continued place for women in the domain of aerial masculinity. Or rather, she redefines the domain of aerial subjectivity as neither male nor female. In this instance, hers is an invasive female agency motivated by the politics of exceptionalist individualism. And, at this particular point in her narrative, Earhart halts the logic of domestication.[6]

Earhart's narrative plays, in most aspects, to the cultural consumption of exceptionalist individualism. That consumption is requisite for her celebrity; her "female" readership will consume her story because of her status as aviator. But the text is also addressed to women as domestic consumers and designed to facilitate the inevitable domestication of flying by making the mass of women more comfortable with the idea of flight. Ultimately, as Anne Hermann notes in her exploration of the gendered double bind within aviation history, Earhart "use[s] her exceptional position as a way of trying to make it more normative" (96). Yet to do so is to transform aviation from an arena of exceptionalist individualism to an arena of comfortable consumerism, thereby colluding in the demise of the mythic celebrity that Earhart's narrative is meant to sustain. As women reimagine themselves as aerial subjects, this thoroughly modern arena of exceptionalist individualism vanishes. The vacuumization of flight disrupts the logic of aerial heroism.

## Orienting Mobility: Anne Morrow Lindbergh Goes "North to the Orient"

> Possibly that feature of aviation which may appeal most
> to thoughtful women is its potentiality for peace. The term is
> not merely an airy phrase.... Anything which tends to annihilate
> distance destroys isolation, and brings the world and its
> peoples closer together.
>
> —Amelia Earhart, *Twenty Hrs. Forty Mins.* (1928)

On July 27, 1931, Anne and Charles Lindbergh set off in a plane called the *Sirius* to survey a new route for commercial aviation. Flying north to the "orient"—from Long Island to Canada, Alaska, the Soviet Union, and China—they traced a route "stretching like a taut string over the top of the globe" (Ware 47). Four years later, Anne Morrow Lindbergh published her account of that journey as *North to the Orient*. Theirs was a division of labor in which each had an appointed domain. Charles piloted the aircraft; Anne wrote the narrative of their flight.

Of course, Charles Lindbergh lends his aura of celebrity to *North*. His is a powerful presence filling the cockpit, even if his voice is rarely invoked. For in the 1930s Charles Lindbergh was indisputably the prince of the air, a cultural icon exemplifying the heroic modern subject. As Lawrence Goldstein notes, after his historic flight in the *Spirit of St. Louis*, Lindbergh was heralded as "the redemptive type of the modern, integrating the devotion to technique represented by Leonardo with the Romantic dream of wings" (134). Lindbergh himself shunned publicity, a behavior that effectively played to this mythic status, as his reticence and inaccessibility established an unbreachable distance between himself as aviator-hero and the mass of earthbound subjects that mobbed him on the ground (144). But if Charles Lindbergh was above communicating with the public, his wife was not.

Like Amelia Earhart, Anne Morrow Lindbergh recognized the uses of narrative for visibility politics. In publishing *North*, she would contribute to the famous aviator's heroic stature by writing a narrative that recorded for posterity his pathbreaking feats and kept him within the imaginative horizons of the public's attention. And by speaking for him, she would sustain the sense of his remoteness from the mass of human beings on the ground. But hers is no slavish tribute to her husband. She does not, for instance, record Charles Lindbergh's version of the flight. Even as she appears to be enacting the dutifulness of the devoted wife, Lindbergh makes claims of her own, identifying herself as a writer first and foremost.

Climbing into the cockpit on Long Island, Lindbergh could not have escaped her associative identity as wife of the famous aviator. In her narrative she alludes specifically to aviation as a masculine enterprise and the cockpit as a masculine domain when she describes the questions reporters ask her husband before takeoff. Questions addressed to Lindy are "vital masculine questions, clean-cut steely technicalities or broad abstractions" (39). Those addressed to her, by contrast, are "feminine" questions, primarily having to do with her aviation couture. With irony, she critiques the cultural identification of women's bodies and the new technology as a relationship of fashion when she notes that the reporters misrepresent her clothing in order to make her over into a stereotypical figure of the female aviator projected through popular iconography.[7] Irony notwithstanding, this aviator was only too aware of the stereotypes that dogged women aviators (Corn 565). Despite this feminization of her appearance in the cockpit, Lindbergh wrests agency as an aviator through two communicative roles she entwines throughout her narrative—her status as radio technician on the flight and her status as writer of the narrative of flight.

*North to the Orient* "takes off," so to speak, with a prefatory address to the reader in which Lindbergh reflects upon writing, in particular the genre of aviator narrative. Exactly what is this narrative she is presenting to the public? she asks. Her query is interesting, given the fact that, like Earhart's, her text incorporates many conventions of aviator narratives. There are extended dramas of dangers encountered: the emergency landing in the Seward Peninsula, the problems with the fog over Japan, the suffocating siege of the sampans on the flooding Yangtze in China. There are descriptions of their receptions upon landing and descriptions of life on the ground. Nonetheless, Lindbergh emphasizes the errancy of "the anomalous collection of chapters before me." Neither guidebook nor technical manual nor geographic survey, the collection "evades classification [and] will not fit the conventional standards and measurements." An anomaly in comparison to more official, scientific, and authoritative genres, her book stands "nameless, awkward and shy, asking to be introduced" (7). Like a feminized woman, the text can claim no identity of its own; it is uncomfortable, reticent, and awaiting recognition.

Lindbergh's troping of the text as feminized woman suggests her acute awareness of the cultural pressures affecting the self-representations of female aviators. As Joseph J. Corn remarks, Lindbergh, like other female aviators, was aware of how important it was for her to act the proper woman as she invaded the skies—that imaginary domain of masculine heroism—even if she did so as sidekick (565). With this language the writer makes her narrative normatively feminine. Her strange aviator narrative, she implies, does other work than that of a guidebook, technical manual, or survey, all instrumental forms of narrative focused on technical skills and activities coded masculine. It does other work than transcribing the adventures of herself as heroic aviator and celebrating the individualism *à l'air* of the new man (who cannot be a woman). Her narrative is, she proposes, a personal tale through which she translates the "essential core" (9) of her experience of extended flight north to the Orient. The turn away from heroic adventure to the personal and communicative is a "properly feminine" turn. The female aviator personalizes for her readers the modern experience that seems so very remote from their everyday lives. With more poetry than Earhart, Lindbergh acts as the translator of flight for the masses secured on the ground.

This role as translator relates to Lindbergh's role as radio operator during the flight. In the opening chapters of *North*, Lindbergh chronicles her struggle to become proficient in radio communication, the advanced technical skill that keeps the aviator attached to the ground rather than entirely free of the terrestrial realm below, the technical skill critical for night flying and long-distance journeys across vast expanses of land. As in the preface, Lindbergh's rhetoric of self-representation here is complex. Dedicating significant narrative attention to her struggle with radio communications, she plays to pervasive cultural stereotypes of the "lady flyer" as "frail, timid, unathletic, and unmechanical" (Corn 560). She emphasizes her utter confusion in making sense of instructions and her lack of familiarity with technical language. Yet even as she reproduces the stereotype of incompetence, she undoes it, for she does learn the technology and thus enters the cockpit not as a fashionable appendage of the famous man but as a crew member responsible for radio communications. Despite the obligatory self-effacement in this vignette, Lindbergh addresses her reader as a woman proficient in a stereotypically masculine (technical) skill and demonstrates her competence again and again in her narration of the journey. Thus, although Lindbergh refuses to promote herself as a model of a thoroughly "modern" woman (for instance, when she contrasts herself to the "new woman" of the Soviet Union), she founds her legitimate authority in the cockpit and in her narrative on her familiarity with critical features of this technology of modernity.

Assigning herself agency in the cockpit, Lindbergh resists the degrading feminization of "Lindy's wife." But she does more. She also demystifies, by disjoining, the masculine association of flight and heroic freedom. Flight, she announces, "rests, firmly supported, on a structure of laws, rules, [and] principles" (24), including careful and often tedious training and planning, what she calls "the back stairs of aviation-magic" (11). The freedom identified with flight thus becomes "contingent," a word she invokes when she describes the kinds of "contingencies" they have to be prepared to meet. To make vivid to the reader the attention to contingency, she includes an appendix that lists all equipment carried on the *Sirius*—emergency equipment, personal flying equipment, radio equipment, navigation equipment—and the log entries for the flight. The resolute specificity of the appendix, which includes the numbers of spoons, plain hooks, gut cords, rounds of ammunition, and tins of army rations, catalogs the mundane objects necessary to flight—the mundane that attaches the plane to *mundus*.

Flight is contingent in another sense as well. As radio operator during the flight, Lindbergh constantly makes contact with people on the ground. That ongoing connection between flight and ground offers her a metaphor for her personal narrative of flight. Writing and radio communication are analogical means of translating what she calls "aviation-magic." Lindbergh seeks in her errant narrative to capture not so much the freedom of the aerial subject flying high above the ground, but rather the radical quality of relationality that aviation enables.

Thus, Lindbergh's narrative takes on the rhythm of cross-cultural encounter. Granted, she organizes the narrative of the journey "north to the Orient" according to the mapped-out legs of the trip, and a map of the leg inaugurates each chapter. But these are Charles Lindbergh's maps, the aviator's means of navigation, rationalizing movement from site to site through the segmentation of geography. The narrator identifies these maps with the masculinist logic of mobility when she puts the following claim in her husband's mouth: "I like to feel that in flying ... I can mark one point on the map for my position and another point for my destination, and that I can draw a straight line between the two, and follow it. I don't like to deviate for possible difficulties en route. I'd rather prepare for the difficulties" (62). Straight lines signal rational control, purposefulness, and functionality. Lindbergh implies that these are masculine tools for organizing flight across the globe, for framing the utility and directionality of flight. Yet these maps offer only one rather limited narrative of the journey, a narrative of instrumental rationality. And straight lines signal only direction, a route.

For Lindbergh, the plane lifts off to fly high above the land below only to touch down for extended interludes on the ground. Thus, she is as attentive to the time on the ground as to the time in the air, narrating the subtle and complicated exchanges with different peoples about the dangers of flight. In this way, Lindbergh wrests her narrative from the maps by getting at the meaning that emerges not out of rationality but out of the relationality of flight and ground. Although she acknowledges the "self-contained insularity" of flight (40), she mitigates the effect of isolated individuality by emphasizing the dialogic communication of the aviator-plane ensemble and the ground. In doing so, she shifts narrative registers, from the celebration of dangerous adventure to the celebration of human cultural exchange.

In this narrative of cross-cultural encounter, Lindbergh focuses on the ways in which she makes connections with diverse people through small exchanges—that of an orange for the doctor's wife in Barrow, of children's photos and laughter in Kamchatka, Russia, of the tea ceremony in Japan. Of the beauty of the tea ceremony, she writes: "If only I could stay here long enough, I thought, going home in the rain, I would learn to see too. And after minutely watching the surface of things I would learn to see below the surface" (193). These delicate exchanges between strangers are not the heroic deeds of exceptional individuals soaring high above the mass of men but, rather, the domestic deeds of women. Culturally coded as feminine, these encounters across difference link local rituals of everyday life to an internationalist message of peace.

In Lindbergh's ethics of relationality, the domestic arts of women become the arts of international diplomacy precisely because they are exercised in an international context. In the 1930s, as Gillian Beer reminds us, the small airplane was identified not only with individualism and

heroism but also with internationalism (276). Rendering all global locations accessible, the small plane brought people together across vast distances. In this way, it held out the promise of peaceful and productive
relations between and among nations. This internationalist promise is
evident in Lindbergh's emphasis on connection with the peoples of the
ground across cultures. The aviator's promissory note to the future lies
in this promotion of peaceful encounter.

The logic that sustains Lindbergh's message of internationalism is
the logic of "the collision of modern methods and old ones; modern
history and ancient; accessibility and isolation" (10). And the vehicle of
that collision is the airplane, master technology of modernity. Overflying
isolated lands and communities at the precise moment when transcontinental flight is about to render the entire globe accessible, the *Sirius*
ascends, maneuvers, banks, and descends in the wedge of time/space that
sutures modern and premodern sites. Lindbergh's focus on this collision links her project to the romance of travelers like Isabelle Eberhardt
and Alexandra David-Neel who moved by foot or horse. Eberhardt and
David-Neel, too, journeyed through "premodern" spaces, seeking respite
from a degraded modernity and a reinvigorated sense of identity. What
distinguishes Lindbergh's projection of the collision between the premodern and the modern from that of Eberhardt and David-Neel, however, is that Lindbergh celebrates the encounter made possible by the
airplane and inserts it into a narrative of progress. She imagines the flight
of the *Sirius* as the twentieth-century fulfillment of the dream of voyage
begun five hundred years earlier when Elizabethan travelers sought a
Northwest Passage to the Indies in their quest for "greater accessibility
and speed" (16). "Travelers are always discoverers," she announces,
"especially those who travel by air" (22).

The residue of imperialist tropes of discovery inflects Lindbergh's
narrative of encounter between the premodern and the modern. The
commercialism motivating the journey is displaced by her romantic
desire for contact with exotic otherness. We see this when she notes
that, in addition to the practical purposes of the flight, she has her own
"minor," personal reasons for desiring to fly to the Orient. She seeks

"*color, glamour, curiosity, magic*, or *mystery*" (20). Through such language Lindbergh invokes the West's enduring fascination with "the Orient" as a destination of "alluring" difference and thus bathes the narrative of this flight in a mist of exoticism and romance. Then too, she figures the aerial couple as subjects of exploration, the latest in a line of adventurers driven by the "allure" of the unknown and the drive for access. "The flier," she writes, "breaks each second into new uncharted seas" (22). To render the aviator subject a sovereign "discoverer," she evacuates history and culture from the space of the premodern. "And for us," she writes, "setting out over unknown country, there would be those austere and breath-taking moments when, looking down on inaccessible territory, one realizes that no one has seen that spot before. It is as fresh, still, and untouched as the night's new-fallen snow. Unchanged from the day it was made" (22). What people they do encounter—in Baker Lake, Aklavik, Point Barrow, and the Seward Peninsula—she presents as living in isolation, expectantly awaiting communication with the outside world. "It was not that we arrived in Baker Lake on August third by plane," she writes as she works to capture the "magic" of their landing at Baker Lake, "but that three hours of flying had brought us from the modern port of Churchill to a place where no white woman had ever been before" (9). Associating the penetration of the modern into premodern outposts with the arrival of white women, Lindbergh figures herself as the delivery sign of modernity.

In the most evocative passage in *North to the Orient*, Lindbergh represents the masses of premodern people as a danger and a threat to the heroic aviator, avatar of modern man. Lindbergh poignantly describes Charles Lindbergh's experience in the disastrous floods in China. Hoping to bring medical relief to thousands of people stranded in sampans in the floodwaters, the modern hero sets his plane down in the midst of the starving people. Immediately, sampans, filled with desperate people whose needs the doctor on board cannot hope to meet, surround the plane. The very press of people comes dangerously close to destroying the plane and all those flyers aboard. With great difficulty, Lindbergh lifts the *Sirius* off the water and escapes from this site of hunger and desperation. "The two worlds," writes the narrator, "were separated by a gulf which, although not wide, was deep, perilous, and unbridgeable. At least it was unbridgeable to the owners of the sampans. The fliers had crossed over from one world to another as easily, as swiftly, as one crosses from the world of nightmare to the world of reality in the flash of waking" (220).

To capture this precarious encounter and to emphasize the risk of heroic flight, Lindbergh contains the Chinese peasants in their condition of premodernity. Narrated with haunting effect, this scene foregrounds the radical disjunction between the modern "world of reality" and the premodern "world of nightmare." Impervious to the arrival of modernity, this seething mass of humanity remains the intransigent premodern that cannot make the leap into modernity even if the aviator can insert his technology of modernity into its midst.

Yet ironically, in a later scene, the *Sirius* goes to a watery grave, destroyed by the implacable force of the Yangtze current as the Lindberghs work to load it onto a British carrier for the return to the States. Before it goes under, a Chinese sampan filled with people comes downstream and drifts perilously close to the plane and its tether. Ultimately, the sampan "skim[s]" under the rope and avoids going under with the wings of the *Sirius*. Here the encounter of premodern peasants with the plane stays the march of progress. The Chinese in the sampan have fooled the three devils always at their backs by slicing death closely. They survive; the *Sirius* sinks.

But, of course, the "magic" moment of these encounters has already passed. The doubled ending of *North* becomes the narrative means through which Lindbergh accepts the passing of an era and recalls the pleasure of the magic that has passed. In the penultimate chapter, entitled "Sayonara," she weaves the word *sayonara* throughout her description of her and Charles's departure for America from the port of Yokohama. Lindbergh is drawn to its meaning—"since it must be so"—as a hauntingly beautiful form of leave-taking: "*Sayonara* says neither too much nor too little. It is a simple acceptance of fact. All understanding of life lies in its limits. All emotion, smoldering, is banked up behind it. But it says nothing" (239). Through exploration of the word, the narrator finds acceptance of the end of an era as the premodern gives way to modernity and global communication. It must be so, because the magic of flight has already passed, by virtue of the very journey she narrates.

Lindbergh does not end *North* with "Sayonara," however. She draws back from this acceptance to luxuriate once again in the magic of flight, but now it is magic experienced in the body and vision of the aviator herself. In her final chapter, Lindbergh takes the reader for one last solo flight of the imagination, offering a poetic tribute to aerial subjectivity. She describes a later flight, one during which she "simply fl[ies]" without recourse to radio, suggesting the experience of flight without attachment to the ground: "There was no limit to what the eye could seize or what the mind hold" (241). The panoramic gaze produces an uncluttered horizon of meaning, free of the limits of grounded perception, perception muddled, perception constrained. The world looked at from above seems a world of "permanency," a world "arrested," a world in which the "trivial" and the "aimless" and the "accidental" dissipate: "For not only is life put in new patterns from the air, but it is somehow arrested, frozen into form" (244). Earlier Lindbergh acknowledged that technologies change both perception and the relationship of persons to place, time, and memory: "We are like the nearsighted man who is not yet used to his new spectacles. We are still trying to look at the stamen of a flower with spectacles made to look at horizons" (48–49). The effect of flight is to change the relationship between the subject and the ground, the subject and time, the subject and memory. The height (spatial distance) of flight becomes synonymous with the distance of time.

In flight the aerial subject becomes a "seeing eye," capable of discerning, beneath the surficial changes and roiling of history, the generalized "essence" of life, its aesthetic forms and inevitabilities. "A glaze is put over life," she explains. "There is no flaw, no crack in the surface; a still reservoir, no ripple on its face" (244). Through the word, Lindbergh celebrates the magic of flight, extracting its aesthetic pleasures from the contingencies of history. Out of this moment of history, Lindbergh has retrieved what she considers to be the durable source of aerial magic.

Technology, vision, and art are joined as the world itself becomes an abstract work of art.

In this, Lindbergh is a thoroughly modernist writer, finding through new technology the aestheticization of experience. By closing her narrative with this poetic testament to the aesthetics of flight, Lindbergh reaffirms her identity as a writer, the one who takes the raw material of her husband's skillful flying and makes it into art by giving it pattern, perspective, and meaning. And she suggests that even though the time of "aviation magic" has passed, the aesthetic perception made possible by the airplane cannot be rendered practical or prosaic.

Moreover, during this flight her body fills with the rhythms of the plane. The roar of the engine is "like music" as the vibrations of the plane rumble through her: "Throbbing with small monotone patterns, the vibration hummed in the soles of my feet, in the hollow of my back. It absorbed some restless side of me, and was satisfying as a hearth fire or rain on the roof. Contented, I could look down at that calm clear world below" (240). Here machine and female body become one interdependent expression of motorized modernity. The word *contented* and the metaphorical invocation of hearth fire and rain on the roof brings the experiential "feel" of flight home, domesticating the effects of this powerful technology for her reader. Leaving us with the figure of a woman alone in the airplane feeling the energy of the engine through her body and celebrating the extension of vision that the aerial panorama provides her, Lindbergh makes her point that technology and woman can be at one, that the prosthetic capacities of the airplane are just as transformative for the modern woman as for the modern man—and transformative for the woman as modern artist as well. For the plane and the technology of flight offer her a vision and an aesthetic through which to capture the magic of the moment.

In *North to the Orient*, Anne Morrow Lindbergh is acutely aware of historical contingency, the slice of time that is hers to narrate: "I must write down my story before it is too late" (13). By making all global locations accessible, aviation brings to an end the romance of the inaccessible. Flights like the Lindberghs' "north to the Orient" ensure that there will be no inaccessible, uncharted places left on the globe. Here is the cultural residue of the romantic myth of the heroic adventurer as the one who traverses the edges of modernity's scope while joined to the very modernist technology that brings an end to the persistence of those edges. There can only be the remains of narrative; thus, to the writer is entrusted the responsibility of capturing the magic of this irrecoverable moment of encounter.

## Beryl Markham Goes "West with the Night"

> Flight is just momentary escape from the eternal custody of earth.
>
> —Beryl Markham, *West with the Night* (1942)

Unlike either Amelia Earhart or Anne Morrow Lindbergh, Beryl Markham begins her travel narrative *West with the Night* in medias res as she recalls a particularly harrowing aerial adventure. Hovering above the apparently barren landscape of the African desert, the aviator surveys the land below, searching intently for a fallen comrade and his plane. Opening in this way, Markham stresses the risk of flight and the deadly vulnerability of the aviator: her comrade Woody may have paid the ultimate price for the exhilaration of flying. So too might the rescuer. In this vignette of rescue, the narrator affirms her technological mastery of the modern machine and her instinctive intelligence in deciphering marks on the land below. She also situates herself in the midst of a particular kind of space, an Africa that is "never dull," because it tests the mettle of the aviator (7). Here we have the ingredients of heroic adventure stories: the inhospitable environment of largely uncharted and unknown land; the courage of the aviator, always vulnerable within "his" plane; the special comradeship of an elite; and the mastery of technology.

Markham's allegiance to this masculinist code of honorable heroism has already been signaled in the triple inscription at the beginning of her narrative. She dedicates the book to "my Father"; expresses "gratitude to Raoul Schumacher for this book"; and cites Shakespeare's *Henry IV*: "I speak of Africa and golden joys" (act 5, scene 3).[8] She proceeds to maintain narrative allegiance to male scripts by means of two powerful fabulations of male heroism that underwrite her text. Looking to the popular mythos of Hollywood films in the late 1930s, she inscribes the narrative equivalent of a swashbuckling adventure film with a female Errol Flynn as hero. Looking back to the heroic world of ancient Greece for authoritative myths with which to ground a modern tale, she entangles her twentieth-century story with Homeric structures of adventure, travel, and contest. As she does so, Markham figures herself an avatar of Athena, the powerful, fleet goddess who emerged full-grown from the head of her father, Zeus.

Markham structures her teleological narrative around her successful completion of three (masculine) tests: her early initiation into the hunting rites of Murani (Nandi) warriors, her conquest of the horse-racing world of Kenya, and her acceptance into the circle of male aviators crisscrossing Kenya during the 1920s and 1930s. Through mythic plotting, Markham recreates a world in which men, and Markham with them, test their courage, intelligence, instinct, and skill against "the elemental forces and purposes of life" (7). In claiming this mythic kinship as an inheritance of modernity, Markham was invoking what, according to Robert Wohl, was a common trope in early narratives of aviation. By drawing upon the models of heroic adventure from classical mythology, Wohl argues, the proponents of aviation effectively "insert[ed] flying machines and aviators into a tradition that reached back at least as far as the Ancient Greeks, their heroes, and their gods. Viewed in this way, aviation was not something new and potentially disruptive or destructive but rather the shining fulfillment of one of humanity's oldest dreams" (262–63). And the aviator himself was acknowledged as a new god of the air.

Through each stage of her adventures, Markham entwines her story and identifies her achievement with that of a male mentor, from her father to Arab Maina to Denys Fynch-Hatton to Tom Black to Bror Blixen, each of whom she ennobles by turns. She allies herself as well with the world of animals, and animals of a particular kind: the horse, the lion, the wild boar, and the elephant with its mammoth tusks. These are willful, proud, powerful, fleet, awesome animals; and she presents herself sometimes as hunter, sometimes as tamer of them. But she is a thoroughly modern hero as well, at home in the world of adventurous aviation, which in the context of Africa had become a modern instrument for colonial expansion in the 1920s and 1930s. Animals of flesh and animals of metallic modernity carry her body swiftly through space, making possible her life as a "wanderer."

They also provide her with powerful antagonists against which to test her heroic mettle. Describing the male honor code of this life early in her narrative, Markham captures both ethos and mythos of her adventurous life: "For all professional pilots there exists a kind of guild, without charter and without by-laws. It demands no requirements for inclusion save an understanding of the wind, the compass, the rudder, and fair fellowship. It is a camaraderie *sans* sentiment of the kind that men who once sailed uncharted seas in wooden ships must have known and lived by" (11–12). In the language of this code, Markham links contemporary and ancient heroism and places herself securely inside the circle of both.

Such masculinist heroism promotes certain narrative orientations toward the world, experience, and subjectivity. First among them is the celebration of her own unique destiny. Manifesting throughout her text what Georges Gusdorf describes as the "conscious awareness of the singularity of each individual life" (29), Markham, privileging her own individuality, makes little effort to decenter her story (as Lindbergh does) or to deflate her own heroism (as Earhart does). Even in that strangest of all passages, where she drops the narrative voice of Beryl Markham to assume the narrative view of the horse Camciscan (109–16), she maintains the young Markham as the center of the horse's "consciousness."

As she foregrounds an idealized individualism, Markham presents herself as an unencumbered subject, an isolated, singular self, purposeful and solitary. Describing her experiences as an aviator, she figures the plane as a mechanical instrument to be manipulated and controlled, but also as a machine that takes her to the limits of a precarious, lonely, "free" existence. "Night envelops me entirely," she writes, "leaving me out of touch with the earth, leaving me within this small moving world of my own, living in space with the stars" (15). She says of the plane that it is "your planet and you are its sole inhabitant" (10). Isolated in the cockpit, the aviator becomes the figure of self-sufficiency, a self-sufficiency that gets translated into the timbre of her narrative voice. Here is subjectivity detached from the ground and from the limiting subjectivity that sessility enforces. Here is subjectivity extended by mechanical prosthesis.

Emphasizing throughout the narrative her ability to "read" the signs on the ground of life, Markham implies that such self-sufficiency derives from an education in hermeneutics. As noted earlier, the narrative begins in medias res as she struggles to interpret signs of the earth—animal tracks, smoke, the silver wings of an airplane—in an effort to rescue the downed flyer Woody in that "vast unmarked desert" of the Serengeti. Circling back to her childhood, she continues by chronicling the education in sign reading she received from the Murani (Nandi) hunters. The narrative of her early experiences as a horse trainer focuses on her ability to "read" the potential in the horse and the rider. The transition between the early education and the later achievements that enable her to leave her mark (on the horse-racing scene, on aviation) follows seamlessly. The airplane that she pilots and about which she writes becomes a machine in which to escape from mapped spaces into what by Western standards are "unmapped" spaces of geography and subjectivity.

In a particularly compelling scene, a scene at the crossroads, Markham reproduces her first meeting with the aviator Tom Black.[9] This meeting brings with it a shift in the arena of her desire. Before meeting Black, the young woman imagines horse racing as the most exhilarating means of a swift traverse of the earth, of speed and escape. After meeting Black, she imagines flight as a more modern means of escape. Black elucidates for her the features of aerial subjectivity:

"When you fly," the young man said, "you get a feeling of possession that you couldn't have if you owned all of Africa. You feel that everything you see belongs to you—all the pieces are put together, and the whole is yours; not that you want it, but because, when you're alone in a plane, there's no one to share it. It's there and it's yours. It makes you feel bigger than you are—closer to being something you've sensed you might be capable of, but never had the courage to seriously imagine." (152–53)

In Black's romantic reverie, the airplane becomes a topographic machine, extending the borders of empire, including the empire of subjectivity.

As with flight, so too with the narrative of flight. In the discursive cockpit of the narrative, Markham celebrates the ethos of Black's romantic and imperial reverie as she enacts the self-magnification of the aerial subject released from social constraints. In the air she discovers the magnification of the self through the prosthetic machine; in the narrative she figures the airplane as an animal straining beneath her: "To me she is alive and to me she speaks. I feel through the soles of my feet on the rudder-bar the willing strain and flex of her muscles. The resonant, guttural voice of her exhausts has a timbre more articulate than wood and steel, more vibrant than wires and sparks and pounding pistons" (16). Body and machine are mutually informing loci of sentience and knowledge.

For Markham, the release of the prosthetic machine is release from the contaminating matter of female embodiment. Thus, her narrative project requires a concomitant diminution of both the "other" woman and the feminine as a way of registering the distance Markham has placed between her aerial self flying high above any domesticated settlements and the embodied drudgery of a sessile life lived on the ground.

At the beginning of chapter 7, "Praise God for the Blood of the Bull," Markham recreates the story of her participation in the initiation rite through which all Nandi boys marked their passage to manhood. In the midst of the narrative, she inserts an exchange with Jebbta, a young Nandi girl who confronts her before she sets out with the Nandi warriors on the hunt for wild boar:

> "The heart of a Murani is like unto stone," she whispered, "and his limbs have the speed of an antelope. Where do you find the strength and the daring to hunt with them, my sister?"
>
> We were as young as each other, Jebbta and I, but she was a Nandi, and if the men of the Nandi were like unto stone, their women were like

unto leaves of grass. They were shy and they were feminine and they did the things that women are meant to do, and they never hunted.

I looked down at the ankle-length skins Jebbta wore, which rustled like taffeta when she moved, and she looked at my khaki shorts and lanky, naked legs.

"Your body is like mine," she said; "it is the same and it is no stronger." She turned, avoiding the men with her eyes, because that too was law, and went quickly away tittering like a small bird. (77–78)

In this scene, Markham positions Jebbta as the other woman who attempts to identify (with) her: "Your body is like mine." Jebbta's undifferentiated sisterhood, posited as it is on a version of identity politics, would essentialize Markham as woman and reduce her autobiographical possibilities to the script of the sexed body. Yet Markham's very narration of the exchange resists Jebbta's insistence on the similarity between white and black girls. Positioning herself as a "boy," she emphasizes the contrast between her own hardy and naked strength and Jebbta's weak, fragile, and demurring femininity.

Throughout, Markham resists a sisterhood of sessility by positioning herself outside the narrative of maternal origins and domesticity, thus erasing the traces of motherhood and mothering, the script embodying traditional femininity. Her mother is elided, her name unspoken, her relationship with Markham unacknowledged. Presenting herself as an unmothered daughter, Markham, echoing the Athena of the *Oresteia*, implies that she is not of woman born. She also erases her own mothering, never mentioning her first or second husband or her son and never positioning herself inside romantic relationships and their consequent social roles. Resisting embeddedness in the arena of domesticity, she divests herself of the textual encumbrances of a selfhood fettered to the female body. Through her embrace of aerial subjectivity, Markham cuts the umbilical cord to Mother Earth and to female embodiment.

But Markham goes beyond erasing the traces of the normative script that would enclose woman in stillborn postures. She goes so far as to position herself discursively as a male speaker. As befits the masculine hero, she adopts the rhetoric of stoic toughness, a stance through which she resists any kind of untidy textual emotion, any maudlin sentimentality—a toughness through which, to use an aerial metaphor, she remains above it all. Thus, the topographic distance in flight functions analogously to her rhetorical distance in narrative voice. Moreover, she locates the feminine in particular textual spaces. To Makula, the Wakamba tracker who refuses to enter her plane, she quotes the proverb "A wise man is not more than a woman—unless he is also brave" (233), miming the cultural invocation of the female body as a sign of emasculated manhood.

More commonly, Markham reproduces modernist tropes that identify the machine to be mastered with a femininity at once passive and potentially fatal in its inconstancy. Talking about another aviator's plane, the *Klemm*, Markham writes: "The silence that belonged to the slender little craft, was . . . a silence holding the spirit of wanton mischief, like the quiet smile of a vain woman exultant over a petty and vicious triumph" (49). She describes the *Klemm* as "frivolous and inconstant," "the sad and discredited figure of an aerial Jezebel" (53) powered by "an hysterical engine" (47). She recalls Woody calling the *Klemm* "a bitch" (54). In such passages, Markham "ventrilocates male ideologies of gender," to use Felicity A. Nussbaum's phrase (149), particularly the ideology of the fallen, contaminating, and potentially disruptive woman, who is as much a threat to man as the plane gone wrong is a threat to the aviator.

Finally, Markham feminizes the Africa over which she flies. A place where she lives "free from the curse of boredom" (10) and constantly finds "a release from routine, a passport to adventure" (198), Markham's rhetorical Africa is a space of mystery, wisdom, wildness, fluidity, virginity, silence, and timelessness, an unknowable space rendered exotic and erotic by the desiring subject of flight. It is virgin land to be conquered, the place where desire saturates the landscape, the field on which the male hero can mark his imperial manhood. A conventionally mythic text, Markham's aviator narrative participates in what Teresa de Lauretis describes as masculinist tropes embedded in the semiology of plotting. "As [the mythic hero] crosses the boundary and 'penetrates' the other space," suggests de Lauretis, "the mythical subject is constructed as human being and as male; he is the active principle of culture, the establisher of distinction, the creator of differences." In this same mythic space, the "untransformable" is marked as "female … an element of plot-space, a topos, a resistance, matrix and matter" (43–44). In this way, "Africa" is figured as a premodern space at the edge of modernity's scope.

*West with the Night* mimes, with haunting elegance and incontestable narrative power, the masculinist logic of traditional Western travel narratives. Surrounding herself in the text with the accoutrements of the heroic figures of Greek mythology and figuring herself textually as "the radiant centre of a transcendent individualism" (Stallybrass and White 21), Markham aestheticizes her identity as (male) bourgeois individual. In this enactment of identity, the gender of performer and performance is distinct from the anatomical sex of the woman whose name appears on the cover. From a certain point of view, then, Markham's narrative of mobility troubles the ideologies through which travel itself is gendered. For the narrative undermines the stability of any essential origin of masculine or feminine identity by "revealing," in Judith Butler's words, "that the original identity after which gender fashions itself is itself an imitation without an origin" (*Trouble* 138).

Moreover, Markham's investment in the masculinist logic of adventure hints at the possible disruption of racial hierarchies as well. As she locates herself within the circle of elite adventurers who test themselves against the elements, she gives credit to and admires the prowess of the male Africans with whom she hunted as a child (Arab Maina, Arab Ruta, and the young Kibii) and later as an adult (the tracker Makula). "Racial purity [and] true aristocracy," she suggests early in the narrative, "devolve not from edict, nor from rote, but from the preservation of kinship with the elemental forces and purposes of life whose understanding is not farther beyond the mind of a Native shepherd than beyond the cultured fumblings of a mortar-board intelligence" (7–8). And she offers slight but stinging critiques of the modernization and bureaucratization of colonial Kenya that ally her with "heroic" natives against the "domesticated" westerners who threaten to empty life of adventure itself. In this romance with adventure, the aristocracy of adventurers appears to be one that joins people across racial differences.

Yet this valorization of the "native" informant—the one who can initiate the westerner into the knowledge requisite for survival on the frontier—is yet another trope of Western adventure narratives that belies the egalitarian romance of an elite brotherhood. Ironically, of course, Markham could identify with a virile masculinity in Africa because, as a white child growing up among black Africans, she had the cultural prerogatives and power to gain access to native male experiences that were inaccessible to the native girl. On a culture's frontiers, formalized arrangements of gender often surrender to practicalities. Life in colonial Kenya offered her the freedom to cross-dress as a young boy and consequently to assume the identity of boy child. As a result she could take from native Africans, all men, the education in courage, prowess, intuition, and camaraderie that was so central to her childhood.

In fact, the Murani warriors are given a major role as educators in her narrative only in her presentation of her childhood. When she moves to the narration of her adult experiences, she accepts a different social and textual contract with the black Africans, as they become her servants. Acknowledging this change with some irony, she nonetheless accepts its inevitability: "What a child does not know and does not want to know of race and colour and class, he learns soon enough as he grows to see each man flipped inexorably into some predestined groove like a penny or a sovereign in a banker's rack" (149). Although her ironic commentary here suggests that she glimpsed the economic dimension of a predestinarian social order, such politically charged commentary is rare in the narrative. It is also compromised by her narrative practice of inserting the African male into Western narrative tropes of the great white hunter and "his" native guide/servant. Markham leaves the cultural economies and narrative tropes of colonial relationships unchallenged. The native Africans are thus doubly servants. In literally serving whites, they also serve the ideological economy of a "masculinity" central to the maintenance of European colonialism, now further entrenched with the aid of the machines that aviators like Markham flew across the lands spread out below.

Moreover, as Markham's text operates to resist the essentializing effects of Jebbta's universal sisterhood, it reproduces that very cultural script of essentialist difference, here displaced onto the body of the African woman. Even as she uncouples her identity from female embodiment, Markham maintains her allegiance both to what Hélène Cixous calls "the white continent" of subjectivity and to the literal white continent by supporting the colonization of the other woman and thus of Africans more generally. The body of the other woman may trouble the edges of this narrative, but Markham keeps the other woman there, at the edges. To incorporate her into the text would be to invite Markham's own identification as woman across the borderland of race and class. It would be to contaminate her identification as aviator in a brotherhood of adventurers. It would be to emasculate and deracinate the "new man" as white man and to contaminate the white continent of Western adventure narratives, in this case the thoroughly modernist version of the aviator narrative. In Markham's narrative we see how the aerial subjectivity introduced through this newest of the technologies of motion could be incorporated into a conservative modernism, a modernism that, in its embrace of the romanticized tropes of mythic adventure, participates in the "imaginative opportunism" that characterizes all kinds of imperial projects.

## The Conclusion to an Era

Even as the proponents of avant-garde modernism hailed the aviator as the new man and flight as a medium of stylistic innovation, in popular modernisms—films, celebrity publicity, and aviator narratives—the figure of the woman in flight became a site around which modernist themes and the ambivalences of modernity circulated. Dorothy Arzner's film *Christopher Strong* capitalizes on and reproduces the female aviator as popular icon, exploiting her celebrity exceptionalism and containing its agency through the logic of the romance plot. The aviatrix is at once an active agent of aerial modernity and the commodified carrier of a more conservative script of domesticated femininity. Yet, through the figure of Lady Cynthia Darrington, Dorothy Arzner insinuates a complex critique of the very logic the film appears to enact. Thus, even as it glamorizes the aviatrix for Hollywood effect, the film participates in the reflexiveness that is so central a component of modernism by encompassing without fully resolving the anxieties of modern social relations provoked by the airplane.

Amelia Earhart, Anne Morrow Lindbergh, and Beryl Markham all negotiated the anxieties of modern social relations generated by the airplane and the transformation of the world inaugurated at Kitty Hawk. Entering the imaginary domain of aerial masculinity, these women became agents of modernity, affirming their right to a place in the skies. Through familiarity with this most modern of modern technologies, these aviators at least momentarily escaped the domestication of women through protocols of proper femininity. They could release themselves from a defining sessility. For them, flight was a redefining mobility.

Yet they encountered in their aerial exploits and the ensuing celebrity the phantasm of the "lady flier" and all the cultural iconography attached to her—from her sleek, boyish, streamlined figure to her perceived incompetence to her radical threat. *Christopher Strong* offered one scenario of celebrity femininity at risk. Sacrificing herself for the sake of normative heterosexual relations, sacrificing herself for the other woman whose marriage she refuses to destroy, sacrificing herself in order to put her beautiful face forward to the camera in her last gesture of restoration, Cynthia Darrington faces the limits of aerial feminism and fails to survive. Earhart, Morrow, and Markham do survive as celebrity figures at risk (at least long enough to tell their stories), yet their narratives reveal how complex a woman's relationship to aerial subjectivity was when she was no longer flying in the skies but putting herself on the page. In their narratives they negotiated the tension between the woman of flight and the woman of the ground. If, as the popular narrative of the doomed aviatrix would have it, there must be either flight without normative femininity or normative femininity without flight, they had to manage their problematic status as "bird women" on the wing.

But the differences in their ways of presenting flight as a defining mobility are fascinating. First, there is a difference in how they position themselves in the narrative. Earhart situates herself as the fun-loving girl next door; Lindbergh as the thoughtful, responsible sidekick to her famous husband; Markham as the remote and exceptional individual. Second, there is a difference in the ways they represent the airplane itself. For Earhart, the airplane is at once a routine machine, a modern convenience like a vacuum cleaner, and a source of fun, a machine not to be feared. Lindbergh represents the airplane as a means of communication between peoples and as a source of tremendous physical and aesthetic pleasure. Markham, manipulating technology to gain height, speed, and heroic distance, represents the airplane as a prosthetic technology extending the borders of imperial subjectivity.

Finally, there is the difference in their narrative logics. Both Earhart and Lindbergh play to the cultural expectation that the female aviator must present herself as properly feminine in order to be allowed the celebrity she requires to fly. Moreover, they assume the role of mediator between the exotic domain of flight and the masses of people on the ground. As translators, they reimagine the domain of flight away from its defining danger, domesticating it for future consumers. Playing the feminized role of social worker and educator, Earhart, "the American girl," promotes an ethics of familiarity. Lindbergh, celebrating the airplane's potential for bringing progress to the edges of modernity's scope, promotes an ethics of relationality and internationalism. Yet she also lapses rhapsodic about the palpable pleasure of the machine, from the aestheticized vision it opens for her to the music of its motion felt at the bone. There's a connection between the two ethics, as both—the aesthetic and the relational—are meant to connect flight to the lives, practices, and bodies of those on the ground. Markham, in contrast, plays to the codes of masculine adventure and comradeship, enforcing the elitism of the aviator willing to confront danger. As she does so, she widens the difference between herself and that other woman with her degraded embodiment. Detaching herself from the sphere of degraded femininity, Markham keeps intact the sense of the skies as a domain of imperial masculinity.

Deeply invested in the masculinist logic of adventure, Markham reproduces an ethics of imperial individualism.

The period of the celebrated female aviator was a short-lived one, spanning from 1927 to 1940. For that brief stretch of years, celebrity was made possible by the agency of the individual aviators who entered the small planes maneuvering through the skies, by the imperatives of an airline industry intent on expansion, and by the spectacular event—the air race, the high-altitude test, the first flight across country, continent, or ocean. In addition to aviator, industry, event, and machine, celebrity was made possible as well by the myth of progress with its imperialist design. Thus, the "lady flier" became an emblem of the most modern of women. But, of course, these aviators were doing cultural work other than merely representing white Western womanhood. If the masses of people, formerly so many dots on the ground, were to rise up into the air, the sky had to be made "safe" for less heroic consumers. The women aviators, by affirming for the masses that flight was safe and comfortable and that it didn't require exceptional heroics, played their role in the transformation of aviation to big business. They made for good advertising copy.

As a last note, we might think again of the narrative of the aviator who ended up paying the ultimate price of the risks of flight. The palpable tensions in Earhart's very popular aviator narrative encompass, without fully resolving, the problems of celebrity feminism in an age of rising consumer culture. Amelia Earhart is at once an active agent of aerial modernity, an avatar of the national modern, and the commodified agent for a more conservative agenda, the domestication of flight in service to big business. It is precisely the remarkable event that assigns Earhart her elevated status, but her role as spokesperson for the emerging commercial aviation industry means that she has to empty the event of its extraordinary and dangerous dimension. Earhart's exceptionalism may not be contained through the logic of the romance plot; it surely is contained through the logic of consumerism. So Earhart's identity itself is placed in transit by this modernist mode of travel and by the contradictory logics of her travel narrative. The American girl, whose winsome image

Isabelle Eberhardt photographed not long before she died in a desert flood in 1904. Reproduced in Kobak.

One of the photographs Alexandra David-Neel included in her published account of her journey to Lhasa (1927). The original caption read: "Madame Alexandra David-Neel, the first foreign woman who has ever entered the forbidden holy city of Lamaism, is seen seated in front of the Potala, the palace of the Dalai Lama. Her face is smeared with black lac according to the custom of the Thibetan women. At her right side Lama Yongden, her adopted son. At her left side a little Lhasa girl."

# FLY

## THE NATIONAL AERONAUTIC MAGAZINE

PAULHAN STARTS HIGH FLIGHT

Vol. II    No. 4    **FEBRUARY, 1910**    Price, 10 cents
$1.00 a Year

The indomitable aviator, alone in his machine. Cover of *Fly* magazine, February 1910.
Courtesy of the Clements Library, University of Michigan.

The "bird men" *(Les hommes-oiseaux)* and their dreams of flight. Engraving from a novel by Restif de La Bretonne, Paris, 1781. Courtesy of the Transportation History Collection Print Collection, Special Collections Library, University of Michigan.

The classical hero in an "Aviators Wanted" advertisement. *Fly* magazine, June 1912. Courtesy of the Clements Library, University of Michigan.

Dressed to fly? Harriet Quimby and Matilde Moisant, the first women in America to obtain pilot licenses, circa 1911. Reprinted with permission of National Air and Space Museum, Smithsonian Institution. SI photo no. A43515.

# Everybody Can Fly!

Learn how at the

## MOISANT AVIATION SCHOOL
### Hempstead Plains, Long Island

## Five Pilots Licensed in August

Miss Harriet Quimby, Miss Matilde Moisant, Mr. F. E. De Murias, Mr. S. S. Jerwan, Mr. Harold Kantner

## MOISANT MONOPLANES USED

Chief Pilot: ANDRE HOUPERT

Licensed by the Aero Club of France

For handsome illustrated booklet address

### HEMPSTEAD PLAINS AVIATION CO.
### Times Building, New York City

"Everybody Can Fly!" advertisement for the Moisant Aviation School. *Fly* magazine, May 1912.

Bessie Coleman with her aviator goggles, circa 1925. Reprinted with permission of National Air and Space Museum, Smithsonian Institution. SI negative no. 92-8943.

The celebrity aviatrix: Katharine Hepburn as Lady Cynthia Darrington in the film *Christopher Strong* (1932). Courtesy of MOMA Film Stills Archive.

Katharine Hepburn dressed up like an insect (a moth?), with Colin Clive, in *Christopher Strong* (1932). Courtesy of MOMA Film Stills Archive.

was broadly reproduced—in her own narrative, in advertisements, and on newsreels—participates in the dismantling of this frontier of defining heroism. Out of expediency and a wily disingenuousness, Earhart traverses values from masculinist exceptionalism to domestic consumerism and the acceptable feminism of her modern admirers. They in turn consume her aerial femininity.

The end of the 1930s marked the end of the era of small aircraft and the individualist heroism associated with flight. In 1935, the year *North to the Orient* was published, the Lindberghs moved to Europe. America's romance with Lindy was waning, and the promise of the new internationalism was fading as a fascist nationalism—with which Lindy was, unfortunately and unwisely, sympathetic—began to threaten international war. Earhart was lost over the Pacific Ocean in 1937. World War II and the rise of commercial aviation brought bigger planes, larger crews, and routine flights. And in the early 1940s, Markham, whose narrative was designed in part to promote a career in Hollywood, failed to find a means to support herself in the film industry and returned to colonial Africa.

# CHAPTER 4

# By Rail: Trains, Tracks, and the Derailments of Identity

To the lady who has a long [train] journey ... let me recommend
that she remove her outdoor garments ... as if she were in her own
drawing room. It will be found a most comfortable plan to take
with one a pair of house-slippers.

—Lillias Campbell Davidson, *Hints to Lady Travellers at
Home and Abroad* (1889)

## Railway Histories

With the invention of the "iron horse" in the early nineteenth century,
trains became both the literal and figurative dynamos of modernity.
They drove the expansion of commercial and communications networks,
thereby accelerating the distribution of commodities across vast distances, the attendant accumulation of capital in metropolitan centers, and
with that accumulation industrialization and urbanization, all defining
conditions of modern nation-states with dreams of preeminence. Their
"capacity to reshape ... environment in order to increase its productivity"
made possible as well the efficient organization of vast colonial empires
from which raw materials could be extracted with cheap labor (Adas 235).

By the late nineteenth century, railway transportation functioned,
according to Michael Adas, as "the measure of men." Their miles of
tracks carved out of rugged and intransigent terrain, railroads signaled
with every whistle and smoke streamer European and American scientific
expertise and the dominance over nature itself. Space could be reorganized, and so could time, with the imposition of World Standard Time
from Greenwich, England. This transformation of space and time but-
tressed belief in the superiority of Western culture and Western "man."
The world of locomotion provided the material basis for and the cultural

sign of Western enlightenment philosophies. Everywhere the railroads stretched there was "enthusiasm for technology as an agent of social change" (Adas 230) and for the moral utility of the civilizing mission that would bring enlightenment to the less "civilized" world.

If trains and train travel were applauded as engines of Western "progress," and with it increased wealth and democratization, they were also condemned as the engines of destruction, cultural intervention, and bankrupt modernity, alienated and routinized. Granted, they could deliver dreams, transporting travelers to all kinds of destinations. But they could also destroy dreams. The expressionist artist Maurice de Vlaminck bemoaned the railway as that "gaping sore which admits infection" into an idyllic landscape, and condemned it as a "wound" through which the infectious disease of industrialization entered the rural body (Freeman 134). Rail beds and tracks cut through hillsides and valleys, slashing the surface of the land, gouging it out, subduing and reorganizing nature for iron purposes. An agent of industrialization, the railway ran over the old ways, radically remaking the rhythm, paths, and purchase of communal life.

In colonized and settler territories, the expansion of the railroad facilitated the exploitation of subject peoples and the radical disruption of communities and cultures. Across the Indian subcontinent, from the north to the south of Africa, through the Australian outback, and across the American and Canadian West, railroads overrode ways of life and reorganized social relations. In Russia, for instance, the railroads transported millions of peasants from the west to the vast tundras of Siberia, thereby facilitating the creation of an entirely new colonial outpost. In India they transported imperial troops expeditiously to sites of unrest, such as the site of the Indian Mutiny of 1857, thereby enforcing violently the might of the home country to quell rebellion. In the American West, they transported hostile settlers through Indian lands to settlements, thereby reshaping the face of the "frontier." In this last instance, the train sometimes became a veritable shooting gallery as settlers shot bison from the windows of railway cars and sometimes shot at the people whose way of life was vanishing with the increasing speed of this engine of national expansion and manifest destiny.[1]

The Sioux activist Zitkala-Ša (Gertrude Bonnin) was only too aware of this effect of the railways. Writing at the turn of the century of her childhood separation from her community in the Dakotas, she ironically invoked the metaphor of the train as an engine of Enlightenment progress when she described her education at a missionary school in Indiana as the "iron routine" through which school authorities tried to remake her into an assimilated American girl. Bonnin condemned the transformative power of the railroad in enforcing a radical remaking of identity. But she was swimming against the metaphorical tide. The cultural expectation that subjects of progress would be radically remade through their relationships with this new technology became a defining myth of the nineteenth century.

That myth became particularly potent in the arena of leisure travel. The railroads changed the everyday relationships of people to organized leisure activity, transforming the nature, reach, expense, and clientele of travel. In England, Thomas Cook recognized the potential early on. According to the lead writer of the *Times* (London) obituary for Cook in 1892, this entrepreneur "saw that the great new invention of the railway might be made, by the help of a new organization, to provide large numbers of people with pleasanter, cheaper, and more varied holidays than they had ever been able to enjoy before" (qtd. in Pudney 19). In the beginning was Cook's first excursion from Derby to Rugby, England, in 1841. At his death there was a vast set of related travel businesses (spanning England, Europe, Africa, India, and America) that he bequeathed to his son. Throughout the second half of the nineteenth century, Cook exploited the desire for and profitability of mass tourism. The middle classes had already begun to organize everyday life around holidays. But inexpensive railway travel meant that people of the working classes could join ready-made excursions and tours as well. Additionally, railway travel provided a relatively safe, clean, comfortable, sheltered, and predictable mode of conveyance for families and for unattended women.

As increasing numbers of travelers took to the rails and created an ever-expanding audience for information about travel, the readily available guidebook became an indispensable marker of the tourist. Karl

Baedeker's *Italy: Handbook for Travelers*, for instance, went through twelve editions by 1896. Guidebooks were targeted at specific niches—Cook's to the middle and working classes, Baedeker's to the wealthier ones. Even Lillias Campbell Davidson's *Hints to Lady Travellers at Home and Abroad*, published in 1889, can be seen as a niche publication geared to the growing number of women traveling by train and steam. Providing useful information such as timetables, historical background, suggested itineraries, daily schedules for visits to important sites, and cautionary advice, the guidebook became a textual chaperon, the mass-produced avatar in the nineteenth and twentieth centuries of the educated traveling companion of the eighteenth century's grand tour. It was servant, tutor, and protector at once.

Guidebooks represented the traveler as a comfortably superior citizen of enlightenment and progress in search of "sacred" sites and the "authentic" artifacts of other cultures.[2] Railroad companies, as well, stimulated the desire for certain destinations and experiences through advertisements and then delivered those destinations comfortably to travelers (Faith 190). For instance, the Santa Fe Railroad in the United States packaged travel to the wild frontier of "the West" (what became Arizona and New Mexico), providing along the route the organized spectacle of "authentic" Indians effectively "pacified" on "reservations," enacting rituals of exotic otherness. Along the tracks, the Sante Fe also advertised the dining and sleeping facilities of Fred Harvey houses, which could deliver "good taste" and "immaculate manners" to the middle-class traveler (Poling-Kempes 37).

Guidebooks, advertisements, and staged spectacles all contributed to cultural understandings of the social utility of travel. In his *Physical, Moral, and Social Aspects of Excursions and Tours*, published in 1860, Thomas Cook quoted one Eliza Cook on the utilitarian merits of travel:

> "It is delightful to see, as we travel on, the breaking down of partition walls of prejudice, the subduing of evil passions and unhappy tempers, the expansion of the intellect, the grasping for information, the desire for books and the eagerness of their perusal, the benevolent sympathies excited by a

more extended knowledge of the circumstances and sufferings of fellow creatures, the improvement in health and prospects, the endurance of fatigue, and perseverance under difficulties." (Qtd. in Pudney 74)

Both Cooks champion the potential for travel to reform the traveler, to make him or her over into a healthier body and a more liberal and enlightened, rather than insular, mind. With increased access to travel, education into an enlightened subject of progress became a possibility for a broader expanse of people. It no longer remained the privilege of the few.

Nowhere perhaps was the identification of train travel with reformation more profound than in northern mid-nineteenth-century America, where abolitionists and escaped slaves such as Harriet Tubman dubbed the succession of safe houses known to protect escaping slaves "the Underground Railroad." For escapees and harborers alike, the railroad offered a powerful metaphor for the progressive transformation of the abject slave into the free subject of American democracy. Some escaping slaves, such as William and Ellen Craft, used the actual railroad as their vehicle of escape north (42). After emancipation, as Houston A. Baker Jr. suggests, railroads continued to signal "the promise of unrestrained mobility and unlimited freedom" (11) to African Americans, immigrants, and backwoodsmen. "To them," writes James Allen McPherson, "the machine might have been loud and frightening, but its whistle and its wheels promised movement. And since a commitment to both freedom and movement was the basic promise of democracy, it was probable that such people would view the locomotive as a challenge to the integrative powers of their imaginations" (6).

Later in America, the trains "loved passionately" by hoboes such as Maury "Steam Train" Graham (93) delivered men and some women, such as "Box-Car Bertha," from the banal conformity and bourgeois repressions of modern life, a delivery they celebrated in their respective narratives of vagabondage. Around the world, in diverse countries and colonies, men and women climbed onto trains to pursue visions of new identities, new relationships, new worlds, new lives. Trains delivered reformers, suffragists, revolutionaries, nationalists, and union organizers to widespread destinations, enabling them to organize networks of supporters for change across national and international boundaries. Trains delivered vast numbers of the devout to pilgrimage sites such as Lourdes, where they sought spiritual reformation. And they delivered to middle-class women a convenient, acceptable means of escape from domesticity. Olive Schreiner's nephew recalls that his aunt "said there was one great thing about living at De Aar, and that was the knowledge that you could always get away, that you could take a train any day" (Gregg 53). People in motion became people transformed. Some aficionados and advocates of steam technologies talked of the impact of locomotion in quasireligious language: the railroad became a "divine" form of intervention in the lives of people (*Locomotion* 1994).

Yet even as the locomotive furthered the agenda of modernity and realigned modern social relations, it also conserved certain features of those relations in the organization, the peopling, and the design of the machine ensemble. Hierarchical systems emerged in the distribution of work roles and identities in railroading and on the train for the people who worked on the railroads and the people who rode them. Around the world, the laborers who blasted the rocks of hill and mountain and picked out the roadbeds came from the poor and oppressed classes. In America, "coolies" brought in from Asia and immigrants from the potato famine in Ireland, as well as unemployed Civil War veterans, built the roadbeds that opened the American West to pervasive settlement; African Americans labored as dining-car stewards and cleaners; white American entrepreneurs assumed positions as engineers and managers of the railway lines, which an elite of white industrialists owned. In Europe and its colonies, passenger cars carried markers of class status ("first-," "second-," and "third-class" carriages and, for the masses, freight wagons); and in America, markers of racial and ethnic hierarchies ("white" and "colored" cars and, across the advancing western frontier, cars marked "immigrants"). Railroad stations, even as they facilitated the mixing of social classes and races, secured the differences between people with their first-, second-, and third-class waiting rooms, their separate station facilities and culinary choices, their marked platforms, their protocols for the purchase of tickets and the quantity of baggage allowed travelers, and their modes of access to the tracks (Richards and MacKenzie 139).

Locomotion incorporated and sustained gender differences in its organization of material, people, and movement as well. Obviously, one of the reasons European and American women began to travel in greater numbers and to range further from home in the nineteenth century had to do with the democratization of travel attendant on the invention of the steam engine. The railroad increased women's mobility, transporting large numbers of women beyond the confines of a domestic life, beyond what Mary Louise Pratt terms the "matrimonialist imperative" (*Eyes* 240), and into public spaces. Later it delivered them cheaply to jobs in major cities. In these instances locomotion enhanced certain women's agency by offering a vehicle through which they could become less sessile, less ignorant, less dependent, and more autonomous.

At the same time, however, the world of locomotion reproduced normatively gendered patterns of work and leisure. As places of work, for instance, railroad companies were organized through highly militaristic traditions (Faith 62–63) and through those traditions forced a hierarchy of locomotive masculinities, from the rugged strength and bravery of the "navvies" who forged the rail beds, to the professional expertise of the engineers and managers, to the entrepreneurial masculinity of the tycoons. Only occasionally did women gain access to railroading jobs on the lines or in the stations—for instance, with the exigencies caused by the dearth of laborers on the railways during World War I—and then often only temporarily. And the kinds of jobs they assumed were jobs coded feminine: service jobs in restaurants and hotels. The "Fred Harvey girl" in the American West is a particularly colorful example of a normatively feminized identity available to women working in railroading.

For travelers as well, the world of locomotion was a gendered domain. The middle and upper classes found locomotive travel an increasingly comfortable and protected mode of transport as railway cars became more and more luxurious. That, of course, was their appeal to women travelers. On the train, these women found themselves enclosed in spaces designed to protect them from the elements and from their own vulnerability as women in transit. In a sense, then, the world of locomotion offered women miniature domestic sites along the rails. As railroad companies encouraged and exploited the identification of traveling women with feminized spaces, with comfort, ease, and safety in travel, they inevitably reinforced cultural stereotypes of women's incapacity for arduous travel.

Even the antibourgeois culture of the itinerant hoboes registered normative spectacles of masculinity and femininity. Male hoboes rode the rails in pursuit of an alternative masculinity differentiated from the routinized and sedentary conformity of bourgeois masculinity. Some of them, such as Steam Train Graham, romanticized the lure and freedom of the road (Carden 98). Identifying the train as their passionate love, they distinguished conventional heterosexual relationships from an outlaw romance joining man and machine. For women hoboes, travel along the rails became a means to escape the degraded arena of bourgeois marriage and to pursue desire outside the conventions of bourgeois femininity. But female hoboes, women moving with no certain destination, also became vulnerable, because they were seen by male hoboes and railroad workers as sexually active and therefore sexually available women. They could not escape the stereotypes linking women in transit with sexual availability. Thus, even as they sought to be remade through the possibilities for mobility that this modern technology offered them, women travelers of all types could not escape the contradictory effects that the world of locomotion generated in modern social relations.

### Railway Envelopes: Interiority, Speed, and Consciousness

Multiple histories move travelers along complex tracks of self-locating. But just as complexly, the semiotics of the railway car and the envelope it places around the traveling subject affect the horizon of transformative self-locating. As Wolfgang Schivelbusch so brilliantly argues, the world of locomotion changed the relationship of the traveler to the world through which she moved. Thus, the impact of the locomotive on modern social relations cannot be understood outside the transformation in consciousness that technology effected.

In exploring how the railway ensemble enforces a particular form of panoramic vision upon the traveler, Schivelbusch suggests that the velocity at which the train moves and the "mathematical directness" of the route sever the direct, sensual relationship of the traveler to the traveled space (53). Because foreground space cannot be absorbed visually, the traveler loses connection with proximate space, concentrating instead upon distant space. This distant space moves by in "a series of . . . pictures or scenes created by the continuously changing perspective." Consequently, "the traveler [sees] the objects, landscape, etc. *through* the apparatus which move[s] him through the world," with the effect that "evanescent reality ha[s] become the new reality" (64). But the evanescent scene functions paradoxically as a fixed scene. For, as Eric Leed notes in elaborating the phenomenon of passage through space in terms of the relationship between an aiming point or point of origin and a vanishing point or point of disappearance, "the motion of the traveler superimposes [a] pattern of outflow and inflow upon an environment," and from this superimposition the traveler "derives . . . an idea of an objective world, of that which does not change as one changes" (75).

In "Railway Navigation," Michel de Certeau translates this phenomenology of train travel in postmodern terms. For de Certeau, there are two sites of immobility put in relationship to one another in train travel. Of the inside of the railway car, he writes: "Only a rationalized cell travels. A bubble of panoptic and classifying power, a module of imprisonment that makes possible the production of an order, a closed and autonomous insularity—that is what can traverse space and make itself independent of local roots" (111). The world outside the railway car reveals another kind of immobility, "that of things, towering mountains, stretches of green field and forest, arrested villages, [and] colonnades of buildings" (111). In this sense there are two locations of immobility: the fixedness of the geographical space through which the traveler passes, and the fixedness of the "rationalized cell" (111) moving through space. Because "vision alone continually undoes and remakes the relationships between these fixed elements" (112), only the eye lies between the immobility of the inside and the immobility of the outside. And transporting the eye, so to speak, is the machine, what de Certeau calls the *primum mobile* (113).

The distance established between the train traveler and the scene beyond; the onrush of impressions that the eye cannot fully process; the monotonous humming of the *primum mobile*—these three defining conditions of locomotive mobility often induce reverie, the withdrawal into personal consciousness, fantasy, and memory. Caught in and by reverie, the subject of train travel imagines herself to have escaped attachment to the literal ground and the figurative grounds of the routine present, to have achieved some kind of freedom as a separate, autonomous subject. In her railway compartment, the traveler experiences a contained individuality held suspended in a perpetual "flow" state, a continuous state of liminality (de Certeau 111–12).

In this experience of mobility, the traveler finds the exhilaration of what de Certeau calls "incarceration-vacation" (114). Incarcerated inside a moving compartment from which she cannot escape, except at great physical risk, the traveler nonetheless finds herself on vacation from habitual consciousness. In this sense the experience of continuous motion through train travel "resolves boundaries into paths, makes thresholds into perceptual tunnels of continuously evolving appearances, converts limits into avenues. Passage, in short, dissolves the realities inseparable from place: the reality of boundaries, the recurrences of time and mortality, all inherited containments within the defining and confining orders of place" (Leed 79). Continuous train travel thus lifts the traveling subject outside her everyday routine as it forces an encounter with evanescence.

Yet the *primum mobile* also projects her along a predetermined route and fixes her points of departure and her destinations. And if it promises to dissolve the reality of boundaries, it effectively secures her in the physical boundaries of glass and steel and the psychological boundaries of an isolated cell of self. Eventually, at the end of the line, there's the entry into the station and the abandonment of the railway car. There, de

Certeau suggests, "the Robinson Crusoe adventure of the travelling noble soul that could believe itself *intact* because it was surrounded by glass and iron" ceases (114).

## Tracking Narratives

When they climb onto the train, women travelers climb into the cultural history of train travel with its politics of gender. On that train they experience mobility through the transformed semiotics of railway perception. When they write about their travels and locate themselves as subjects of locomotion, they contribute to the long history of cultural representations of the railroad. Since the first chug of the locomotive across man-made terrain, narratives of locomotion have permeated popular- and high-cultural venues, from paintings and prints to songs, novels, and films.

Visual artists in the middle and late nineteenth century turned their eyes with fascination on the railroad as it transected the landscape and announced the achievements of modernity with every grunt and whistle. In England, J. M. W. Turner exploded color across the canvas as he captured the atmospheric effects of light, landscape, and forward motion in his famous *Rain, Steam, and Speed* (1844). Other English painters rendered locomotion with less atmospheric and more narrative effect than did Turner. Along the tracks, and particularly at the railway station, they found endless opportunities to paint scenes that combined stunning visual detail with the grandness and emotional power of spectacle. Thus the popularity of scenes filled with the bustling energy of stations, their preparations, departures, and arrivals—scenes such as the one W. P. Frith captured in *The Railroad Station* (1862). Later there would be paintings capturing the mass good-byes of troops off to the war front, a spectacle charged with the threat of death.

In France the railway was everywhere in the canvases of the impressionists, marking the landscape with an insurgent thrust of modernity and providing stark contrast between bucolic scenes and the engine of the future. In a series of successive canvases depicting Gare Saint-Lazare (ca. 1877), Claude Monet worked to render in visual terms the awesome energy of steam power and the synergy of vapor and hard steel. In the first decades of the twentieth century, the futurists continued to find visual subjects in the dynamism and monumentality of the locomotive. In his 1909 futurist manifesto, F. T. Marinetti announced that the futurists would "exalt aggressive action, a feverish insomnia, the racer's stride, the mortal leap, the punch and the lap" as they would "sing" of "deep-chested locomotives whose wheels paw the tracks like the hooves of enormous steel horses bridled by tubing; and the sleek flight of planes whose propellers chatter in the wind like banners and seem to cheer like an enthusiastic crowd" ("Founding" 41–42). Like the airplane, the train symbolized for the futurists a thoroughly virile modernity, energetic, mobile, violent, noisy, and confident.

In these early years and decades of the twentieth century, the music of African Americans filled with references to trains, tracks, depots, and the desire to go "down the line." In blues performances across the northern and southern United States, travel was, as Angela Davis emphasizes, "one of the most salient of [the] imaginary themes" of the blues (66). For former slaves and the sons and daughters of former slaves, the railway, as has been noted, signified some modicum of freedom—and the personal liberation to earn a living elsewhere, to escape the reach of "the man," and to pursue adventures, including amorous ones. For bluesmen, and blueswomen, the sound of the whistle and rumble of the tracks became a familiar leitmotiv of possibility in mobility.

There were cultural representations that attended to the dark side of locomotion as well. The first train narratives, the stuff of folk art and folk songs, were the nineteenth-century ballads chronicling train disasters and their violent devastation and loss of life. Trains also rolled through the pages of the great realist novels of the nineteenth century, often serving as background engines of change, carrying peoples into and out of class positions, into and out of communities, and into and out of plots of great expectations and great failures. Sometimes the station was a central site of desire, desperation, death, and destiny, as it was in the pages of Dickens and Trollope and Tolstoy, all of whom stage climactic suicides in train stations. In their novels the locomotive becomes the deus ex machina of bourgeois modernity. This connection of locomotion and danger continued into the twentieth century, when the train became a site of murder, intrigue, and sexual excess. Early in the century, Maurice Dekobra's *The Madonna of the Sleeping Cars* (1927) combined death, desire, and detection in a plot of violent motion. More recently, Paulette Giles's *Sitting in the Club Car Drinking Rum and Karma-Kola: A Manual of Etiquette for Ladies Crossing Canada by Train* (1986) reimagines detection and desire through the parodic treatment of film-noir versions of brief encounters.

And then there is the relationship of film and locomotion. Recall that the Lumière brothers' *Arrival of a Train at La Ciotat Station*, shown in December 1895, marks the beginning of the film era. Like the impressionists, the Lumière brothers recognized the visually dramatic spectacle of steam and steel. Not long after this inaugural event, *The Romance of the Rails* and *The Great Train Robbery* appeared in America (1903). As with aviator narratives, train narratives immediately became popular in the emerging film industry. From Buster Keaton's silent-era film *The General* (1927), to Jean Renoir's *La Bête Humaine* (1938), to David Lean's *Brief Encounter* (1946), to Alfred Hitchcock's *North by Northwest* (1959) with its famous kiss on the train, to Sidney Lumet's *Murder on the Orient Express* (1974) and all the other murder-on-the-train films, filmmakers have exploited the romance with trains and the kinds of narratives and visual effects trains make possible. Sometimes it's terrifying motion the films engage, sometimes the dangerously claustrophobic enclosure and latent violence, sometimes the steel brutality of modern industrialization, sometimes the exotic locales through which the trains race, and sometimes brief encounters between strangers. Trains and their destinations have been identified with fleeting romance, with escape from the constraining circumstances of everyday life, with brute realism, with violence and sexual intrigue, with desperation, with mass murder, with mass political mobilization, and now with nostalgia. The train in motion offers a multivalent site for human drama, perhaps because its rhythm of pulling out of a station, journeying through the landscape, and pulling into a destination bears the marks of narrative itself, or perhaps because it is simultaneously a potentially liberating and constraining vehicle for identity and its discontents.

What about the representational possibilities for women and the locomotive? The figure of woman has been integral to the plots of fleeting romance, intrigue, violence, sexuality, and death in motion. Just recall two extremely popular melodramatic series from the early days of American film: *The Perils of Pauline* and *The Hazards of Helen*. These melodramas turned on the vulnerability of dependent, sessile women incapacitated before the brute machine. Pauline, tied to the track, facing death under the iron wheels of the phallic engine, waits passively for her heroic liberator. If subsequent filmic women have not been literally tied to the tracks, they have been bound to the narrative tracks of heteronormative plots, no matter where they've been headed. The brief encounters on trains and in stations that recur throughout twentieth-century films offer moments of respite from the banal relationships of everyday life; but the respite is limited to the heterosexual plot of romance, however inflected with intrigue or exoticism or danger. The spectacle of arrivals and partings, so central a theme of nineteenth-century narrative painting, returns in the twentieth-century film to provide an intensification of the stakes of romance.

And then there is the titillation of a stranger's exotic sexuality—the look of a Greta Garbo passing along the corridor, or a glimpse of Lauren Bacall withdrawn into her sleeping compartment, or the wholesomeness of a Janet Leigh kissed in the darkness of a tunnel. In so many popular films, the train is projected as an imaginary domain inhabited by exotic and dangerous women posing a threat to men or sexually repressed or expectant women awaiting awakening by a man. Whatever their differences, they are women contained through the technologies of narrative and the technologies of mobility that identify that locomotive as excessively phallic. Heterosexual romance, provocative sexuality, and the engine as phallic destiny—no wonder that in the great realist novels of the nineteenth century and in the many popular films of the twentieth century, woman and train have had a limited repertoire of relational possibilities.

But this is to erase the possibilities for railway agency that come from other cultural locations, for instance, the lyrics of the blueswomen. Through their lyrics and voices, the blueswomen registered for their audiences the possibilities of black women's locomotive agency. As Davis suggests, "the ability to travel implied a measure of autonomy, an ability to shun passivity and acquiescence in the face of mistreatment and injustice and to exercise some control over the circumstances of their lives, especially over their sexual lives" (74). The lyrics of Ma Rainey's "Traveling Blues" reimagine the itinerary of black womanhood from the sessility of the bed and house to the openness of the road (Davis 74). Through their engagement with the trope of the traveling man (the privileged trope of the bluesmen), blueswomen such as Rainey and Bessie Smith took up the train and remade it for their own purposes.

It is this remaking of locomotion for greater female agency that I want to explore in three late-twentieth-century narratives of train travel. But before turning to the narratives of Mary Morris, Linda Niemann, and Daphne Marlatt and Betsy Warland, I look back to the 1920s, to an essay Virginia Woolf wrote about traveling on a train.

## Modernism's Locomotive Manifesto:
## Woolf's "Mr. Bennett and Mrs. Brown"

In May 1924, Virginia Woolf addressed the Heretics Club in Cambridge, England, giving her talk with the alliterative title "Mr. Bennett and Mrs. Brown." To enliven her meditation on the rupturing difference of the modern writer, Woolf narrates a story of everyday train travel in a third-class carriage that takes her from Richmond to Waterloo, not a far distance at all, but in this case a distance registered through profound questions about "representation, history, and sexual difference" (Bowlby 2).

Entering the railway carriage, Woolf observes an anonymous elderly woman, whom she calls Mrs. Brown, talking with a man, whom Woolf calls Mr. Smith. Mr. Smith seems vaguely threatening in his exchanges with Mrs. Brown, but he eventually gets off. Not long after, Mrs. Brown climbs down from the car and walks away. The plot is simple: woman gets on train, woman talks to man, man gets off train, woman gets off train.

Yet if Mrs. Brown passes out of the frame of the scene, she does not pass out of Woolf's imagination. Having observed the comings, exchanges, and goings in the railway compartment, the writer makes out of Mrs. Brown, an anonymous stranger encountered on a train, a character in a story she wants to tell of the transition from the literary culture of Edwardian to Georgian England—a transition, she notes, that took place "in or about December, 1910," when "human character changed" (320), or rather, when the aesthetics of representing human nature changed. It seems that Mrs. Brown commands narration. We have here a common trope of railway narratives, the "brief encounter" that forces strangers into one another's lives. In this particular iteration of the trope, the artist, fascinated with the scene playing out before her, uses the occasion of a train narrative to meditate on the mystery of human character and the aesthetics of representation.

As Rachel Bowlby notes in her study of Woolf (and as was noted in the preceding section), by the early 1900s the railway carriage had become a commonplace metaphor for the materialist aesthetic of and in realist fiction (3). References to and scenes located in stations and railway cars figured the displacements and alienation of industrialization, the ruthlessness and sheer force of the conditions of modernity, and the inescapable material conditions thwarting human desire and imagination. Dwarfed by the conditions of modernity, the human subject in the third-class compartment signified a degraded humanity.

For Woolf, this realist aesthetic—and the generic forms it produced in the late nineteenth and early twentieth centuries—is embodied in the work of Messrs. Bennett, Wells, and Galsworthy. This trio of Edwardian writers direct their gazes only to the outside of the railway carriage, away from the specificity of Mrs. Brown to the dystopian world into which they insert Mrs. Brown as a pliable figure through whom the forces of modernity enact their exacting scenarios. In such scenarios Mrs. Brown becomes merely a functional component of the narrative, a "sign" of some larger force. She might, for instance, figure as a sign of "progress," the woman who can travel on her own on the train (Bowlby 200). As Woolf's light but deft critique makes clear, the problem with such a functionalist approach to character, which pays attention almost entirely to the material conditions of existence, is that it erases the pressure of the character. Directing her harshest critique at Bennett, Woolf accuses him of "never once look[ing] at Mrs. Brown in her corner" (330). He does not look; he cannot see.

Edwardians exhaust themselves, the reader, and "the truth itself," because "so much strength is spent on finding a way of telling the truth" (335). But for Woolf, the Georgians, as well, in their efforts to shed the aesthetics of the Edwardians, end up "smashing and crashing" their object of representation, their Mrs. Browns, enacting a violence of representation every bit as ominous as the threatening posture of Mr. Smith in the carriage. Yet, Woolf assures her reader, Mrs. Brown persists: "There she sits in the corner of the carriage travelling not from Richmond to Waterloo, but from one age of English literature to the next, for Mrs. Brown is eternal, Mrs. Brown is human nature, Mrs. Brown changes only on the surface, it is the novelists who get in and out—there she sits and not one of the Edwardian writers has so much as looked at her" (330). As "an old lady of unlimited capacity and infinite variety" (336), the stranger Woolf encounters on a train is the figure of the ineffable and the durable in human character.

For Bowlby, the critical gesture in Woolf's manifesto is her reading of Mrs. Brown as a stranger, insisting on her "difference from the way she is presently dealt with" (11), that is, her difference from contemporary representations of her. In her sheer persistence, this Mrs. Brown dissipates an outdated convention that "ceases to be a means of communication between writer and reader" (Woolf 334) and generates instead a new mode of address, a new relationship to words, a new concept of time, a new contract between writer and reader, a new covenant of truth-telling. The modern artist who seeks the truth of character must shift her focus from the externalities of character—character situated primarily in the material world—to the interiority of character. She must imagine how it feels to be a subject in and of everyday life. She must ponder and probe the elusive, the ineffable, the mysterious, the evanescent, the partial, and the fluid nature of the strangers of and in her imagination.

Woolf's journey from Richmond to Waterloo is a journey that "tracks" the transition from an outdated environmental realism and a materialist poetics of character to a modernist poetics of psychological innerscapes, a poetics she genders feminine. Only too aware of the limited ways in which woman has been represented, the modernist writer projects a new representational logic. In doing so, she uses the train as both material site and metaphor. She presents it as the literal engine of motion driving the march of an everyday modernity and as the metaphorical engine of transition from one age to the next. In this latter sense, the train serves as a vehicle of artistic vision in which the woman, "Mrs. Brown," is imagined through another representational relationship to the engine of modernity.

Woolf's strategic use of the railway journey in "Mr. Bennett and Mrs. Brown" is highly suggestive for the contemporary narratives of train travel to which I now turn. Woolf invokes the technological engine identified with her male predecessors and their materialist aesthetics. She then identifies their practices as masculinist conventions that have denied women characters a viable subjectivity. She consigns those conventions and those writers to the past. Finally, she situates a new ethics of character and a new representational logic in the midst of the very vehicle associated with those predecessors. In this way she empties the railway carriage of its masculinist logic and fills it instead with the mystery of the ineffable Mrs. Brown. In their recent narratives of train travel, Mary Morris, Linda Niemann, and Daphne Marlatt and Betsy Warland engage the limited repertoire of relations that women have had to locomotion. Presenting themselves as agents of locomotive feminism, they explore the ways in which the woman mobilized through locomotion rides the rails of identity through her discontents. And, like Woolf, they remake the instrumentality of the train and its phallic engineering to their own purposes.

## Locating the Past

In *Wall to Wall: From Beijing to Berlin by Rail* (1992), Mary Morris reconstructs her 1986 train journey from Beijing to Berlin via the Trans-Siberian Express, a journey she undertook in order to visit the home of her maternal grandmother in Ukraine. Morris's journey across China, Mongolia, the Soviet Union, and Eastern Europe is precisely the kind of journey that train travel first made possible in the mid-nineteenth century. Offering independent women a relatively safe and comfortable mode of mobility, it saved them problems with language, speed, and expanse that travel by foot or by automobile would entail. In fact, in Morris's case those modes of mobility were impossible; they could not deliver her to her destination. And flight would have taken her too far above the memorial ground she wanted to cover. Locomotion, in this instance, coincides with the itinerant purposes of the woman in motion.

The rail line, reproduced in a prefatory map, serves as the linear spine of Morris's narrative. To flesh out this narrative spine, Morris reconstructs the everyday details of the trip, based on the diary she kept. After all, like other professional travel writers, she wants to entertain her reader with vignettes of people encountered and sketches of exotic locales. But throughout these descriptive and anecdotal details of her journey, Morris weaves a far more personal narrative that includes the anatomy of a disintegrating romance, a family chronicle of immigration to America, a series of minihistories of famous walls she encounters on the journey, and a meditation on the meaning of travel for the independent woman. This personal narrative has everything to do with Morris's relationship to locomotive mobility and the identity of traveler she has shaped for herself.

"The windowglass and the iron [rail] line," de Certeau writes, "divide, on the one hand, the traveler's [the putative narrator's] interiority, and on the other, the power of being, constituted as an object without discourses, the strength of the exterior silence." Paradoxically, it is "the silence of these things put at a distance, behind the windowpane, which, from a great distance, makes our memories speak or draws out of the shadows the dreams of our secrets" (112). As the traveler looks out of the panes of glass, she reads not some mute "reality" out there but her own interiorscape, her past. Into the distance that railway travel enforces, the traveler pours herself, filling it with her own memories.

We see the residue of railway reverie in Morris's narrative practice.

She presents herself as a traveler reading her own state of affairs—more the history inside than the history outside—self-referentially across the face of the country she passes by. From the train, the narrator reads geography as personal history and history as personal geography. Of the Siberian landscape she writes:

> All my life I had imagined this terrain, a country as much within me as without, a landscape that seemed almost of my own making. I could not look at this land and not think about its history. And I could not think of its history without thinking of my own. We crossed frozen ground, ice-trimmed lakes. Peering through the open shade, I saw a world outside that seemed no different from the one I carried within. Cold, hungry, empty, and vast. (97)

Because the external landscape and lives through which the train hurls her cannot and do not speak back to her, she can project upon them roles through which she articulates her defining story.

That story is about the way that, for Morris, mobility has been self-defining. "I have never bought sheets for myself" (88), she tells her reader. To be a woman in motion, a "moving body," is, the narrator claims, to be "a woman in control" (152). To be a woman in stasis, a woman at home, is to be woman controlled. The woman in control is Morris's feminist ideal, an ideal the narrator tells the reader she fabricated as a child to cope with the emotional turmoil of being chastised for failing to perform any task adequately. It is also the compensatory identity she imagines to extract herself from the narratives of female long-suffering recited by her mother during her childhood and adolescence. Her mother's "master narrative," which this daughter incorporates into the text, centers upon her great-grandmother, who buried her children alive in order to outwit the Cossacks intent on pogrom, and on her grandmother, who was buried alive: "Women, my mother said when she told me this story, lived terrible lives. They were abused, but who would listen. They suffered, my mother said, but whom could they tell" (50). Gagged, buried alive—the maternal legacy is a too-familiar legacy of mute victimization from which the woman in motion flees.

Thus Morris's investment in the identity of "the traveler." That figure of mobility has embodied Morris's mythic ideal of the woman in control: she travels where she wills, she proceeds purposefully, she maintains her independence. As Julia Watson suggests when discussing Morris's earlier travel narrative, *Nothing to Declare* (1988), for Morris, the woman who travels becomes "a moving point of perception" who in this way works "to elude the strictures of definition as 'woman' that would immobilize her" (159). Ever on the move, the traveler remains unfixable as woman. By becoming the traveler, the narrator implies, Morris has resisted being reproduced as her mother, an immobilized woman. Travel transports Morris beyond degraded femininity, the identity her parents enforced through socially instituted norms.

But there has been a price to pay for such defining mobility; and so, throughout *Wall to Wall*, Morris assesses that price: the rootlessness and restlessness of the unattached wanderer of the diaspora. Attentive to this burden of rootlessness, she identifies herself with other figures of mobility, figures for whom travel is a dislocation and an isolation rather than a liberating mobilization: "I am orphaned, disenfranchised, removed. A *desdichada*, a Jew, a lost one, searching for my clan. I have not been able to find my mate, my place. Like most Americans I dwell far removed from the source—in deserts where no one knows where we've come from, in cities where no one cares" (87). Wandering Jew and immigrant exile in America—these are "nomadic" figures, figures disconnected from their past.

Thus, too, the urgency of Morris's journey to her grandmother's home in Ukraine. Yoking the wandering Jew and the immigrant exile in America, the narrator explores her desire to return to her roots, equating a return to her grandmother's ancestral home with the recovery of a matrilineal anchorage in "community, family, the place to belong" (87). Paradoxically, it is this compulsive dream of going home that sets her in motion. If, she suggests, "my dark Russian soul, plunked down in the Midwest, has been exiled, banished, relegated to another place," then "I thought that by coming to Russia, by traveling to the country my grandmother called home, I would somehow find an answer. I would recognize what I had been looking for all along" (138). Like Isabelle Eberhardt in the North African desert, Morris leaves home to go "home" to a memorial point of reference.

Initially, train travel seems perfectly suited to her project of reconnection. Find a map. Find grandmother's home. Then find the rail line that can get her where she wants to go. Her destination sets her on a particular itinerary and puts her on a particular train; and the dependable forward movement of the train across the geographic expanse of Asia and the Soviet Union seems to register the progress toward her goal. With its purposeful movement and its promise of delivery to stipulated destinations, passage by train seems perfectly matched to the narrator's desire to reach the sacralized city of maternal origins (112, 118).

Moreover, as it rushes through space, the passenger train catapults Morris across borders and into relationships through which she makes contact across walls of various kinds (linguistic, national, ethnic, etc.). In her vignettes Morris celebrates those connections. Some people give her gifts. The cook gives her a beautiful comb (124). A fellow passenger, Dmitri, cries at parting (124). She in turn gives other travelers sardines (123). They connect.

But the narrative also reveals that train travel places "barriers" between the traveler and others. If people get on, they also get off. Differential destinations render connections temporary, intense but short-lived. Although it offers the illusion of connection, then, the train is instrumentally an engine of disconnection. It delivers relationships without roots in the past, without issue in the future, and thus with only present and fleeting possibilities. Consequently, Morris's narrative is full of connections never made, information not fully processed, relationships stalled. In effect, the train compartment enforces self-containment, a privatized interiority, a carapace of isolated individualism. And the traveler remains a moving point of perception whose motion ensures her disconnection.

Remembering locomotive mobility, Morris recognizes that trains foster personal isolation, thereby heightening the effects of incarcerated individualism: "On the inside I have had encounters as well.... I've been invited off trains into homes, into beds, asked to walk into people's lives, all I am sure because people know a train traveler will never leave the train" (67). One stays comfortably inside, does not descend into the unknown, does not connect. Train travel promises but does not deliver connection. Thus, the engine of progress and independent mobility becomes the engine of dislocation and incarceration. Train travel, Morris writes, keeps her "trapped in an itinerary," a situation she has tried to "avoid all my life." It keeps her "encaged by my journey" (83). By the time she gets to Moscow, she feels she is a prisoner of her own destination. Locomotion becomes incarceration. Travel becomes less and less progressive: "For the first time in my life I found myself backtracking, taking a route I'd already taken, returning the way I'd come" (215).

Incorporating anecdotal allusions to other train travelers, both fictional and real, the narrator presents trains as engines of death for people isolated and homeless. At one point she recalls that Tolstoy died alone in a train station, in flight from his family. She remembers Anna Karenina, the doomed lover, in flight from the impossibilities of her outlaw desire, falling under the iron wheels of convention. She recalls Jewish parents, waving from the platform in Berlin as they send sons and daughters into orphanhood elsewhere. And she recalls most powerfully the millions of Jews herded into boxcars and carried off to concentration camps. This technology, so implicated in instrumental and brutal rationality, is, for the writer, the lover, and the Jew—that is, for Mary Morris—a vehicle of abandonment, separation, loss, and mass murder: "In this train station where my journey had ended, other people's nightmares had begun" (248). By the close of the narrative, the promise of train travel has been redefined as danger.

The technology of mobility ultimately cannot take Morris where she wants to go, because, paradoxically, its instrumentality is undone by the very materiality of the traveler's body. Early in her trip, Morris recognizes that "something was wrong with my body" (35). At first there is inconvenience, exhaustion, and hunger. Then she perceives her body as "foreign" (163). Then she discovers she's pregnant: "We lay there together for the first time, one inside the other, inside the bed, inside the alcove, the room, like those Russian dolls I carried with me as gifts, each one smaller and smaller, tucked inside the other" (186). The child grows within her body. The man she loves refuses her desire for marriage. The nuclear winds across Ukraine threaten her unborn child. Morris decides against locating her grandmother's home, too close to Chernobyl for comfort. And so she remains captive of and in the railway car from which she cannot disembark because of the destructive effects of modern nuclear technology. Sneaking "like a thief in the night across this tainted land" (231), the train rushes its passenger past the threatening nuclear dust of Chernobyl, past the tense border of the USSR and Poland, and delivers her finally to the railway station in West Berlin. Maps and itineraries have failed her. Timetables have proved ineffective. The body disorganizes the imaginative phantasm of the woman in control.

But Morris proposes through her narrative of the train journey an alternative way of connecting with her grandmother and her own past, an alternative route to self-recovery. The very permeability of the female body in pregnancy, the growth of another within the skin-walls of the body, forces Morris to displace the figure of the traveler who would escape the spectacles of degraded femininity with the figure of "the mother/child." Speaking as "mother," the narrator claims self-recovery as the motivation for her search for her grandmother's home. "My grandmother," she writes,

> had been buried alive as a child and I understood now, carrying my own child within me, why this image had stayed with me all this time, why it had sent me on this trip. I thought how we all bury the child within us or have it buried for us. . . . In my own way I had buried a child of my own. Not the one I was going to have, but the one I had been. Now I felt her within me, scraping at the edges of her grave, beginning to dig her way out. (239)

Morris turns her grandmother's literal burial as a child into her own psychological burial of the child within. Thus, the child growing within her functions metaphorically as the forgotten child buried deep inside her.

Morris remembers how as a child she buried unacceptable desires and disidentifications with socially enforced norms of proper femininity in the goodness that was required by an oppressive patriarchal household and the message of woman's long-suffering. That is, she walled up (repressed) the abject child within, what she calls her "buried treasure" (152).[3] The promise that she identifies with pregnancy is the possibility of recovering and unburying that child within. Morris thus shifts her compass from the geographical to the psychological axis, imagining a return to a state of innocence before the fall into socially enforced norms: "Perhaps, with a child of my own, this might be possible once again," this "gazing up at the night sky, innocent again" (258).

If the excess in her body undoes her sense of control, the narrator suggests that it also undoes some of the mechanisms through which she keeps walls in place—the walls, for instance, between herself and her parents, whom she has defined in fixed terms. (When she calls them to tell them of her pregnancy, they are accepting rather than disapproving.) The narrator closes with a scene before the Berlin Wall. The stirring of the child within encourages her to touch the cold wall, to reach for the end of walls, "because any boy now was someone's child to me" (259).

The romance of self-recovery through pregnancy displaces the romance of geographical return through locomotion as a vehicle of self-knowledge. At "the end of the line"—the line of tracks, the line of words that have become Morris's text—the narrator muses: "I think that perhaps home is not a place. Perhaps, it is what we remember" (253). The narrative of remembering that Morris makes out of this railway journey is the only return she can claim, the only home available. Through an act of remembering, she ultimately un-becomes the rootless traveler through reconnecting with the child within. Invoking a Graham Greene quotation, "Childhood is a non-cerebral, thus mapless little journey" (9), she counters the certitudes of mapped itineraries. Now, instead of positing train travel and itinerant mobility as the vehicle for achieving connection, she posits the new subjectivity of the mother as the defining connection. In effect, the steel instrumentality of locomotion is displaced through the materiality of the moving body. Writing afterward of her failed journey, the narrator shifts the meaning of locomotion away from the defining logic of a liberatory mobility.

Morris's journey as originally conceived was a failure. But the second journey, the journey of narration, becomes a quest narrative through which Morris explores the cultural logic of defining mobility. The story Morris tells of "walls" is the story she tells of her own personal journey. The Great Wall of China, the Forbidden City, the Kremlin, the Berlin Wall—these edifices are barriers obstructing exchange, barriers disconnecting peoples. Marking landscape and cityscape, they signify as well an interior geography of walls—between people, between the narrator herself and others, and within herself. In the interior of the nation and the interior of the subject, borders are secured and walls are erected. But she discovers the other side of walls. They are breachable. They fail to hold out the enemy. For the narrator, the evidence of history suggests that material walls are never secure. Projects designed to hold back the abject, to wall some identity in and some other out, are always ineffective. That which has been contained leaks out, and that which has been held at bay leaks in. Total control is impossible.

What Morris discovers in her train journey and represents in her train narrative is that the engine of modernity cannot do for her what she wants it to do. For Morris the traveler, the woman in control turns out to be a myth of identity that train travel undoes as female embodiment catches her up. But for Morris the narrator, the myth of the train as an engine of phallic instrumentality can be undone through her refiguration as pregnant woman. Ultimately Morris looks through the window of embodiment rather than the window of technological instrumentality.

## The Boomer

> I was a Doctor of Philosophy and I knew what was in the books.... The boxcars in the freightyard reminded me of those books.... They were thirty-ton books on iron guillotine wheels; they had origins and destinations; they had histories along the way.
>
> —Linda Niemann, *Boomer* (1990)

There are locations on trains other than the passenger cars in which Morris rides. There are the working cars, the engines and cabooses, a reminder to the reader that locomotion depends upon laborers to deliver goods to their destinations and people to their desires for connection or escape. It was in these cars that Linda Niemann rode the rails for better than eight years in the 1980s, working as a boomer, one of the itinerant brakemen who follow "the rush periods of work in different parts of the country" (15). *Boomer* (1990) is her narrative of life on the rails.

Niemann's is a working railroad, not the train of reverie Morris rides. Yet, like Morris, Niemann would be a woman in control. She announces to her reader at the beginning of her narrative that "the railroad transformed the metaphor of my life" (3): "When I saw the ad in the Sunday paper—BRAKEMEN WANTED—I thought of it as a chance to clean up my act and to get away. In a strategy of extreme imitation, I felt that by doing work this dangerous, I would have to make a decision to live, to protect myself. I would have to choose to stay alive every day, to hang on to the sides of those freightcars for dear life" (3). Reading the paper for its metaphors, Niemann responds to the want ad as a message directed at her wants. The narrator represents this reading practice and the decision to become a boomer as a gesture designed to displace the psychological danger of her life with literal danger. Muscular mobility she reads as potentially lifesaving, a survivalist necessity. By literally putting brakes on in dangerous circumstances, by exerting physical control over matter, the boomer rehearses the satisfactions of starting and stopping, the everyday reiteration of control. She also places herself in an environment of danger, one in which death can no longer be romanticized as a desirable end to personal angst. Death becomes the palpable possibility of everyday life. By becoming a brakeman, Niemann puts her life on the line in an embrace of motorized modernity. By pumping this kind of iron, she enacts everyday control over the chaos of self-destructive habits.

If this is the reading Niemann originally applies to the advertisement of life on the rails, her narrative of that life offers a far more complex reading of life in locomotion, for it participates in various generic intentionalities. It is by turns a descriptive manual of dangerous and demanding work (complete with a glossary of terms); a nostalgic tribute to a fast-fading way of life; and a survivalist's celebration of rugged individualism with its stamina, endurance, grit, and courage. Registering the vicissitudes of muscular masculinity and the demise of a masculine way of life dependent upon the great engines of modernity, Niemann makes explicit the identification of the railroad ethos as masculine, an ethos forged in the spectacles of muscular masculinity associated with the *primum mobile*. Jumping onto the side of the train, Niemann climbs onto a man's machine.[4] She works the brakes, moves freight cars back and forth, and ensures the continued movement of the train along the tracks, the continued allegiance to a timetable. She depends upon the other brakemen for her survival, and they depend upon her. Through these generic intentionalities, Niemann registers her "outlaw" positionality as a woman joined to the phallic power identified with technology, the mastery and control of machines, time, and space.

This outlaw identification is signaled in the name she takes on the rails. "Gypsy" signifies her nomadic mobility, her freedom from the defining spectacles of sessile femininity, her capacious sexuality and desire. The name also registers the ambiguity of identity. "Gypsy" can be both a masculine and a feminine signifier. Her narrative of life on the rails reveals the category crisis of the woman who participates in defining spectacles of muscular masculinity. Throughout, the narrator alludes to the persistent refrain that women don't belong on the rails (128) and dramatizes the everyday discrimination against women who work them. But she also explores the ways in which rigid and fixed sexual differentiations become blurred in the camaraderie of dangerous work. If you act dependably and if you do your work, then you are accepted, if grudgingly.

The women boomers break the connection between the masculine subject and masculinist travel tropes, between what a body is and what a body does. But even as they break that connection, they remain subject to the pressures of normative spectacles of gendered identity. Whereas some of the women, like Niemann, erase their sexual difference by becoming "one of the guys" (35), others dress in working-class femininity. The narrator captures the complexity of the sexual politics of cross-dressing when she describes the purchase of her first pair of boots. Attentively reconstructing her search for the right boots (131–33), the narrator comments: "Women don't wear them much, unless they need to for a specific reason," and one of those reasons is to signal "that they have a male-identified power in the world" (132). In buying her boots, she dresses for success.

Instead of the immobilities de Certeau assigns to the traveling subject inside the car and the scene outside the car, here we have a drama of radical mobility. Life on the rails, even as it promises the sheer muscle of dominating masculinity, forces Niemann to the limits of identity through the multiple cross-dressings of gender, class, and sexuality. For the railroader's scene is an intense arena of homophobia, sexism, masculine privilege, racism, anti-intellectualism, and survivalist fundamentalism, an arena that constantly contests the intelligibility of the various identities she presents to others in the freight yard. Thus, Niemann crosses over a variety of identity borders and enters an arena in which identities cohere and dissolve, a landscape where the freight of stipulated identities is all mixed up. "The hurricane ambience of Houston brought to the surface all my old struggles to fit in, to feel located in an identity," she writes. "I had never found a niche where I didn't violate some of the membership rules. I was an intellectual, and I looked like an all-American bimbo. I was bisexual, but lesbians thought I looked straight, and straights thought I looked gay. I was middle class, but I was living a working-class life. I was extremely ambitious, but in a curiously spiritual sense" (33–34). The narrator understands herself to exceed definitions that would fix her in some kind of secure position. Getting on and off the tracks, putting on and taking off the brakes, Niemann constantly discovers the shifting grounds of identity. Sometimes, to conform to the screens of identity through which she materializes in other people's gazes, she puts on feminine drag or her "porcupine identity" (37) or her "Pasadena" persona (85). But always she acknowledges the insufficiency of identity categories to anchor her in any meaningful location.

Instead of anchoring her sense of identity securely inside the glass and steel of the *primum mobile*, train travel untethers Niemann. Instead of providing her with what de Certeau calls "a module of imprisonment that makes possible the production of an order, a closed and autonomous insularity" (111), train travel sets her adrift in disorder, taking her to the limits of intelligibility: "I found my borders disappearing. The simplest questions were gnomic. Self-image, sexual-preference, profession, family, history. I wasn't sure about any of them" (134). The imposed systems that secure people in identity locations, that attach the identities of bodies to what they do or what they look like or where they've come from or whose they are, no longer hold. Her life on the rails is a life of liminality, a life of perpetual displacement that captures her sense of herself as always exceeding fixed identifications. It is as if she moves into and out of depots of identity.

Niemann's representation of the world of locomotion captures this random drift of identity. The narrative itinerary moves randomly with the trains across the Southwest, from one destination to another. People move randomly into the narrative frame, then disappear. The tough, colloquial, and ironic narrative voice invokes the gritty rhetoric of life on the rails. The staccato pace of the prose captures the restlessness and perpetual spatial displacement of that life, the movement of the boomers from one yard to another in search of work, the continual movement in and out of relationships, in and out of towns, in and out of bars, the restlessness of the endlessly unfolding tracks. It captures as well the frenzied fragility of a way of life characterized by exacting labor, fatigue, sudden layoffs, insecurity, and the desperation of workers caught in the vicissitudes of a postindustrial economy: directionless travel, directionless identity, frenetic movement for movement's sake.

Midway through *Boomer*, however, the narrative voice of restless mobility gradually begins to give way to another, more poetic and less frenzied voice as Niemann begins to weave through the episodic, itinerant narrative the mythic journey out of the abyss and the subsequent ascent into a new life, a way of life whose determining metaphor is the river. This transition—or conversion, if you will—occurs when the narrator claims a specific identity in the midst of radical dislocation, that is, when she claims her "I" as an alcoholic "I."

Gradually the multiple genres incorporated in Niemann's narrative of restless train travel give way to the master narrative of the twelve-step recovery program of Alcoholics Anonymous (AA). A "retrospective narrative designed to reinterpret the past in the light of a more enlightened present identity" (Warhol and Michie 330), *Boomer* is structured around the AA "coherence system," involving a "drunkologue" followed by a sobriety story that gives attention to a transforming spiritual force. Writing her narrative after "recovery," Niemann assesses her brakeman's life as symptomatic of her drinking life. The first half of the narrative, then, is seen as being preoccupied with inventorying her unmanageable life, her life as "a runaway boxcar" (62). In her life before sobriety, she was a woman out of control (77) who needed to "get a brake on" (62). Thus, the variety of symptoms she reads in her past are all signs of the alcoholic subject: failed relationships, alcoholic binges, loneliness, emptiness, self-duplicity, and her insistence on her difference as an outlaw. From this point of view, the central ritual of masculine command and control, buying boots, becomes a symptom of her denial of her "true" identity as alcoholic. She therefore mocks her participation in that defining ritual, critically assessing the meaning of her eagerness to try on and to buy the right pair of boots. The boots function for the narrator as a substitute fetish for sobriety.

According to formula, Niemann's drunkologue gives way to a sobriety story and her search for a "new mythology" (134). As in the normative AA narrative, the alcoholic subject finds a way to renewal through a "greater power," which Niemann identifies as the "river" flowing through her. "When Westerners want to find themselves," she reflects, "they go look at the land; they travel. They find a mirror that looks outward and describe the geography of a certain frontier. Even today, like Major Powell, we seek the blank space on all the existing maps, knowing, as no doubt he did, that the unknown river is in the mind, and all we seek is the empty space to discover it in" (110). As with Mary Morris, the incarceration that is integrally a part of life in motion within the *primum mobile* inaugurates reverie, the personal fantasy of a place of belonging. Niemann reflects that it was in the "panoramic emptiness from the window of a moving train that I began my slow understanding of what serenity could be" (131). Watching the Colorado River pass by, the restless traveler feels it running inside her; and in that gesture of interiorization she "discovers" the metaphor of the river of the mind. From this turning point in her narrative, Niemann tracks her recovery. Fleeing the house of an alcoholic friend and its pervasive sense of hopelessness, the narrator recognizes "the final resonance of my drinking life, gasping in a waterless pool like the brakeman's craft itself, not at all what it had been like. And impossible to go back to, to do anything more than remember it as it had been" (242–43). Concluding her narrative, Niemann announces to her reader that "a gentler river moves me now on its way to the sea" (245). The natural movement of water displaces the engineered movement of the *primum mobile* and the railroad track as productive of self-knowledge.

Ultimately, Niemann finds a representational home in the master narrative of the twelve-step program for sobriety and the coherent, universal "I" of the alcoholic. In fact, her act of telling, as Robyn Warhol and Helena Michie argue of the sobriety tale, "is itself evidence of sobriety" (348). To testify is to find a way

> to become my own story, as Dickens puts it, to find out who was the hero of my own life. I had told my story many times in bars, elaborating the fantastic, the grotesque, the dangerous. I had traveled in the manner of embellishment, knew all the side roads where one stopped at small wineries to taste, to lose days and weekends, to create a parallel life—a life of dreams into which my lifeblood and spiritual river was slowly draining away. (111)

In writing her narrative, Niemann attempts to "become one with her story" (111), to become coherent and unified in the autobiographical "I"—and the conforming "eye"—of AA.

In remembering life on the rails, Niemann interprets her immersion in locomotion as immersion in the world of itinerant difference. Life lived on the working cars of the railroads offered her an arena of rugged individualism, an arena for the enactment of an outlaw identity—outside the norms of femininity, normative heterosexuality, and middle-class respectability. In chronicling her participation in these defining spectacles, the narrator registers her identification with the cultural script of a masculinity of excesses—of mobility, bravado, language, liquor, and sex. Hers is a late-twentieth-century iteration of the masculine myth of the romantic artist flirting with self-destruction, the frenzied itinerary of a latter-day Jack Kerouac. Returning to her home in southern California, she asks: "Was it all some kind of circle I was feeling the return to now, here where I went into the world and found drinking and poetry and the desire to consume more and more life?" (238).

According to the AA master narrative, this preoccupation with difference is itself a symptom of alcoholism. Thus, when Niemann claims the identity of alcoholic, she claims as well a corporate (and anonymous) identity through which her radical difference is rejected. The sign of her rejection of radical difference from social norms is her identification of self-recovery as the recovery of "the feminine side of my god-consciousness" (207). As she identifies with the natural terrain outside the train window, Niemann turns from the phallic instrumentality of the locomotive and the life of "masculine" excess to the abjected femininity within that her life on the rails has encouraged her to brake.

## Doubling Women, Doubling the Negative

The final text I take up in this chapter is a doubly authored poetry collection cum travel narrative, Daphne Marlatt and Betsy Warland's *Double Negative* (1988). In May 1986, Marlatt and Warland rode the train across the Australian landscape from Sydney to Perth. They purposefully "chose this steel line" (9), they recall, in order to journey "through" Australia rather than merely fly "over" Australia. That journey through initiates a poetic engagement with the progressive logic of train travel, which they explicitly gender masculine. Moving across the postcolonial Australian landscape, these lesbian lovers explicitly "rewrit[e] the train experience from a female perspective" (38).

*Double Negative* is divided into three sections. It opens with a series of poems, then introduces a transcript of a conversation between the two poets, and concludes with a series of poems that riff seriatim on a line from each of the poems in the first series. The first section, "Double Negative," follows the linear trajectory of the train moving progressively across the landscape of Australia. Names of sites on the map—the cities and towns through which the train passes or in which the train stops—provide titles for the poems, thereby registering movement toward Perth. As the poems mark the progress of the train across the landscape, the speakers attend to the details of train culture: the initiatory commands of the conductor issuing instructions about dining arrangements, the protocol of stops along the way, the rushed recovery of glasses from cabins during the final push into the station in Perth. And they capture the rhythm of the progressive movement along the tracks in such poems as "past Menindee."

But the "syntax" of train travel, the poets propose, must be reorganized through the logic of metaphor. The train may be a "train of thought," pushing rationally and instrumentally toward conclusion, destination, and destiny; but the speaker of "Zanthus" wants "no syntax only syllables" (28). That is, she wants to resist the linear progression of the train and all that it signifies in Australian colonial and postcolonial history. For the railroad functioned as a force of modernity overwriting Aboriginal lands with the march of progress. Thus, this engine of modernity signifies the force with which the white explorers and settlers pressed across the continent, which they labeled *terra nullius* (empty land), devastating in their wake the landscape and the indigenous peoples and cultures inhabiting it. Riding the rails across Australia, the lovers cannot escape this specific history of colonization, a history captured in the very titles of the poems. Mixing English and indigenous Aboriginal place-names, the titles signal the complex cultural history of encounter, displacement, and persistence written across the land. Playing on the etymology of the word *train*, the lovers find a way to resist the locomotive as a train of thought or a train of progress by focusing on another meaning of *train*. They seek, they say, to "traine" the train, that is, "to feminize (part of a[d]dress)" by carving a linguistic and imaginary space for lesbian desire within the realpolitik of the train. They would do this by joining the body of woman to the material body of Australia, "go[ing] inside out into the womb of the continent" (13). To do so, the speakers of the poems seek to recover the unseen landscape (the womb) of this overwritten locale by attending to the flora and fauna past which the train moves. They fill the poems with the natural world of Australia—the trees, flowers, birds, and animals—bringing an "ab/original" Australia into being by naming this flora and fauna in the "ab/original" languages (14–15). In "Forrest," they catalog the richness of the Nullarbor—the Latinate name white Australians gave to the vast desert they saw as a land without trees—and thus affirm that there is "thriving outside The Gaze" of the westerner who would see only emptiness (24). They populate with life forms an environment ruthlessly labeled *terra nullius*.

Further, they find the language of this *terra nullius* rich with possibilities for capturing their experiences of one another. The land and the female body are joined (18) as they reimagine the other's body through this new landscape, through new words, scenes, and senses. In "Port Pirie," woman as "negative feminine space" is identified with the Australian desert, also labeled empty space. "Woomera," named for the weapons-testing range, offers an opportunity to play on the idea of a "prohibited zone," which the speaker rewrites as the V of her lover's body. "Deakin," a poem describing the journey across the Nullarbor, becomes an occasion to dismiss the representation of the great western plain as "nothing" (as woman is "nothing") and to identify the ubiquitous "saltbush" of the plain with the salty taste of the lover's body. In "Rawlinna," the speaker remembers lovemaking as the skin contact of emu and kangaroo, because "the dream they are / we are":

> Touching you
> i touch kangaroo
> lick my way through
> your red fur. (27)

Punning on the word *emu* ("me/you") and the "not" of *knot*, the speaker in "Kalgoorlie" announces:

we will do
the walk the emus do
the me/you train that doubles us
into the not. (31)

For the lovers, the desert through which they journey becomes "the feminine" as they yoke *terra nullius*, the Nullarbor plain, and the negative that is woman (22).

In their linguistic playfulness with syllables rather than syntax, the lovers would "reinvent" "the matter of language" (28) as a *féminine écriture*. The indigenous words they invoke become "a magnetic field of sounds" (16), disrupting any unified train of thought. The doubled negatives they sprinkle through the syntax disrupt meaning at the same time that they capture lesbian pleasure, a pleasure they situate outside the logic of phallic pleasure:

sentences as waves
o contractions ("she didn't say nothing")
of double negatives. (29)

This self-reflexive experimentation with language outside the normative rules of syntax, an experimentation coded feminine, wrenches certain of the masculinist meanings of locomotion into new purposes. Thus, by the end of the line, the very steel wheels that carry the great engine of modernity toward its destination are transformed into

a gradual sensation
of the Great Wheel rolling under us
of the Great Womb we call earth
not solid not still
but an ever turning threshold. (33)

The second section of *Double Negative*, "Crossing Loop," takes its title from a particular site along the railway tracks. The crossing loop is the place where the forward progress of the train is interrupted, its thrust into the future momentarily halted. Here trains come to a stop while they wait for other trains to pass or change tracks. And here, in the middle of their text, Marlatt and Warland interrupt their poetic engagement with train travel to enter a dialogue about what they have included and what they have excluded in the poems they have written about the journey "through" Australia. Critically, they interrogate their relationship to this technology of modernity and the relationship of that technology to writing itself.

"D" (Marlatt) notes that they "didn't admit any of the tradition of [the way] trains have been depicted" in the cultural imaginary as a "powerful industrial monster whose rhythms and approach are seen as very much like the male orgasm" (36). For Marlatt, the power of the cultural imaginary to represent locomotion through sexualized images and metaphors must be held at bay, for in such a scenario of locomotion the train is the engine of phallic desire. It forces itself through the landscape on its inflexible iron tracks, bearing down on the station in its forward drive toward the relief of a destination reached. The only positioning available to woman is that of the passive figure tied cruelly to the rails, awaiting the advancing engine of desire. In this imaginary scenario, woman remains passive victim, an object fastened to the track. She is Pauline in peril. She has no desire of her own.

The domain of the technological, according to Marlatt, is the domain of the masculine. Thus, even as she critiques the phallic associations of train travel, she remains caught inside the web of the cultural imaginary. For, characterizing the movement of the train as "the on-track crescendo of male orgasm" (37), she reproduces the very tropes of the train as phallic. She cannot think the train other than through its phallic identifications.

In contrast, "B" (Warland) resists Marlatt's preoccupation with the linearity and unidirectionality of the locomotive and its track, arguing instead for the regenerative possibilities of train travel. Refusing to be subjected to the cultural imaginary's identification of locomotion with phallic power, she deploys new metaphors for locomotion, remaking the track into an "umbilical cord." For her, the track "represent[s] our continuous dependence on the earth which we're never really cut free from" (37). Moreover, she foregrounds the cyclical rather than progressive trajectory of train travel, invoking the rhythms of arrival and departure, of stopping and starting. This poetic move enables Warland to identify locomotion with "the cyclical nature of the female orgasm" (37).

Warland's strategic move encourages Marlatt to shift her focus away from the linearity of the track to the encapsulating and rhythmic rocking of the train and to join Warland in taking locomotion's defining terms and playing with them. In that play of language, the poets proliferate the meanings of this engine of modernity. "Born again in this very encapsuled and intimate experience" (36), they find a new birth in their berth. Within the web of this metaphorical move, the tracks become a birth canal. Through linguistic play, the double-negative narrator inhabits this engine of modernity in order to evacuate the signifier of its identifications with masculinist power and to rethink its imaginative possibilities for a poetics of female desire.

Yet by the end of "Crossing Loop," the lovers admit that they "want to get off the train, get off the narrative track, and move out into the desert in a different way" (38). In the third section, then, entitled "Real 2," they revisit the desert through which they have journeyed. In each of the twelve highly stylized and experimental reflections in this section, they cycle back to a poem in the first section, taking for the title a line out of that poem. But now, Marlatt and Warland refuse the surface narrative of the journey organized around the linear movement down the track and focus instead on the power of a "feminine" language to rescript the movement of women through the male domain of the Australian outback.

Writing against the containment of the train compartment, the lovers speak of and to the feminine as an excess in the phallic train. In exploring the relationship of woman and the Nullarbor Plain, Marlatt and Warland make three simultaneous moves. They imagine the straitened lives of women who, isolated in the desert, try to carve out a meaningful domestic space in the midst of such hostility:

setting bread on the
table it's plain Jane we've been here before making a
home in the desert dreaming more than survival
dreaming domestic paradise in the heart of the lost. (45)

They merge female body and the body of the earth to put woman
back into the landscape from which she has been banished by the march
of Australian national spread:

this shared weather does
not mean the mixedgrey of our coast monumental
thighs breasts slide into (islands touching under the
water). (43)

They imagine another relationship to the desert as they attempt to
see through the eyes of "ab/original" Australians:

whatever it is they see
differently until them i had not known the power of a
culture shapes the substance of our eyes makes us
citizens on a cellular level. (44)

Acknowledging female genealogy, bonding desert to female body,
imagining an alternative way of seeing—all these imaginative gestures
are acts of merging: of woman to woman across time, of female body
and landscape, and of subjects across cultural divides. For Marlatt and
Warland, such merging evidences the resistance of woman to her status
as isolated object of an imperial (masculine) gaze.

As lovers and as writers, Marlatt and Warland enact, to play on
Luce Irigaray's philosophical reverie, the "two lips in continuous contact"
(24). The doubleness of the signature on the title page and the anonymity
of the speaker in the poetic pieces signal the merging of the one and the
other in an imaginary domain of collaborative travel narrating. Through

their collaborative encounter in and through a train, the lovers refuse narrativity that necessitates "Law and History," and refuse the male quest story, which is a narrative of "escape from the metaphorical womb and the / conquering of it" (54). With "her desire to untrain herself / undermine every prop(er) deafinition," the narrator of "he says we got to stay on track" announces that

> she throws the
> switch on train as phallus ("bound for glory") train as
> salvation leaves it behind at the crossing loop. (51)

Having left the traditional metaphors and associations of the train ensemble behind at the geographical crossing loop and the section of the text entitled "Crossing Loop," the speakers write the "null" (28) and the "negative"(20)—that is, they write outside of masculinist logic.

In myriad ways, Marlatt and Warland rupture the logic of the rail lines (the logic of the phallic metanarrative) by refusing the sentence and the syntax of paternal narrative. The speakers interrupt idea segments to start new idea segments. They play riffs on words, phrases, and associations. They wrench words out of normal syntax. They improvise on the very letters of the alphabet, breaking them off from their attachment to words. Often there is no punctuation to signal beginnings, middles, and ends, no capital letters to indicate the beginning of a sentence. Sometimes there is punctuation without sense, punctuation arbitrarily inserted. Sometimes there is no period that announces the conclusion of a sentence, a thought, a poem, that is, the arrival of the idea at the station. Sometimes there is only the conclusion of a question and its mark. In all these ways—playing with words, refusing common sense constructions, breaking syntax, punning, and interrupting text with visual traces—the lovers resist traditional narrative and its investment in phallic power, rupturing the symbolic with the play of the nonsensical and the errant. As the title line of the first poem in "Real 2" announces, they are figuratively "travelling backwards through Australia" (12), traveling backward from "progress" through the imaginary domain of lesbian erotics:

and the train begins to roll as her hand moves across the page
spiral movement (imagin-a-nation) here she can rest
here she can play encounter her anima(l) self pre-sign
pre-time touching you i touch kangaroo words forming
then shifting desert dunes her desire to untrain herself. (51)

The "ecstasy" of lesbian desire renders the mouth a site of sexual and linguistic pleasure:

Lingual tongue in alkaline caves succeeds accedes to the
pre (prairie free) symbolic flowers here a desert's
standing sea the ocean in us throbs to meet. (56)

*Double Negative* is at once a meditation on writing and on locomotion. As "double negatives," Marlatt and Warland would resist the repertoire of meanings assigned to locomotion in the "mainstream literary tradition" (38). They would take this technology of motion, this engine of modernity, and inhabit it from the inside to disengage its identifications with phallic power. Celebrating "female coming" (37) rather than the male engine bearing down on the woman tied to the tracks, they site their lesbian sexuality inside the *primum mobile* in order to explode the ease with which the locomotive engine can be identified with normative heterosexuality. Circling back around to the sites and the poems in the first section, they produce a poem cycle to affirm the cyclic nature of return rather than the driving journey to closure.

## Conclusion

Locomotion involves travelers in a complex machine ensemble. Narrating travel by locomotion implicates narrators in a complex meaning ensemble. Morris, Niemann, and Marlatt and Warland all track meaning along the rails of identity. As they ride the rails of narrative, they ride histories of railway travel. They may come from different cultural locations when they enter the train and move to different locations on the train, but they all redefine the utility of the technology of locomotion as they change representational logic, that is, the logic of woman's relationship to locomotion. Like Woolf in the 1920s, they reframe representational possibilities from inside locomotion, in effect assessing what kinds of mobility locomotion makes possible for women and what price must be paid for that mobility.

Unlike the aviators and unlike the women who travel by foot, these women of locomotive mobility turn on the very mode of mobility that keeps them in motion. Of course, locomotion puts them in motion, offering them some kind of escape from the norms of sessile femininity. But there is far more to this locomotion than the escape from degraded femininity that mobility affords. There is also trouble with plots, trouble with machines, and trouble with destinations. Their narratives suggest just how much trouble they find with locomotion and how complicated it is being an agent of locomotion.

For one thing, popular narratives of women in locomotion confine the traveling woman to the plot of normatively heterosexual romance (whether as encounter, as heterosexual intrigue, or as melodrama of perilous vulnerability) and to a normatively feminized identity. For the plot to unfold, she must be or become suitably partnered up. But Morris, Niemann, and Marlatt and Warland all present themselves as unpartnered women, women outside any defining relationship with a man. They are errant women, "bad girls" of some kind. And they are particularly bad in the sense that they position themselves outside heterosexuality's preferred patterns of engagement. Morris's journey and her narrative begin with the rupture of romance and then unfold as the story of an independent pregnant woman. Niemann presents herself as bisexual. Marlatt and Warland speak as lesbian lovers who rewrite the romance of the rails in lesbian desire. These are sexually active women, but sexually active in ways that defy normative expectations.

In addition to resisting the plot of heterosexual romance that popular culture identifies with locomotion, these travel narrators also resist the myth of locomotion as engine of beneficent mobility, a mobility of comfort and protection. In their narratives of women and locomotion, the train serves as an enforcer of instrumental rationality, a site of phallic power, a force of subjugation, and an engine of disconnection. As the *primum mobile* propels Morris along a predetermined route, fixing her points of departure and her destination, it promises to dissolve the reality of boundaries, to take her home again. But the narrator of *Wall to Wall* represents herself as a captive of the locomotive car. Caught inside an itinerary of return, she's trapped inside a self-defining myth that joins mobility and masculinity (independence, freedom, purposefulness), and the unforeseen effects of nuclear technology render her destination a danger rather than a point of delivery and reconnection. The train cannot take her where she wants to go. Its instrumental rationality fails her as locomotion fosters disconnection rather than connection.

In *Double Negative*, Marlatt and Warland explicitly confront the phallic identification of the locomotive. Invoking the troubles of Pauline on the track, they seek ways to resist the engine bearing down on them. Through their double-voiced narrative, the lover-narrators join sources, forces, and language to destabilize the phallic machine ensemble from inside its driving rhythms. Situating lesbian desire within the *primum mobile*, Marlatt and Warland refigure the engine of modernity as an engine of cyclical pleasure. Niemann, as well, puts an errant body inside the working cars of the *primum mobile*. In *Boomer*, she breaks the connection between the masculine subject and masculinist travel tropes, between what a body looks like and what a body does. She simultaneously affirms and disrupts the narrative identification of excessive (and self-destructive) masculinity and mobility.

Troubles with destination get played out in the logic of reclamation that characterizes all three of these narratives. Shifting representational logics away from locomotion, all four travelers incorporate in their narratives strategies for escaping the kind of mobility locomotion enforces. For Niemann, the engine of modernity generates a postmodern proliferation of subject positions. Out of this proliferation Niemann becomes multiple, as the mobility of the trains serves as a metaphor for her own unfixable status as subject. Yet, if she initially embraces the muscular masculinity of locomotion and the narrative itineraries and cultural metaphors that constitute the Western subject as (male) individualist (thereby affirming the normative relationship of masculine subjects to travel narratives), she eventually shifts to a metaphor coded feminine. Reflected in the metaphor of the calmer river running through her, Niemann remakes herself through the narrative of recovery offered by Alcoholics Anonymous. Its rhetoric of a unified alcoholic subject gives her a way to represent her life of itinerant locomotion as symptomatic of her drinking life, a descent into the chaos of fragmented subjectivity, a descent from which she finally recovers.

To resist the cultural construction of woman's vulnerability before the locomotive and the landscape through which the locomotive moves, Marlatt and Warland invoke the discourse of French feminism, which provides them with a vocabulary, a reading strategy, and the analytic of two lips in continuous contact to read woman against the common readings of her in the railway car. Through their "feminine" writing, they come down off the train and return to the vast land of settlement, in this way recovering from their constitutive negativity and from their alienation in land claimed as male territory. Like Marlatt and Warland, Morris finds a source of resistence in female embodiment, for it is through a celebration of pregnancy as a force for self-recovery that she undoes the brutal instrumentality and the radical danger of locomotion. Turning what she describes as the "fictive mode" of train travel to her own purposes, Morris reads her own drama of homelessness across the landscape beyond the pane of glass. Through that drama, she seeks to understand the meaning of pregnancy, a sign of the woman in stasis, for the "prodigal traveler." Being with child, the one inside her body and the one she remembers of herself, she seeks an alternative route home. The train cannot be a mode of communication to the past, but pregnancy can.

Yet in two of the three narratives there's a residue of discontent. The very mode of motion through which Morris engages in reverie and through which she would make connection with the past, with the child within, exacerbates the effects of walls, sustaining what de Certeau describes as the partition between the inside and the outside. The travel narrator cannot get to the buried treasure, the more authentic child self, before walls constitute identities and differences. A failed quest, Morris's is what de Certeau calls "a fable of our private stories" (112). It is ultimately a melancholy journey.⁵ It is as if the reverie of train travel continues to affect the narrator long after the train fails to deliver her to her desired destination. The reverie of train travel turns the traveler inward, promoting and reproducing the psychological landscape of nostalgic desire. Morris has presented herself as a kind of noble soul on a journey of self-recovery, but the end of the narrative, like the end of the journey, reminds us how provisional such noble pursuits can be.

In *Boomer*, the residue—the afterimage—of the narrative of muscular mobility haunts the foreclosure of the ending, that "home" of the twelve-step narrative and the coherent, recovering "alcoholic" subject. Niemann's text testifies to the ways identities coalesce, disperse, reform, and transform one another contextually. As Bella Brodzki suggests in a blurb on the dust jacket of the hardbound edition of *Boomer*, it is this excessive subjectivity, evidenced in Niemann's multiple marginalities, that opens the space of critical knowing and accounting that in turn motivates Niemann to describe with humor, irony, and anguish the homophobia, sexism, racism, and class antagonisms she experiences in her life on the rails and in the rail yards. By implication, this critical knowing contains a critique of the myth of unified selfhood even as it forces the closure of a recovery from alcoholism.

Morris and Niemann turn on locomotion by displacing the promises of iron mobility with myths of recovery. But the metaphor of derailment persists in both narratives, because nostalgia for the ambience and empowerment of radical dislocation persists.

# CHAPTER 5

# On the Road:
# (Auto)Mobility and Gendered Detours

Those who have taken the pains to search below the
surface for the great tendencies of the age, know what a giant
industry is struggling into being there. All signs point to the
motor vehicle as the necessary sequence of methods of
locomotion already established and approved. The growing
needs of our civilization demand it; the public believe in it,
and await with lively interest its practical application to the
daily business of the world.

—"Salutatory," *Horseless Age* (1895)

The intoxication of great speeds in cars is nothing but the
joy of feeling oneself fused with the only *divinity*.

—F. T. Marinetti,
"The Founding and Manifesto of Futurism" (1909)

Throughout the nineteenth century, railroad tracks spread over the
landscape, carving out rational routes of "progress." To secure the locomotive purchase on that spread, railway companies in the United States
and Europe exerted pressure upon politicians to enact laws that would
curb experimentation with other technologies of motion. In the long
run, of course, they were unsuccessful, especially in the United States.
The explosion of the bicycle craze in the 1890s created the desire for
flexible transportation, hard road surfaces, and individualized routes
(Flink 7–8). Growing discontent with railroad monopolies created pressure for the development of a good highway system as an alternative way
to transport farm commodities and industrial goods expeditiously over
long distances.

These forces generated enthusiasm for a new form of mobility, the automobile. When the internal combustion engine was perfected by the end of the century, inventors, manufacturers, and customers rushed to embrace the promise of a small engine to empower individuals through their own explosive mobility. Carl Benz and Gottlieb Daimler in Germany, Emile Levassor in France, and Charles E. and J. Frank Duryea in the United States left their undeniable legacy to the world—the century of automobility.

From the elevation of the airplane, automobiles far below seemed more like black ants than powerful engines of progress. But on the ground, these ants multiplied with abandon. As with locomotive interests in the nineteenth century, the commercial interests promoting and producing automobility "joined forces at a key moment to close off all other options and ensure that henceforth investment would be channeled into automobile technology" (Wajcman 128).[1] They were far more successful than their predecessors in the locomotive sector had been. This individualized mode of mobility became the transport of choice in the industrialized West. Below the soaring airplanes and around the chugging locomotives, automobiles hummed along at a bracing pace.

The automobile transformed everyday life, making individuals instantly and comfortably mobile. No planning and no tickets were needed. Eventually no excessive wealth was needed either. The mass production of the auto, made possible through Fordist principles, fostered increasingly widespread ownership. The effect of that widespread ownership was the gradual reorganization of social relations. Life in cities and countryside, in families and communities, and in public and private spaces changed radically. Witness the emergence of the suburban experience. People could work in the city and then take refuge in a home surrounded by lawns, trees, and countryside—an organized and accessible nature distant enough from the bustle, noise, danger, and confusion of the urban metropolis to give ready access to jobs *and* countryside leisure. The auto, notes Wolfgang Sachs, simultaneously created and satisfied this desire for escape in proximity. One could "get away" without having to go too far (106).

The reorganization of living patterns into urban work districts and suburban retreats for middle-class and working-class families began long before World War II, but two decades of the Depression and war kept the pace of change a modest one. World War II brought with it the strict rationing of gasoline and other commodities that forestalled the expansion of highways. Afterward, however, expansion could not be stayed. A new "super highway" system reached out across the land, facilitating postwar industrial booms. New "shopping centers" brought mass-produced consumer goods to people living in communities distant from city centers. With goods so easily accessible, the home of the 1950s and 1960s became the "privileged site of individual consumption" (Ross 4–5).

The automobile became a necessity of everyday life in consumer culture, and one of the most prized items of consumption. In the long history of this century of the automobile, three arenas of technological innovation sustained one another: the road, the assembly line, and the home as consumer retreat. In car culture, motorized modernity came right into the home. Yet even as the mass-produced automobile functioned as the engine driving the routines of middle-class life and norms, it simultaneously functioned as a vehicle of escape. In their automobiles people sped away from the domestic constraints of home and the deadening routines of a rampant consumerism, and headed out across the land in search of new experiences.

## Automobility and Perception

Automobile travel multiplies destinations, routes, and the pleasures of perspective. As with railway travel, it collapses space and time, producing the experience of evanescent reality. "The automobile and the motion it creates," observes Kristin Ross, "become integrated into the driver's perception: he or she can see only things in motion—as in motion pictures. Evanescent reality, the perception of a detached world fleeting by a relatively passive viewer, becomes the norm, and not the exception it still was in the nineteenth century" (39). Although this sense of an evanescent reality characterizes the effect of locomotive travel as well, the traveler's experience of it in an automobile is different from the experience of gazing through the rigid frame of the train window. From the automobile, suggests Sachs, "the landscape [becomes] accessible from all angles, so that fixed perspectives [dissolve] into an abundance of views, a multitude of vantage points" (155). Evanescent reality becomes kaleidoscopic. Inside the automobile, the traveler absorbs continually shifting perspectives, viewing some scenes from close up, others from mid-range, and still others from a great distance. In the early decades of the twentieth century, the futurists, celebrating speed, motion, and continuous flux (Silk 58–59), embraced this continuous change of perspective as the quintessential expression of the dynamism of the modern age.

Furthermore, unlike locomotive travel, automobility fosters an intimate relationship of traveler to technology of motion. Not confined by schedules, tracks, and prepackaged destinations, the traveler, with hands on the wheel, can change the course, speed, and rhythm of encounter and perspective. Nestled inside the cab, the automobilist thus experiences an insular, autonomous individuality and an exhilarating freedom of movement. As a result, the metallic carapace becomes a prosthetic device (as did the small plane in the early days of aviation), an extension of the body into and through space.

This fusion of body and machine facilitates speedy escape—from the past, from the static routines of domesticity, and from an outmoded identity. Physical freedom translates into psychological freedom. Extending the reach and maneuverability of the traveler's gaze, this prosthesis "transforms" travelers into "explorer[s]" who, according to Sachs, can "set new goals and approach the old in a fresh manner." They can experience the new powers and pleasures of "penetrat[ing] even the most distant corners" (155). And if they need directions, they can always find road maps to guide them as they pursue the sensation of motion.

This object, the automobile, promises to take individuals where they please, even if they don't always know where that is. It is, after all, the perception of being in motion, being "on the road," that is the prized experience. Arguing that the automobiles that have "tamed" urban and country environments are the very engines that generate fantasies of the exotic, the wild, and the sexual that travelers pursue in their odysseys of the road, Judy Wajcman recognizes that the desire for speed, mobility, and escape from routine is a gendered desire (134).[2] Thus, we are required to consider how the culture of automobility has always been organized around and through a complex set of gender relations and identities that affect the woman traveler's relationship to the prosthesis that is the automobile.

## The Gender of Car Culture

> If women could realize the exhilaration that comes from being
> able to handle a 60-horse-power touring car, the sight of a woman
> driver would be anything but a novelty.
>
> —Mrs. Andrew Cuneo, "Why There Are So Few
> Women Automobilists" (1908)

In his 1896 lithograph *The Automobilist*, Henri de Toulouse-Lautrec fills the diagonal foreground with the figure of the new automobilist, fusing driver and machine as an expression of motorized modernity. In the background a woman, her back to the viewer, parades with her tiny dog. This female figure, sketchily drawn, faces away from us; the automobilist, dramatically drawn, comes toward us. Gerald Silk suggests that in this litho "the centuries confront one another: the tranquil nineteenth-century world of Impressionist imagery is pitted against the tumultuous vision of twentieth-century technological invention" (37). The man in his machine is the figure of modernity, the woman a figure of backwardness and relative stasis.

Like the early aviators, the early inventors, engineers, and manufacturers of the automobile were identified as doggedly masculine types—inveterate tinkerers, daring dynamos of speed, gritty visionaries (Scharff 10). The drivers were imagined as men of wealth and daring. Racing the automobile "made the man" as a hero of prosthetic masculinity. Owning an auto, especially one of the expensive models, made the man as the privileged subject of modernity.

Women's relationship to this object of modern masculinity was an ambivalent one. In the early years, observes Bayla Singer, "women who motored did so strictly as passengers" (32). Access to the passenger seat affirmed their prominence as wealthy women and their status as modern wives and daughters. But it reinforced their stereotypical frailty and passivity as well. In complicated ways the woman in the passenger seat was at once the same "old woman" (passive within the carriage) and the disturbingly "new woman" (transgressive in her movement through public spaces in this newest of technologies).

But, of course, it wasn't long before upper-class women, having become habituated to motoring as passengers, began to "take the wheel" from the hands of chauffeurs and to experience the release of independent mobility. Independent women of the middle classes followed them into the driver's seat. Behind the wheel, these women began to understand the possibilities loosed with the independent mobility of the automobile. Thus, as did women in so many other fields, they pushed into the realm of motorized masculinity. In 1909, Alice Huyler Ramsey became the first woman to make an automobile trip across the United States. Blanche Stuart Scott, in 1910, and Anita King, in 1915, followed her. The most daring of these early automobilists participated in races that were open to women. Elsewhere, women took up automobiling in pursuit of political and social goals. Suffragists used automobility as a means to reach an increasingly widespread audience in their organizing efforts on behalf of the movement (Scharff 78). When World War I came along, daughters of the privileged classes and single women volunteered to transport wounded soldiers to hospitals. The ambulance service offered these women an arena in which to gain confidence and competence by assuming control of an expensive, complex, thoroughly modern machine. (Remember, for instance, how Gertrude Stein, as she tells us in *The Autobiography of Alice B. Toklas*, learned to drive—if only in the forward gears— during World War I in France.)

According to Virginia Scharff, this "journey from back to front seat, from passengerhood to control of a vehicle deeply identified with men, began in public and entailed repeated confrontations with popular manners, morals, and expectations" (17). Cultural perceptions of the female automobilist were inflected with moral judgments. Scharff notes how, in the rhetoric that emerged around motoring, to be caught in traffic was tantamont to being caught in flagrante delicto. Motoring women appeared to be flagrantly undomesticated and thus flagrantly available, conspicuous, and indiscrete. They might even become notorious. Moreover, the fact that working-class men, virile in their maneuvering masculinity, chauffeured women of wealth in public made the automobile carriage a site of a potentially transgressive cross-class liaison. Women in motion, even if only as passengers, became identified with sexual display, technological power, and pleasurable excess. We see the figuration of this identification in certain artworks of the period. In 1915, the cubist artist Francis Picabia, recognizing during a visit to the United States that "the genius of the modern world is in machinery" (Silk 77), drew a series of five "object portraits" for Alfred Stieglitz's periodical *291*. One of the portraits he titled *Portrait of a Young American Woman in a State of Nudity*. Picabia represents the nude American woman as a spark plug, thereby inviting the identification of the woman automobilist as a "'hot woman' able to ignite flames of passion" (Silk 77).

When women took the wheel, they added emphasis to their radical displacement from the home. A woman out for a drive was a woman out of place. Early women motorists, adds Scharff, "terrified traditionalists … with their public exhibition of spending power, and with their refusal to see constraint as protection, choice as a 'nightmare.' Climbing into an automobile a woman rejected the cloister, certainly, and potentially also the female sphere of hearth and home" (24). But the ferocity of the arguments about woman's conspicuous display and her errant femininity only testified to a fait accompli. "Independent mobility" (Scharff 24) offered women a means to travel into and through public spaces with ease; and embrace it they did.

Recognizing the trend, automobile manufacturers identified women as a potential market for their product, but a market with a difference. Since the beginnings of production in the 1890s, automobile technologies and marketing strategies have reproduced normative gender identifications by ascribing to men and women different tastes in cars. These ascriptions influenced the pace and direction of change in automobile design. Actually there were two early modes of automobility, the gasoline-driven car and the electric car. Electric cars were cleaner, easier to handle, less noisy, and far less powerful than gasoline-driven vehicles, but they had a much narrower range, because they had to be recharged. Like women, they had to be kept close to home. In marketing the electric car, manufacturers turned the difference in engine capacity into sexual difference. The electric model began to be identified as the "woman's car" (Singer 33), designed specifically to meet the needs of the newly motoring woman. The two markets—the electric and the gas-driven—provided a tidy differentiation between motorized femininity and motorized masculinity, maintaining in yet another form a differentiation of separate spheres. "By designating the electric as a 'woman's car,'" observes Singer, "men at one stroke reinforced their definition of proper femininity and attempted to confine women even more strictly within it" (34).

The increasing influence of motorized modernity, however, stimulated desires in women for speed and distance, desires the electric car could not satisfy. They too began to prefer the power of the gasoline engine. "The time has gone by when motor cars had sex," wrote C. H. Claudy in 1912, "when the gasolene [sic] car was preeminently for the man, and the electric, because of its simplicity, for the women" (36). Furthermore, the increasingly sophisticated design of motor vehicles had the effect of eliminating the expectation of hands-on knowledge on the part of all drivers, male and female. Automobiles were soon too complicated for any driver to repair; mechanics had to be hired. Thus, knowledge of the intricacies of the internal combustion engine no longer served as a marker differentiating motoring as a masculine domain of expertise.

The demise of the electric car meant that the technology could no longer be used to differentiate motoring masculinity and femininity. The demise of the technician-motorist as normative driver meant that neither could a set of behaviors so easily be used to differentiate motoring masculinity and femininity. But new means of distinguishing motoring masculinity and femininity emerged during the 1930s, 1940s, and 1950s as the expansion of automobile ownership made the automobile a necessity of everyday life, at once an item of consumption and a vehicle fostering the consuming habits of the family. Large numbers of women had become drivers. Now their easy access to autos and obvious proficiency in driving, both of which eroded the certitudes attached to the masculinist logic of travel, got absorbed and reinterpreted as necessities of a normative femininity in consumer culture. Women's was mobility in service of homemaking. Their uses of automobility had to do with the well-being and smooth running of the domestic sphere.

Additionally, women's driving continued to be feminized as it had been in the very early days of motoring when articles and letters filled magazine and newspaper columns about women's incompetence with the new technology of motion. Through various forms of popular culture, from comics to jokes to editorials, women's behavior behind the wheel was represented as ab-normative, errant. As drivers, they were less proficient and more dangerous, or hopelessly incompetent and hesitant. The way they drove offered a means to continue differentiating virile from timid automobility.

Women's relationship to automobility may have been—and may continue to be—represented through gender stereotypes. Their position within the grid of relations constituting automobile culture may have been organized through conventional gender assignments. And the machines themselves, down to "the very nuts and bolts" that held them together, may have had "ideas of masculinity, femininity and proper family life built into them" (Clarsen 2). Nonetheless, women used automobiles as vehicles of resistance to conventional gender roles and the strictures of a normative femininity. Autos provided access to jobs and continuing education. They provided access to recreational travel. These opportunities for activities outside domesticity offered new identities for women. We see this association of automobile with independent woman in Tamara de Lempicka's *Self-Portrait* (1925). In her racing hat and leather gloves, the female automobilist looks at home behind the wheel. With her piercing eyes, elegant femininity, and arrogant self-presentation, she exudes independence, competence, and calm self-discipline. Lempicka's fashionable and confident self-portraiture is part of what Scharff describes as the "minute adjustments of private negotiation" that characterize the history of twentieth-century automobility. "Through the small changes of personal life, leading to larger transformations on a social scale," she suggests, "activities and entities assigned to one sphere or the other, considered appropriate for either women or men, sometimes lost or recast their gendered meanings. When women refused to conform to expectations, when new technologies unsettled traditional assumptions, when entrepreneurs defied common wisdom in search of profits, change accelerated" (40).

## Narratives of Motorized Masculinity

> A car-driver, always speeding across space, like a tempest
> or a cyclone, is something of a superman.
>
> —Octave Mirbeau, *La 628–E8* (1908)

Even with these "minute adjustments of private negotiation," however, the automobile has continued to be a technological vehicle through which mobile masculinity gets enacted in modernity. We can read this persistence in car fetishism. "For men," Wajcman contends, "cars afford a means of escape from domestic responsibilities, from family commitment, into a realm of private fantasy, autonomy and control" (134). To own a particular kind of car, to "soup it up" after a particular fashion, to drive it in a particular way, to take it to particular destinations—all these psycho/auto/motive behaviors provide male motorists with ways to get a masculine kind of life and to be a masculine kind of guy.

Narratives of automobility have been one of the cultural vehicles for imagining the relationship of men to this phallic prosthesis of mobility. This has been particularly the case with film. The gangster films of the 1930s, for instance, identified the car with the violent masculinity of mob men. Films with dramatic chase scenes, such as *The French Connection* (1971) and *Cannonball Run* (1980), identified the car with renegade masculinity. Road films, such as *Easy Rider* (1969) and *Kings of the Road* (1976), identified the car with the sexual prowess of a countercultural masculinity. Fictional and nonfictional road narratives have also enacted myths of American masculinity in romantic, transcendental, picaresque, and pastoral modes, as Kris Lackey suggests in *RoadFrames: The American Highway Narrative* (24). From Theodore Dreiser's *A Hoosier Holiday* (1916) to Henry Miller's *The Air-Conditioned Nightmare* (1945) to William Least Heat-Moon's *Blue Highways* (1984), mobile men have pursued self-discovery, expanded consciousness, profligate consumption, sexual release, and nostalgic return. But Jack Kerouac's 1957 novel *On the Road* comes immediately to mind as the quintessential tale (at least the quintessential North American tale) of man, auto, motion, and masculinity. Kerouac's protagonist, Sal, romps across the United States in an ecstatic odyssey of renegade masculinity for which the automobile is an absolute necessity. This is a motorized masculinity Kerouac flings in the face of the new organization man, the sedentary, "feminized" bourgeois businessman of the late 1940s and 1950s. Moreover, this is a kind of mobility through which Beats like Kerouac could compete with the heroic masculinity identified with the returning soldier and the veteran.

Turning a cold eye on the unmanning of an America returned to peacetime, Kerouac sends his heroes across the country in search of renewable identities. Through these subversive scripts of masculinity, the road crew seeks to reman, remake, and rewrite postwar masculinity in America. To drive away is to escape work, obligation, conventional commitments, and domesticity. To drive hard and fast is to enact one's independence. In Kerouac's odyssey, Sal goes where mobility takes him, bounded in his destinations only by the limits of the two oceans, the domesticities of New Jersey and San Francisco. Speed, drift and impulsive movement, momentary desire and inconsequential abandonment—all are identified with automotive masculinity. It is a masculinity whose trajectory is unplanned, undirected, unruly.

The excessive maneuverability of cars and their relative accessibility even to the down-and-out makes for socially fluid spaces. People get in cars. They get out of cars. They pick up hitchhikers. They hitch rides with other drivers. Sal and his friends race through days and nights, connecting and disconnecting with a diverse assortment of people. Sal identifies his version of motorized masculinity with this perpetual movement, with the fringe cultures of America—the hoboes, the migrant workers, the African Americans in jazz clubs—and with a cavalier attitude toward "possessions." (Cars are stolen, women exchanged.) Individuals are on the move, breaking away from communities and forming temporary communities of motorists without alliances. The continuous change of venues multiplies the performative possibilities of a masculinity rescued from bourgeois repetition.

In trying to escape the dehumanizing consumer culture of 1950s prosperity, Sal and his friends displace the site of consumerism to the realm of the appetites. Eschewing the accumulation of things, they seek on the road the accumulation of frenetic "experience"—the next high, the next exotic locale, the next woman. On the road, they court women who are attracted to them by sheet-metal desires. "Girls" enter the narrative as passengers in automobiles, passengers in the ride of life. Seduced into the automobile, they attest to a central performative act of riderly masculinity: the ability to get girls to ride in your car with you. This is masculinity by invitational largesse. Thus, for Sal and his friends, the interior of the automobile is decidedly a masculine interior. Men saturate the inside of the machine ensemble with their words and their desires. Women may get in, but they do so as silent passengers whose own sedentariness is only momentarily interrupted, whose bodies are readily available to men, whose own desires are unimaginable. They are momentary points of sessility that bracket mobility, or they are pawns to be maneuvered in the game of male bonding, a bonding central to renegade masculinity.

At the end of *On the Road*, Sal sits, redomesticated, in the spacious limousine of his upwardly mobile friend. He's returned to New York and to middle-class respectability; but he has made his journeys through the margins of middle-class respectability, and he's narrated them. An integral part of those journeys and that narrative is the "making" of girls. Girls, cars, and sex make for prosthetic masculinity, and prosthetic masculinity is implicated in the politics of class. It is through the gender politics of class that I want to explore how automobility stimulated, satisfied, or blocked the realization of desires in the women who have been subject to its fascinations and for whom it has been the subject of narrative.

## Motor-Flying with Edith Wharton

At the beginning of the twentieth century, the intrepid traveler Edith Wharton captured the excitement of the new automobile travel and its shifting perspectives in a series of magazine articles she wrote about her journeys through France. The articles were subsequently collected and published in the United States in 1908 as *A Motor-Flight through France*, a title suggesting the imaginative association of flight and automobility in the early decades of the century. Because airplanes were the most exotic and astonishing of the new technologies of motion, Wharton and her contemporaries turned to flight as the metaphor for the movement of the new automobiles through space. These earthbound flying machines delivered to travelers on the ground a modicum of the speed and maneuverability that flight delivered to the elite travelers of the air.

Maneuverability, that freedom of direction the new technology promised, distinguishes automobile travel from the more established technology of locomotion. In an automobile, Wharton announces in her opening celebration, the traveler can escape the "compulsions and contacts of the railway, the bondage of fixed hours and the beaten track" (1). Here is travel without enforced timetables, without fixed itineraries and destinations. A far more individualizing mode of mobility than locomotion, the automobile responds to the traveler's desire, imagination, and energy. And so, to the degree that "the motor-car has restored the romance of travel" (1), it serves as a vehicle for a regenerative romantic individualism. "Restoring" the individualizing logic to travel, automobility distinguishes the true traveler from the mere tourist, who proceeds by railway. Locomotive travel directs travelers to particular attractions over well-worn rails. It determines their destinations and contributes to the pernicious effects of tourism, what Wharton describes as the "secularised, museumised aspect of the monument" (150–51). By contrast, the automobile carries the true traveler away from museumized (prepackaged) sites.

The automobile not only enables the traveler to go where she wills, it also rescues her from the dissatisfying prospects of locomotive travel. Traversing back roads that take her through ever-changing environments, the traveler meets one picturesque scene after another (15). "Taking" places "unawares," she finds the unknown and inaccessible suddenly visible (1). Then too, the automobile enables the traveler to maximize the aesthetic pleasure of travel by avoiding the ugly, impoverished, "unpicturesque" quarters of cities and towns (172). Circumvented as well is the dreary ugliness of the station, which locomotive travel inevitably leaves as its last impression. Integral to the romantic individualism restored by the automobile is immersion in the succession of impressions that intensify aesthetic pleasure.

Furthermore, the automobile shifts the relationship of the passenger to the organization of space—geographic, architectural, and human. In automobile travel, space becomes a product of time, or rather time's passage. Thus, the maneuverability of the automobile proliferates the aesthetic pleasures that attend "the sense of continuity," what Wharton describes as "the truest initiation of travel." She means by this "the sense ... of relation between different districts, of familiarity with the unnamed, unhistoried region stretching between successive centres of human history, and exerting, in deep unnoticed ways, so persistent an influence on the turn that history takes" (37). Contemplating the successive images that the automobile has delivered to her, Wharton comments at Comminges that "the finger-tailed monster of Chauvigny, the plaintively real bat of the choir-stall at Poitiers, and these silent evocations of a classic past group themselves curiously in the mind as embodiments of successive phases of human fancy, imaginative interpretations of life" (116).

Because the automobile provides access to roads leading everywhere, it carries the traveler through successive histories inscribed in the geography, demographics, economics, and cultural practices of specific locales (58). In her prosthetic vehicle, the traveler comprehends more clearly than the traveler on a train the relationship of place to the unfolding of historical time. Carrying her through the countryside, the automobile offers Wharton endless opportunities to come upon scenes where history returns to inform the present and where the people of the present can be imaginatively remade into historical figures. Recalling her visit to the home of George Sand, Wharton describes the young girl she sees at the entrance to Nohant as a young woman stepping right out of a Sand novel (42). The automobile, for Wharton, is an engine of surprise and delight (32), both of which derive from the seductive interpenetration of past and present that the machine seems to invite.

Writing in the early decades of the twentieth century, Wharton celebrated automobility precisely because such motion promised to deliver her from the ravages of the rampant modernization she identified with America, the home she left behind. Throughout her narrative, she represents America as a nation where unbridled growth, industrialization, urbanization, democratization, instrumental architecture, and mass culture have impoverished, if not eviscerated, the aesthetic imagination by destroying beautiful scenes and buildings. America, she writes, is "a country where the last new grain-elevator or office building is the only monument that receives homage from the surrounding architecture" (32). In contrast, she represents France as a place where the aestheticization of everyday life is integral to the "enjoyment of living" (28–29), a place where the romance of history generates ever renewable pleasures. Wharton's narrative of her "motor-flight" through France becomes a commentary on the cultural poverty of America.

Wharton's aesthetic of travel is an effect of a new mode of mobility that inspires a new, modernist aesthetic. The proliferation of points of view, the imprinting of multiple layers of time, the preoccupation with formal qualities abstracted from the passing landscape—these are features of the modernist aesthetic in the early decades of the century. These features of mobility suggest how implicated new modes of technology are in new modes of representation.

If Wharton anticipates the futurists in her celebration of the changing vistas of automobile travel, she certainly does not share their identification of the automobile with speed, dynamism, and the future. Her identification of this modernist aesthetic with a premodern France rather than a modern America reveals her class privilege and its concomitant privileging of "travel-as-culture" (Schriber 196). Like other women in

the early decades of motoring, Wharton enters the automobile an independently wealthy woman. Her privilege gives her access to the new
automobile and to the leisure required to develop what Mary Suzanne
Schriber describes as her "formidable intellectual credentials" (192).
These credentials sustain her identity as modern woman, scholar, and
artist. Paradoxically, the modern woman becomes the woman who looks
backward to the picturesque remnants of a premodern past that motoring brings into view for her. How this dynamic reverses that of Toulouse-
Lautrec's *Automobilist*!

Wharton's narrative represents the automobile as a vehicle of
romance for the elite traveler who differentiates herself from the hordes
of tourists still captive to the railway and the museumized sites along that
way. Time, the mass production of the automobile, and the expansion of
touristic travel would, over the century, open the romance of travel to the
mass of tourists fanning out over the countryside. Like Wharton, but often
without her "credentials," these tourists, as Sachs has argued, would turn
a sentimental, romanticized gaze upon landscape and peoplescape, both
of which they bathed in the imaginary glow of time past and time quaint.

There have been more recent narratives of automobility that turn
anything but a romanticized gaze on the automobile and on woman as
motoring subject. It is to two of these narratives—Beverly Donofrio's
*Riding in Cars with Boys* and Irma Kurtz's *The Great American Bus Ride*—
that I now turn.

## Sheet Metal and Bad Girls

> Unlike a gas range, a car has sex.

—Bill Mitchell, head of styling staff at General Motors in the late 1950s

In her narrative of life "off the road" with Neal Cassady, Carolyn Cassady
includes a photograph album. One of the photos, taken by someone in
the backseat of a rather beat-up automobile, catches Neal Cassady at the
wheel and a young woman in the passenger seat. His right arm holds the
top of the steering wheel. His face, in profile, bears his distinct aquiline

Amelia Earhart in 1928: the iconography of the woman aviator. Reprinted with permission of National Air and Space Museum, Smithsonian Institution. SI photo no. 78-16945.

Charles Lindbergh and Anne Morrow Lindbergh, circa 1931, standing before the *Sirius*. Reprinted with permission of National Air and Space Museum, Smithsonian Institution. SI negative no. 13 A4818-B.

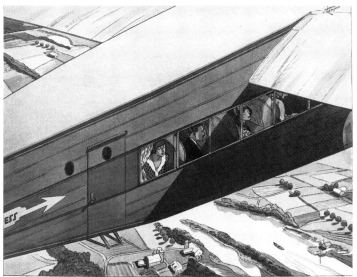

*Illustrated in a Fokker F-10-A Super-Tri-Motor, which carries 12 passengers and 2 pilots.*

# GENERAL MOTORS CHOSE FOKKER

The commercialization of flight. *Fortune* magazine advertisement for Fokker Aircraft, General Motors Corp., June 1930. Author's collection.

*Eisenbahnbrücke bei Trachau.*

The transformation of the landscape: the railroad line at Trachau, Germany, 1840. Courtesy of the Transportation History Collection Print Collection, Special Collections Library, University of Michigan.

Map cover of "The World's Grandest One Day Trip" (circa 1890). Courtesy of the Clements Library, University of Michigan.

L.N.E.R. STREAMLINED ENGINE "SILVER LINK"

Force, direction, speed: the "Silver Link" locomotive of the Silver Jubilee train, looking ever so phallic along its route from King's Cross to Newcastle, England (1936). Courtesy of the Transportation History Collection Print Collection, Special Collections Library, University of Michigan.

Speed, mobility, and auto-femininity: an early-twentieth-century vision of woman in motion.

On the road with Alice Huyler Ramsey, the first woman to drive a car across the United States, in 1909.

Advertising the elegance and stylishness of "Milady's Choice" in *Scribner's* magazine advertiser, circa 1912. Courtesy of the Transportation History Collection Print Collection, Special Collections Library, University of Michigan.

Selling automobility as "Confort Elégance" in a Delahaye advertisement in *L'Illustration*, February 11, 1933. Author's collection.

# ...the Engine is Mobiloil Clean!

"More Miles per Gal. More Smiles per Gal." Selling the postwar proliferation of highways and automobile culture with a sweet smile and a wholesome sexuality in a Mobiloil advertisement in *Time* magazine, June 10, 1946. Author's collection.

The chauffeur and the lady: an early-twentieth-century instance of the danger of "riding in cars with boys."

Once upon a time: selling Greyhound sexuality in the 1930s (June 11, 1935). Courtesy of the Transportation History Collection Print Collection, Special Collections Library, University of Michigan.

The anonymity of the generic Greyhound station in Windsor, Ontario— photographed in the 1930s, but looking just as familiar at the beginning of the twenty-first century. Courtesy of the Transportation History Collection Print Collection, Special Collections Library, University of Michigan.

nose, his rugged and gaunt cheeks. His mouth open, he seems engrossed in his own conversation. Clearly this virile man controls the conversation and the automobile. The young woman in the passenger seat turns her face slightly toward him. We see nothing specific of the face except the partial, light-blazed profile. To this photograph Carolyn Cassady adds the following caption: "Neal in heaven—a car and a girl, any time any place. (Actually with Anne Murphy, 1960.)" Her use of the generic descriptor "girl" suggests that the girl's identity doesn't much matter, although Cassady adds it in parentheses. "Girl" is only a placeholder for adoring femininity, an accoutrement, like the automobile, that constitutes the "heaven" of mobile masculinity. The "girl" gains her identity as "actually Anne Murphy" only by riding in a car with this particular "boy."

The automobile ensemble in this photo—machine, persons, occasion, and location—functions as a site of gender production. Far more than any other form of transportation, the automobile has been associated with male sexual prowess. The arc of desire and the mark of sexual prowess find their aerodynamic contours in the coupé or sedan, the sports car or pickup, the low rider or high-priced Mercedes. In the imagination, the automobile itself is bisexual. Men often imagine their cars as female; they are possessions. But they also imagine them as prosthetic extensions of the sexual organ. They are, in this sense, possessed of phallic power. And certainly as a mobile cabin, the automobile has provided men with a ready-made place for sexual conquest. If the automobile represented a venue for self-display in its early days, it very soon became a venue for secretive behaviors. Autos can be hidden from view or driven out of range of police of all kinds. With cars, men can pick women up, feel them up, knock them up. In front seats and backseats they can assert their attractiveness to women and their power over them. At the least, they can imagine keeping women in their place through the conventional gender arrangement of (male) driver and (female) passenger (Singer 35).

Driving a car as a "boy" signifies empowered masculinity, whether it's the elegant masculinity of the corporate subject in his Mercedes or BMW, or the ethnically marked masculinity of the low rider, or the working-class masculinity of the muscle car. The automobile itself often functions as a second skin of identity, down to the condensed inscriptions of bumper stickers. And driving that car becomes a performative act through which men stake their claims to defining masculinity. Riding in a car as a "girl," however, is another matter altogether. Girls who climb too readily into cars find themselves assigned the identity of the "bad girl" out for a ride, for getting in cars with boys implies getting into trouble of various kinds. And "trouble" means engaging in unbecoming behaviors—including smoking, drinking, taking drugs, having sex, and getting pregnant—defining what it is to be a bad girl. Bad girls ride in cars with boys. They are trouble; they have trouble; they mean trouble, and they get into trouble. In the cultural imaginary, bad girls are assigned lower-class status, differentiating them from the proper girls of the middle and upper classes. In the automobile, bad and good gender identities get reproduced as class identities.

The identification of automobiles and illicit or outlaw female sexuality has a long history, going back to the early days of motoring. As Scharff notes, the wealthy women who sped through city streets and country roads with their chauffeurs at the wheel were suspect women. Out for a ride, they were also taken to be out for another kind of ride. Later on, automobiles came to provide, and, critically, were understood to provide, a space for sex outside the more guarded domestic space. Providing easy access to sexual encounters without high cost or inconvenience and without identification with the traffic in sex (of prostitutes) on the streets, automobiles were sites of rebellious sexuality, aligning sheet metal, women, and sexual excess.

It is with this troubling history of "invitations to ride" that Beverly Donofrio opens her recent "confession," entitled *Riding in Cars with Boys*.[3] The photo on the cover of the paperback edition captures the erotic dynamics of this auto locale and invokes a whole history of advertising that attaches a sexualized female body to the body of the newest make of car. A teenage girl, her back to the reader, holds herself on the left front fender of an old, dented car. Her legs are spread open, her knees stick out to both sides, and her arms hug her sides. From one point of view, she spreads her legs open to the car in a gesture of compliant and available sexuality. It is as if, in a strange way, the car is driving right between her legs. Thus, the photo presents a metaphor for bad-girl availability and bad-girl acts. But there are other ways to read the photo. This girl mounts the auto, her back defiantly to the reader. She has taken control of the automobile, obstructing the view of the driver's seat. Hers is a solo mobility. The provocative ambivalence of the cover photo might lead us to wonder whether Donofrio is free to choose her presentational posture or bound to ride in this way, to paraphrase Rachel Bowlby (198).

Automobiles are ubiquitous in the pages of Donofrio's memoir. They literally and figuratively drive her narrative. The narrator continuously invokes cars, their names and colors, their defining characteristics, the status of their drivers, their social implications. Hardly a page passes without reference to a car of some sort and for some purpose. In *Riding*, the automobile is inextricably linked to self-making and self-representing. To get an auto is to get an (auto)biography. To have an auto is to have an identity. *Riding in Cars with Boys* engages the diverse cultural meanings and the material implications of automobility in America.

There is much about *Riding in Cars with Boys* that harkens back to Kerouac's *On the Road*: the staccato prose, the cast of characters, the sense of restlessness, the critique of middle-class norms of propriety, the celebration of badness. But the critical difference of Donofrio's text is the way in which the automobile itself is never assumed as being merely a vehicle for getting from one location to another. Automobility in its broadest sense—the configuration of people, machines, landscape, urban geography, and culture that attends the increasing dependence upon the gas engine for transport in industrial and postindustrial societies—is the thematic core of her narrative. *Riding in Cars with Boys* foregrounds how the automobile must be understood as a machine for the production and reproduction of masculinity and femininity; and it foregrounds, as well, the ways in which the automobile structures class relationships and underwrites certain myths of national identity. It is Donofrio's engagement, both explicit and implicit, with the larger cultural meanings of automobility that distinguishes her narrative from other road narratives.

Because (auto)biography is a class act, Donofrio negotiates myths of self-making in the class geography of American modernity. Thus, she is careful to define her own family's liminal class position. The Donofrios are solidly working-class but live in the marginal neighborhood contiguous to a public-housing project. Her father is a policeman. Her mother is a housewife preoccupied with cleanliness, food, appropriate behavior, and responsibility. Through promotion of these behavioral markers, her mother defines her own class aspirations, the differentiating behaviors that separate her from the people in the projects on welfare and that bolster her image of herself as really middle-class. The larger community surrounding the Donofrios is solidly working-class, made up of the families of factory workers. This class identity is reinforced for students in the attitudes of the schoolteachers, who define them as the children of factory workers, that is, children with no place to go but the same assembly line as their fathers. Effectively, the social history of Fordism and mass industrialization with its alienated labor becomes the background noise in Donofrio's narrative.

Paradoxically, the very product that is produced on the assembly line—the automobile—becomes the marker of identity, in complex and contradictory ways. Donofrio captures how identities in America are car-born and car-generated, and how they engender desires—the sexual desires of teenagers and later the desire for a certain social status. As David Gartman suggests, it is paradoxical that the mass-produced automobile, a reified product of consumer capitalism, becomes a defining sign of individuality and rebellion against corporate culture (7). Auto access is equivalent to access to the defining American value of individuality. "Americans of all classes," notes Gartman, "wanted cars that lent them some distinction in a Fordist world where the work of even bourgeois businessmen and professionals was subject to the leveling logic of rationalization" (170).

But there are differences in the meaning of access to automobiles for girls and for boys. To climb into the driver's seat, for a young boy, has been to get an identity as manly and desirable. To get into an auto, for a young girl, has often been to get into trouble. "Trouble began in 1963,"

Donofrio declares as she opens her narrative, trouble "as in pregnant." To be bad is precisely to "get pregnant in high school." The alternative to being bad is being good, which means not having fun. If, as her mother tries to warn her, a good girl makes sure her legs are always crossed, especially in critical situations, then a bad girl opens her legs to give the jocks "crotch shots" or to have sex. But Donofrio suggests that trouble really begins when she takes up "riding in cars with boys" which, she confesses, starts at the age of fourteen: "I was speeding around Wallingford[, Connecticut,] in crowded cars with guys who took corners on two wheels" (17).

Renegade automobility marked rebellious adolescence in the early 1960s. Yet renegade automobility, as she and her friends understood too well, is a masculine prerogative. Donofrio describes how she and her friends, in order to have the kind of fun that boys have, in order to rebel against the strictures of goodness, start "acting like" boys through their participation in "hood" culture. "We got drunk in the parking lot before school dances," she writes, "and rode real low in cars, elbows stuck out windows, tossing beer cans, flicking butts, and occasionally pulling down our pants and shaking our fannies at passing vehicles" (20). Here is performative badness, the adoption of behaviors constitutive of working-class masculinity. If the bad girl is one who gets into cars with boys, the female hood is one who enacts certain kinds of behaviors inside the automobile in mimicry of (auto)masculinity. Donofrio identifies how her relationship to the automobile functions in her rebellion against normative standards of behavior. But she also explores the price she pays for her rebelliousness, especially as it relates to (auto)biography. Bad-girlness is synonymous with bad-daughterhood. Bad-girlness leads to motherhood and, in Donofrio's case, to bad-motherhood—yet another form of resistance to the normative femininity required for middle-class respectability.

Donofrio explores how automobility has implications for the social and economic life of young girls and young mothers, and how relationships to automobiles organize desire and its discontents. For one thing, relationships to men are organized around cars. Her initial fascination with Ray Bouchard (who becomes her husband) is a fascination with his renegade identity as a greaser—"he could probably fix cars because that's why hoods were called greasers" (27)—and his possession of "a yellow Bonneville with a black roof and . . . plenty of money for beer" (97). The Bonneville, a working-class muscle car of the mid 1960s, signifies renegade working-class virility. It exudes an aura of metallic masculinity. Because styles of automobility function as styles of identity, the Bonneville stands for the man in the aesthetics of modern desire. It promises the satisfaction of erotic desires. Aptly, Donofrio imagines the trajectory of her erotic relationship with Ray through the romance plot of *On the Waterfront*. Ray and Marlon Brando merge in the young girl's imagination.

The automobile remains an object defining Donofrio and Ray's sexual and familial relationship as conventional. Normative gender assignments determine access to wheels. When Ray gets a job, he uses the car, leaving Donofrio home all day with her son, stationary and bored (83). When he gets tired of domestic responsibilities, he drives off, leaving behind his wife and child. In this gesture of escape, he enacts a normative scenario of vagrant masculinity. "Why did he always get the car?" the narrator queries (84). And when he eventually abandons her, Ray takes the car with him, leaving her with a child and without a car. In this state of affairs, there is only one plot for Donofrio's life script: the slippery slide into welfare dependence. Riding in cars with boys has gotten her a ticket to marriage and then to the center of the projects. Ironically, Donofrio has materialized her family's fear of the slide from respectability to the socially abject.

Stranded in welfare dependence, Donofrio's identity is determined by the presence and absence of automobiles in her life. The narrator explores how, at a particularly low point in her period of bad-motherhood, her reputation, and more critically her legal status, is affected by the cars parked in front of her home. A policeman, a friend of her father, warns her that she will get busted for prostitution if he sees more cars in her driveway. In other words, the policeman constructs a particular kind of sexual biography for Donofrio, assigning her the script of promiscuous young mother based on the objects surrounding her. "I should've known," she writes. "It wasn't the drugs, it was sex" (120).

But the absence of an automobile equally defines her autobiographical possibilities. In the economy of automobility, to be without a car is to be trapped in welfare dependence. To be with a car, Donofrio suggests, is to be "free" (95). When she and her roommate Fay venture into an Italian club, in an odyssey that combines both sexual revenge and sexual neediness, they find themselves "damsels in distress," precisely because they have lost their wheels. "Soon after we'd found the club," she writes, "Fay's creep of an ex-husband sneaked up in the night and stole back the yellow Dodge, leaving us carless and furious—because it had been men who'd knocked us up, men who'd left us with kids, and men who got the cars" (109). To be dependent and sessile is to remain outside motorized modernity; it is to have no place and no way to go. Home, in this case, is a site not of leisure, consumption, and pleasure but of dead-end dreams and captivity. In their compensatory daydreams, Donofrio and Fay dream of returning to the site of abandonment in a red Ferrari (113), a muscle car for the very rich. The metallic fantasy provides compensatory escape from the degraded everyday reality of Donofrio's life as a too-young, divorced welfare mother without a future.[4] Relieving the monotony of everyday life, dreams of Ferraris provide her with the exhilaration of power, projection, and pleasure (see Gartman 152).

The culture of the automobile in America strands people without cars, most notably the poorest members of society, a large proportion of whom are women with children. Without cars, they're also without a future. Judy Wajcman notes that women have less mobility than men in automobile cultures and that they remain more dependent upon public transportation. Thus, she concludes, "the organization of the transportation system compounds women's inequality, virtually locking them into a world of very limited physical space, and exacerbates the unequal allocation of resources within the city" (131). In this context, transportation becomes an obligation and a struggle rather than a pleasure. Donofrio's memoir critiques the way in which the automobile, heralded in the early part of the twentieth century as the motor of democratic capitalism, by the last third of the century became a sure marker of class divisions and identities.

Donofrio's critique of the welfare system and institutionalized poverty has everything to do with the pressures and effects of automobility on women's lives. An unsympathetic welfare officer warns her, "You're not going to get a free ride here," invoking one common metaphor of automobility used to denigrate those who find themselves living on welfare (143). But a young welfare mother without a car remains a bad girl who can get neither an education nor a job. To take courses at the community college—a commuter institution—Donofrio needs a car. To continue at college, she needs a car. Those without a ride remain future-less. In the late twentieth century, the upward mobility of self-making, the American myth of bootstrapping your way out of poverty and into the middle class, required an automobile.

Even as Donofrio turns her brash wit and staccato prose to a cultural critique of automobility for working-class girls and young women, she tells a quintessentially American story of self-making in a feminist key. This working-class daughter, once a welfare mother, earns an education first at a community college and then at a prestigious Ivy League institution. Upon graduation, she moves to a new job and a new life in New York City. There she raises a son who continues on to college himself. The working-class "hood" raises herself and her family into middle-class respectability. Appropriately, her narrative of bad-girlhood and bad-motherhood is framed at beginning and end by the automobile ride she takes with her son as she drops him off at college. Yet repeatedly she makes clear how, in America, the automobile is a material necessity in this drama of self-making. Only with the aid of her sidekick Cupcake, the "beautiful fourteen-year-old with-a-rebuilt-engine emerald-green Volkswagen" that she purchased "after four years without a car" (144), can she "join the human race" (147). The automobile is one of the material objects, if not the only object, that mediates the social relationships of class in America.

## "Greyhounding," or The Politics of Riding Otherwise

> Whereas [John Clellon Holmes, in his introduction to a new
> edition of his novel *Go*,] scrupulously matches each of the male
> characters in his roman a clef to their originals, the "girls" are
> variously "amalgams of several people"; "accurate to the young
> women of the time"; "a type rather than an individual." He can't
> quite remember them—they were mere anonymous passengers
> on the big Greyhound bus of experience. Lacking centers, how
> could they burn with the fever that infected his young men?
> What they did, I guess, was fill up the seats.
>
> —Joyce Johnson, *Minor Characters*

Joyce Johnson's offhand remark about representations of young women as "passengers on the big Greyhound bus of experience" links women and bus travel in an intriguing way. Acutely aware of the way in which women of the Beat coterie were always represented as "minor characters," and never as central players in the game of postwar hip rebellion, Johnson emphasizes how, in the narratives of the Beats and their promoters, young women remain "anonymous passengers" who merely "fill up the seats" on the bus ride of life (79). Johnson's metaphor joins women, cultural anonymity, and disempowered ridership. It is precisely this conjunction of gender, anonymity, marginality, and bus culture that Irma Kurtz's *The Great American Bus Ride* negotiates.

In the early 1990s, Irma Kurtz returned from London to the United States to spend ten months traveling around her country of birth. *The Great American Bus Ride* (1993) is her narrative of that journey across America by Greyhound. Kurtz organizes her narrative around the legs of her bus rides, using the route numbers of the buses she takes as section markers. Her peripatetic journey through America seems unplanned, spontaneous, and offbeat. And it seems to go nowhere in particular; there is no "progress" to her itinerary. She follows her instincts, her interests, and her whims in searching out "unknown" America. As she listens to other travelers talking about their journeys, she puts names of places to go on her own list (29). At other times she uses even less rational ways to choose her destinations. "I was going to Dinosaur[,Colorado]," she writes, "simply to make up for dereliction of a traveler's duty every so often to go somewhere for no reason but the sound of it" (199). Hers is a serendipitous route through which she resists "forward planning" (180).

Even the more purposeful trip Kurtz embeds in her narrative of Greyhounding fails to take her where she wants to go and fails to register progress. This more personal narrative has to do with a journey of return to her land of origin and to places where members of her family lived. She visits her mother's hometown of Elwood, Indiana, where her mother's Jewish identity ran afoul of an America imagined by the local Ku Klux Klan. Here Kurtz discovers the fragility of memory and self-narrating. Visiting a local graveyard, she seeks out the grave of one of her mother's teachers, a woman whom the daughter remembers her mother describing as hostile and bigoted. But, as her mother later clarifies, the person she has berated in the cemetery is not her mother's teacher. Memory has failed her. The past has a way of disappearing on her at the very moment when she would hold it accountable. In Denver she searches for a trace of her mother's childhood that she might find meaningful: "For once I was trying not to prepare arguments, and not to be too rational, only to let myself feel if anything was there on that street waiting for me to catch up with it: a piece of my picture, I mean, a loop of Irma's timeprint unique among the infinite, a clue, a hint, a trace of something planted in the American past for me, and me alone" (192). She finds those pieces when she locates the place where her grandfather died and the very books he bequeathed to a local institution (194). In Los Angeles she visits her brother and realizes how quickly relatives wish bus travelers back on the bus. With its fits and starts, this personal odyssey cannot be organized as a progressive journey of recovery. The journey of return, a journey in ways similar to Mary Morris's train journey, turns into a journey of itinerant wandering.

Kurtz's itinerant wandering puts her in the midst of the down-and-out. In this sense, perhaps, she can be read as a latter-day avatar of the boys on the road. In fact, the ghost of Kerouac haunts this narrative of Greyhound mobility. Rummaging through a bookstore in Louisville, Kentucky, Kurtz finds an old copy of *On the Road,* which she purchases and reads during her travels (167). An expatriate, Kurtz presents herself as a traveler on the road to "my unknown homeland" (22), "my unknown America" (107). It is a journey as peripatetic as the journey of Sal and his comrades across the continent, a journey through which, like these young men, Kurtz encounters habitués of an America outside the mainstream of modernity.

This journey to the "obscure" America beyond the sacralized sites of organized tourism requires a particular kind of mobility. Trains, for instance, cannot deliver that obscure America to Kurtz. "I soon discovered," Kurtz writes, "American trains would not take me anywhere obscure, or anywhere much at all it seemed, unless I kept going to Chicago first" (21). The routes of trains, in an America of superhighways, cheap gas, and underfunded public-transportation systems, are far too limiting. Only automobility can take her where she wants to go—to the far reaches of the country, across its back roads, and into the obscure recesses of the nation. But a rented car will not do for her. Refusing to put herself behind the wheel of an individualized driving machine that would isolate her from obscure America, she climbs into a Greyhound bus, a form of transportation within automobile culture but positioned at its margins. For Kurtz, the Greyhound is itself the site of the traveler's exploration. *The Great American Bus Ride* is fundamentally a travel narrative about Greyhounding.

In the age of automobility, the Greyhound bus has come to fill a particular niche for travelers in America. Stretching across the entire continent, Greyhound bus lines join urban centers with the smallest of small towns huddled on prairies or deserts or mountainsides, and with the people isolated in those spaces. They provide cheap transportation for masses of people who cannot afford to travel in style. They cater to a clientele that has few possessions and few alternatives. In a land of privatized mobility, Greyhound buses offer a modicum of mobility to the marginalized: young people without money, older women on small pensions, the relatively homeless, the directionless, and the downright poor.

Kurtz is well aware of the meanings of Greyhound travel in her country of birth: "Buses and bus depots scare the wits out of genteel Americans (*America* scares the wits out of genteel Americans) and the Greyhound depot defines the wrong side of the tracks" (19). The Greyhound bus is the vehicle of and for the abject in motion. "America is a road country," she remarks. "To be without wheels in America is to be lame" (21). To have an auto, as we discovered in reading Donofrio's *Riding in Cars with Boys*, is to have an (auto)biography, to possess an identity, a destiny, a vehicle of self-making. To ride the Greyhound bus, by contrast, is to ride as one of the "lame." It is to ride in the "wrong" way. In the cultural imaginary of America, bus travel is the last resort of the down-and-out, the errant, the dispossessed, the poor, and the "nut cases" (20). The Greyhound bus and the public stations servicing bus travel have become identified in the cultural imaginary as the domain of the excluded.

Thus, there was no better place to go if one was after the exotic underside of American postmodernity in the automobile century than to the very form of automobility identified with the down-and-out. "'You've got to remember,'" a bookstore owner in Fargo, North Dakota, advises Kurtz, "'that by and large towns in America are places being passed through. Most of America is being passed through or flown over most of the time'" (110). In a postmodern world of speed without attachment to the ground, signified by the transcontinental plane, Greyhounding promises to deliver the "real America" to the traveler who is prepared to take on its demands. Travel by Greyhound in postmodern America is equivalent, Kurtz suggests toward the end of her narrative, to traveling the Nile by barge or the Sahara by camel. It is a "primitive" form of travel in a modern land.

As a Greyhound traveler, Kurtz identifies herself with a particular kind of mobile femininity when she implies that only a certain kind of woman chooses Greyhounding as a mode of travel (if she doesn't have to). Hers is a version of middle-aged bad-girl femininity, sexualized around the desire for down-and-out experiences. "The truth is," she confesses early on, "I am a hussy of low appetites who always yearns shamelessly for rough travel, and I grab the chance whenever I can to arrive at my destination exhausted, knowing I've earned my goal the hard way. Greyhound and I were made for each other" (22). Kurtz's "low appetites," suited to "rough travel," even become a kind of addiction: "I had become a Greyhound junkie, an addict, who couldn't bear to hang around anywhere for long without a fix, not even in Louisville, where there was, like, lots of historical stuff" (168). In late-twentieth- and early-twenty-first-century postmodernity, Greyhounding functions as a form of arduous travel and exacting travail. It is a mode of mobility through which the woman who chooses it differentiates herself from the tourist who is after comfort in mobility, from the traveler addicted to the repertoires of a far more genteel femininity.

Figuring herself as a "hussy" of "low appetites," Kurtz masquerades as one of the excluded and marginalized who travel the Greyhound by necessity. Like Alexandra David-Neel, who traveled as the "common *arjopa*" in her journey to Lhasa, Kurtz culturally "cross-dresses." And, like that of David-Neel's journey, the meaning of Kurtz's journey is dependent upon the successful enactment of the other, in this case, the Greyhound "type." On the bus, Kurtz becomes and remains an anonymous passenger, a middle-aged woman in rather eclectic yet nondescript clothing, wearing one item from here, one item from there. "It is a peculiarity of the solitary woman in her fifties," she notes, "that she can for long periods of time believe herself to be invisible. I count anonymity as a chief virtue of middle age" (27). Acutely self-reflexive, Kurtz acknowledges that she is too old for femininity as "to-be-looked-at-ness." Describing an experience in the Chicago Greyhound terminal, Kurtz recalls advising a young girl who seeks her protection from a man who seems to be tracking her: "'You know you've got to get used to that kind of thing when you're young and pretty. God knows at my age,' I told her, 'a woman has to get used to doing without it.' She looked at me blankly. 'What I mean is, young people, when you travel, well, you are bound to be seen by the world. Later in life you can travel and see the world without anyone paying much attention to you'" (76).

In this cloak of anonymity, Kurtz finds the freedom to ride and observe precisely because the inconspicuous identity she assumes enables her to blend into the indistinct interior of the bus and to listen to others without being an object of undue attention or speculation. The anonymity that Joyce Johnson bemoans as the lot of the women of the Beat generation is precisely the screen of invisibility that this middle-aged traveler embraces as desirable for the kind of journey she wants to take as one of the "lame."

Anonymity facilitates eavesdropping, which Kurtz calls "a longtime avocation of mine. Most of America is an eavesdropper's paradise, which puts it as close as a whisker to hell" (33). Deploying this screen of invisibility, Kurtz listens to and then records the itinerant logic of Greyhounding, the rhythms of encounter and exchange that characterize this "obscure" America. In this way, she becomes a backyard ethnographer of sorts, attentive to the organization of space, the human and material architecture of the depot, the unspoken code of conduct among riders, the distinctive Greyhound behaviors, and the demographics of ridership.

Kurtz captures the rhythms of exchange in Greyhounding by weaving together the voices of anonymous riders and their fleeting conversations without adding her own commentary. The rhythm of her prose captures the conversations begun, interrupted, and overheard as she gets on, rides, gets off, and rests from one ride to the next. Exchanges come out of nowhere, often go nowhere, and eventually return to silence. Through this narrative strategy, Kurtz captures the multivoicedness of Greyhounding, incorporating partial, cryptic exchanges, sometimes even nonconversations. Combined, these patches of dialogue become a discursive ledger of communication in bus-time America, the background chatter of the anonymous riders who move through days of displacement in postmodernity.

Kurtz also incorporates condensed sketches of people she meets during her rides, people such as the nineteen-year-old Geena in her "stabbing heels," a young woman "already past most happiness" (125), and the "Iron Lady," an "expat to hot, cheap countries … trapped south of the border by a diminishing fixed income"(254–55). These sketches of strangers entering and exiting Kurtz's sphere of eavesdropping project the "raw identities" of habitués of the Greyhound: the lonely, hardened, impoverished, sometimes strange, and often needy. Her recourse to such epithets as "Iron Lady" reinforces her assertion that such projected portraits substitute for genuine connection; as she notes, "Bus travelers hardly ever exchange names, not even when they have been steeped in each other's intimate spaces for hours through the day and night … and as long as bus passengers are on the road, it is by raw identities that they know each other" (121).

Kurtz listens to, observes, and records what the "litmus paper" of the Greyhound has to reveal about modern social relations in America. She labels the Greyhound bus as it rides across America's roads "the state without a zipcode" (138) and thinks of it as a political entity that reproduces and reflects the political organization of life in the United States. As the bus crosses from the Lower to the Upper Peninsula of Michigan, she notes that the ridership becomes entirely white. "Greyhound's routes," she reflects, "run like litmus paper throughout America, reacting without judgment to what they find: when we pulled out of Clare with new passengers on board, for example, there was not a black person among us, and we had a white driver too" (82). Acutely aware of the ways in which the bus culture itself becomes a hierarchal culture, Kurtz records the social stratifications encoded in the spatial organization of difference on the bus. She delineates the code for decisions about where to sit—decisions made according to race, sex, class, and age (78). She tries to sit no further than halfway back, "right at the point where genteel passengers panic and take the first empty seat they come to rather than move on any closer to the back, where the habitual smokers, and goodness knows what else, congregate" (54). The back of the bus she characterizes as the nether region of disorder, disease, distemper, and dissipation. It is a predominately masculine site. And the depot she describes as "a sort of thermometer in the nether orifice of any city" (135).

In *Bus Ride*, Kurtz ultimately recognizes that there are at least two different kinds of travel by Greyhound. There is the travel that the people she observes do by Greyhound, the kind of travel that is left to the dispossessed, the disempowered, and the displaced in America who are not on the way to upward mobility. And then there is Greyhounding, the kind of travel of choice by certain travelers out for a particular kind of experience. Reflecting upon a black British man she meets in the Bayside, Florida, depot, Kurtz comments on the differential attraction of public conveyance at home and abroad:

> When he was in London, I'd wager, he would not dream of taking public transport. But he understood perfectly the cachet of traveling by Greyhound around America: it was like doing the Nile on a barge or joining a caravan across the Sahara. On one level Greyhounding was more than just cheap and efficient; it was authentic, it was the real Yankee Doodle way to travel, as endorsed by bluesmen in their songs and featured in chewing-gum commercials. Especially if one did not actually need to go by bus, it was a grand way to see America, and really very high style. (294)

"To Greyhound" is to travel to the America commonly passed by, the unseen, the "primitive," and therefore the "authentic" America (here in an imperialist trope identified with North Africa). In making a verb out of the noun, Kurtz captures with irony the way in which the traveler turns a material object of transportation that signifies an entire way of life on the margins into a grammatical figure, an infinitive, that signifies the accumulation of "authentic experiences" on the part of the traveler. As Sachs says of the automobile and its stimulation of desires, it "transformed the traveler into a potential explorer, who could set new goals and approach the old in a fresh manner; now, with active probing, the tourist's gaze could penetrate even the most distant corners" (155).

The accumulation of experiences brings us back to the ghost of Jack Kerouac. Like Kerouac's young men, Kurtz seeks out the habitués of America's margins. But hers is a narrative of observation rather than immersion, and of searing self-reflexiveness. Kerouac's young men embrace life at the margins; accumulate experiences, including the sexual conquest of young women whom they love and leave; and come to express a renegade masculinity. Kurtz, a middle-aged woman, understanding her anonymity *as* middle-aged woman, finds her own way to an enabling identity as "low hussy," a hussy out for overheard conversations rather than sexual conquests. It is through gendered anonymity that Kurtz can assess the limits of social mobility that riding the Greyhound signals.

## Conclusion: The Fear of the Road

At the beginning of the century of the automobile, Edith Wharton celebrated the ways in which automobile travel, as it enhanced the aestheticization of everyday life for the elite traveler, restored the romance of travel. Taking her access to the automobile for granted, Wharton set off across the French countryside seeking out the pleasures of "taking scenes unawares." For Wharton, the automobile enabled the traveler to turn a romanticized gaze upon landscape and peoplescape. According to Sachs, this "attraction" to the "real" country "grows in direct proportion to its distance from the conditions of the tourist's own life. The contrast with daily life allows romantic feelings to sprout" (154). Paradoxically, of course, the automobile, which restores the romance of travel for Wharton, is the technological expression (product and cultural effect) of Western modernity and progress Wharton decries. It is only from within modernity that the picturesqueness of the French countryside, as opposed to the American landscape, achieves its value as desirable; for it is only from within modernity that the picturesque can be imagined as premodern and thus outside ravaging modernity's scope.

At the end of the century, Donofrio and Kurtz resist the romance of automobility, only too aware of the ways in which the culture of the automobile organizes gender, sexuality, and class in everyday life. Donofrio's narrative registers the centrality of the automobile for upward mobility in America, whereas Kurtz's expatriate narrative registers the alternative mobility of those left behind on the road of postmodernity.

For Donofrio, (auto)motion is both the site of the reproduction of the class politics of gender in postmodern America and the site of social resistance and social mobility. In her hard-boiled feminist odyssey, the former "hood" explores how riding in cars alone gains her access to an (auto)biography as it takes her into another terrain of class. As she understands only too well, the symbolic value of the automobile has to do with what Gartman describes as "social mobility and belongingness" (154). Cupcake takes her for a ride out of welfare dependence. Along the way, the former "bad girl" learns to refuse to ride in cars with men whose motoring masculinity requires that women remain down-and-out at home (Donofrio 174).

In Kurtz's narrative, automobility becomes a lens through which to glimpse the disconnections and dispossessions of a culture organized around the ubiquity of mobility and displacement. The expatriate takes home to her reader an America through which she deconstructs certain myths of automobility and modernity. Hers is no nostalgic drive through the premodern American past identified with idealized childhoods. Hers is no solitary odyssey of return to her origins. Hers is, rather, a travel narrative about the mode of travel she chooses, a travel narrative about Greyhounding. And Greyhounding, by the end of the twentieth century, had become, in its own way, a mode of mobility as arduous and exotic as the modes of mobility chosen by Alexandra David-Neel and Isabelle Eberhardt at the beginning of the century.

Donofrio's analysis of the automobile as a signifier of upward mobility and Kurtz's analysis of the racial and class organization of life on the Greyhound bus remind us that the meaning of twentieth-century automobility must always be contextualized. For people of color in the United States, for instance, possession of an automobile has fostered a sense of belonging, a sense of ownership in the founding myths of American national identity. James van der Zee's 1932 photograph of an African American couple posing with their car in Harlem captures this pleasure of possession. The man sits in the passenger seat of a shiny new Cadillac; the woman stands beside the car. Both wear resplendent raccoon coats. Looking directly at the camera's eye, they come across as elegant and confident, in the midst of the Depression.[5]

There is also the narrative of automobility Maya Angelou embeds in her first autobiographical narrative, *I Know Why the Caged Bird Sings*

(1970). Unable to live with her father and his second wife, yet unable to return to her mother's home, Angelou finds a month of stability and friendship in an abandoned car lot. In wartime Los Angeles, she joins other homeless children who huddle together for support, sharing their earnings and their trust. In the midst of poverty and displacement, by-products of the motorized modernity made possible by the automobile, the refuse of the production line provides respite from the street. If possession of an automobile signifies the owner's participation in the American dream and the good life attributed to American dynamism, in Angelou's case possession of an abandoned automobile signifies the resourcefulness of children displaced by a culture of isolation and racism. Here, too, the automobile is a defining object of modernity, offering temporary housing to the abandoned and the abused, the destitute and the mentally unstable, the addicted and the itinerant, even as it clutters up the landscape.

Not everyone has been free to ride, however, not even free to ride buses as they please. Private and public forms of automobility, for instance, were contested sites in the Jim Crow South of the United States. Public buses, as well as trains, organized interior spaces according to racial hierarchies—whites in front and blacks in back. Refusing to sit in her assigned seat, Rosa Parks, tired after a long day's labor, opted for forward mobility, thereby inspiring a widespread civil rights movement. For others, to be on the road in a private automobile could be a matter of life and death. The possession could be a site of dispossession. In *The Sweeter the Juice* (1994), Shirlee Taylor Haizlip recalls how careful her parents were to position themselves properly in the family automobile when they took trips to see relatives in the Deep South during the 1940s. With her father being dark-skinned and her mother light enough to pass for white, they knew only too well the danger of appearing to be an interracial couple out for a drive. As Lackey suggests in his discussion of African American road narratives, the traveler "is not freed into neutral self-examination by anonymity, the absence of bosses, and the power to consume. Instead, the driver becomes a product offered for the scrutiny of other consumers" (113–14). Vigilant about the stakes of visibility, the traveler of color negotiates the history of race, racism, and racialized identities.

At the turn of a century, being caught "on the road" continues to bring with it dangers unto death for some people, especially people of color living in a white world. As bell hooks cautions in her deconstruction of conventional notions of travel: "To travel is to encounter the terrorizing force of white supremacy" (344). In "Fences against Freedom" (1994), Leslie Marmon Silko provides a dark tale of the road as she documents how "race policies" in the United States permeate the everyday life of people of color as they head out on the road. Silko vividly reveals how certain people ride along certain roads at their peril. Along the highways of the Southwest, people of color become suspect and suspects at "checkpoints," those quintessential sites of race politics that the border patrol sets up along the interstate highways and back roads of Arizona and New Mexico to prevent "illegal aliens" from entering the body politic. At these points American citizens who happen to be people of color are policed by the force of badges, guns, and search dogs. They are stopped, searched, made to tremble. Silko traumatically remembers her fear of detainment as palpable.

Silko uses the freedom to ride highways as a register of the freedom to be an American. Thus, she invokes the common understanding among Americans that the freedom to ride is constitutive of American national identity. "We citizens of the United States," she writes,

> grew up believing this freedom of the open road to be our inalienable right. The freedom of the open road meant we could travel freely from state to state without special papers or threat of detainment; this was a 'right' citizens of Communist and totalitarian governments did not possess. That wide open highway was what told us we were U.S. citizens. Indeed, some say, this freedom to travel is an integral part of the American identity. (59)

To be stopped and "checked" is to be confronted with one's otherness in the body politic. It is to be checked of an inalienable, defining right. The border patrol's checkpoint, an interruption of automobility, is tantamount to a check on (auto)biography. At the redefining moment of the checkpoint, the traveler is made to understand herself as other in and to America.

# Electronic Transport
# in Cyberspace

> As writing yields to flickering signifiers underwritten by
> binary digits, the narrator becomes not so much a scribe as
> a cyborg authorized to access the relevant codes.
>
> —N. Katherine Hayles, "Virtual Bodies and Flickering Signifiers"

As a coda to this discussion of women's travel narratives and technologies of motion, I want to offer a very brief and provisional meditation on the kinds of travel narratives that might emerge as women become more involved in traveling along the electronic highway. For, undoubtedly, new kinds of travel narratives will emerge with this new technology of postmodernity. In fact, they already are emerging, as we can see from such narratives as Melanie McGrath's *Hard, Soft, and Wet: The Digital Generation Comes of Age* (1997). I don't mean to suggest here that cyberspace travel is the next, most advanced or avant-garde form of travel, although it is apparently the latest fashion. But it may be that in thinking about the condition of travel in cyberspace and the relationship of time to space, and space to identity, and identity to body, and body to imagination in motion, we may come to appreciate how this newest technology of travel might be used by mobile women to undefining effect.

One way to think about travel in cyberspace is to look to the realm of business travel in the late twentieth century. Business travel transports people from one geographic location to another at high speeds. Planes set travelers down in airport hubs, where they exit into terminals hermetically sealed off from the everyday disturbances of life in the cities and countries around them. Shuttles transport them to international hotel chains, where multinational corporations deliver the same conveniences to them whether they're in Bangkok or Paris or Chicago or Tokyo. After a while, planes return them home via the same controlled routing. From a certain perspective, such travel becomes "virtual."

Airplane travel with its network of routes, hubs, terminals, and homes away from home, maps global space in ways analogous to the geography of the communications networks that take people from their computer terminals into cyberspace. Electrons move along optic fibers at unimaginable speeds, taking users into virtual realities, cyberspaces that are no spaces. Here electrons set in motion imaginary encounters of armchair travelers who sit at their terminals and don't move, except at their fingertips. In this virtual reality, time and space collapse, folding into one another; and travelers move along routes that multiply in a virtual world of information.

There are, of course, different kinds of traveling a woman might do with her computer, which is yet another object through which postmodern social relations are negotiated in everyday life. "Surfing the Internet," she might become a vagabond, following first one path and then another through the excesses of information available on the Net, much as Irma Kurtz moved by Greyhound across America. Or she might decide to wander along hypertextual routes on a CD-ROM. Or she might enter a virtual world of relationships by taking up a conversation in a "Multiuser Dungeon," where she would join an anonymous collectivity in the shared production of a virtual world of relational experiences. Or she might enter the imaginary world of virtual reality, where graphics programs "create a three-dimensional computer-generated space that a user/participant interacts with and manipulates via wired peripherals" (Balsamo, *Technologies* 120). As a traveler in virtual reality, she might don a new kind of mechanical prosthesis, the properly wired gloves, suit, and/or headgear necessary for virtual motion.

Of course, at the beginning of the twenty-first century, only certain women can do this kind of traveling. Access to the Net and to cyberspace is still the prerogative of a relatively privileged group of people: the highly educated and computer-literate population of the industrialized West and the burgeoning Pacific Rim countries. The electrons that speed along the information highway are electrons of the elect, who are the beneficiaries of this newest revolution of modernity. There is little to no access to computer technologies, let alone networks and cyberspace, for millions of women and men across the globe. Habitués of Greyhound buses, and their equivalents around the world, can't get to cyberspace.

Cyberspace travel not only reproduces unequal relations of class and caste, it also reproduces the gendered social relations of (post)modernity. For the terrain of entry is not an alternative terrain, an elsewhere to the cultural relations of "real" space. The objects that are made for this kind of mobility and the environment surrounding those objects are fully inflected with codes and spectacles of masculinity and femininity that permeate the real world. Think, for instance, of the gendered arrangements of the world of hackers, those with unlimited access to the Net. Judy Wajcman, Anne Balsamo, and Allucquère Rosanne Stone all explore the various ways in which the cyberculture of computer engineering, programming, hacking, and surfing is a masculinist culture, a culture organized around certain values—instrumental and disembodied rationality being primary among them.

Because embodiment and disembodiment play such a critical role in the coding of femininity as sessile and of masculinity as mobile, we might think further about what happens to the body as the traveler moves via electrons. Flight lifted Amelia Earhart's body off the earth in a miracle of heavier-than-air transport. Her body remained with her nonetheless, suited up and strapped in. Subject to accident, it could be incinerated, dismembered, crushed; it was, in the end, lost. But in cyberspace the body effectively disappears as meaningful to travel. This apparent disappearance releases the cybertraveler into a state of anonymity. With much less hassle than Kurtz faced in riding the Greyhound, she can eavesdrop on the conversations that hum along the information highway. Or, like Alexandra David-Neel crossing the Himalayas, she can become an inconspicuous *arjopa* by taking on a "character," "as close or far away from [her] 'real self' as [she] choose[s]" (Turkle 355).

The cyberspace traveler can fabricate identities to defy, evade, or confuse the constitutive constraints of normative femininity in the world outside the Net. She can take a man's name, for instance, or a gender-neutral name, as she traverses the multiple itineraries available to her on the Net. Or she can assume the identity of someone from an entirely different culture. In all these ways she can experiment, as Sherry Turkle suggests, with alternative identities through sophisticated role-playing (357–59). Identity in this context becomes fluid, provisional, adaptable, postmodern (Stone 43–44). Here is travel with radically undefining effects.

The disembodiment at the heart of cyberculture and cybertravel is also at the heart of travel in virtual reality. Although this kind of travel requires a bodily apparatus, whether visor or helmet or bodysuit or lenses for the eyes, the apparatus effects a repression of the body in cyberspace. "In most programs," suggests Balsamo,

> a user experiences VR [virtual reality] through a disembodied gaze—a floating moving "perspective"—that mimes the movement of a disembodied camera eye.... The repression of the body is technologically naturalized. I think this happens because we have internalized the technological gaze to such an extent that "perspective" is a naturalized organizing locus of sense knowledge. As a consequence, "the body," as a sense apparatus, is nothing more than excess baggage for the cyberspace traveler. (*Technologies* 126)

The traveler becomes a disembodied eyeball that meets, challenges, succumbs to, or defeats cyborgs, exotic morphs, and robotic fantasms. "With virtual reality," Balsamo concludes, "we are offered the vision of a body-free universe" (128).

But this does not mean that travel in virtual reality and cyberspace is travel without the constitutive constraints of a defining femininity attached to embodiment. Journeys into cyberspace may, on the one hand, promise release from messy embodiment, because they exert control over what Balsamo describes as "the unruly, gender- and race-marked, essentially mortal body" (*Technologies* 128). But this dream of disembodiment may, on the other hand, be the reiteration in our postmodern time of a predominant narrative of modernity in the West: the elevation of mind over body/matter. In this way, the anonymity of cyberspace "belies a gender bias in the supposedly disembodied (and genderless) world of virtual reality" (125). It is precisely that suspicion and devaluing of embodiment that has kept the place of woman a place of sessility.

Moreover, to move anonymously with the electrons is to journey through gendered spaces much like the other spaces traversed in this study. The disembodied subject, in its material absence, remains a virtual presence. This unmarked body, here in its avatar as cybersubject, is the latest manifestation of the privileged subject of Western enlightenment and progress, carrying the marks of that privilege in anonymity. This unmarked body of the virtual world is the normative subject of travel, empowered, masculine, and white. He is an Odysseus of the virtual.

Inevitably, embodied codes and behaviors get transported into virtual environments (Balsamo, "Feminism" 694, 695). The promises of radical disembodiment and pliable identity in Net traveling must therefore be qualified by the recognition that this newest technology and its uses are infiltrated by social relations that structure the real world outside the virtual world. Like the air of early aviation, virtual air is saturated with the values of the larger society.

Journeys through electrons are as complicated as journeys by foot or plane or train or automobile. As opportunities for "exploring, constructing, and reconstructing … identities" (Turkle 363), they facilitate experimentation with encounter, pace, itinerary, and the multiple pleasures of mobility. But as a new generation of women puts such journeys together, it must beware the dangers of underestimating how travel in this postmodern mode of mobility might catch women out and return them home via the masculinist logic of travel. The challenge cybertravelers face is how to negotiate virtual journeying so that women become resistors along the circuits. Balsamo points to the undefining possibilities of cybertravel when she reminds us that "people engage technologies in many ways that are not simply determined by the form of the technology itself: subjectively, expressively, and bodily" (*Technologies* 125). Turkle, a most hopeful theorist of the new age, emphasizes how this kind of traveling "throws issues of the impact of gender on human relations into high relief and brings the issue home" (362).

Now that the woman traveler can travel without leaving home, she must beware what electrons she rides and where those electrons take her. If she doesn't have to go anywhere to go anywhere, then mobility and sessility become indistinguishable. But that doesn't necessarily mean that they are inconsequential.

# Notes

## Introduction: Vehicular Gender

1. For a fascinating tracking of the etymological roots of the words for travel in Indo-European languages, see Eric Leed, (5–14).

2. See my "Cheesecake," "Memory," *Poetics*, "Reciting," *Subjectivity*, and *Where I'm Bound.*

3. For a discussion of Lopez's hybrid road narrative, see Laura Laffrado on the thematics of road agency.

## 1. The Logic of Travel and Technologies of Motion

1. Christianity, suggests Mary B. Campbell, is "the first Western religion in which the sacred territory is located emphatically Elsewhere. As a result, Christian pilgrimages are the first to lead pilgrims abroad on their religious travels" (18).

2. Mary Louise Pratt argues that "as Christianity had set in motion a global labor of religious conversion that asserted itself at every point of contact with other societies, so natural history set in motion a secular, global labor that, among other things, made contact zones a site of intellectual as well as manual labor, and installed there the distinction between the two" (*Eyes* 27).

3. Pratt calls the travel narratives that emerged out of this global and encyclopedic project "anti-conquest" narratives (*Eyes* 7).

4. As Dennis Porter notes, comparison of one European homeland with another has a long history (29).

5. In biracial love there is harmony across the cultural and racial divide:

"As an ideology, romantic love, like capitalist commerce, understands itself as reciprocal. Reciprocity, love requited between individuals worthy of each other, is its ideal state. The failure of reciprocity, or of equivalence between parties, is its central tragedy and scandal" (Pratt, *Eyes* 97).

6. "The larger the degree of *financial* involvement in the non-European world," suggests Peter Hulme, "the more determinedly *non*-financial European adventure stories become" (183).

7. For a discussion of late medieval and Renaissance responses to vagabonds, see Eric Leed (155–57).

8. The need for prostitutes was particularly urgent in places, such as the Cape Colony in South Africa after 1685, where prohibitions against intermarriage between Europeans and indigenous peoples were instituted (Pratt, *Eyes* 40). Cross-cultural mating on the frontier became a very destabilizing activity, for, according to Jean Comaroff and John Comaroff, "such intercourse, and its half-caste product, breached the physical separation of white and black and mocked the sense of European distinction that was the *sine qua non* of colonialism" (195).

9. As Pratt notes (*Eyes*) there were aristocratic women who sponsored naturalists, providing the financial support that underwrote voyage and narrative. In this way certain wealthy women were second-order facilitators of travel narratives not their own, as the duchess of Strathmore was of William Paterson's *Narrative of Four Journeys into the Country of the Hottentots, and Caffraria* (1789).

10. These prints are part of the collection assembled by the National Museum of Women in the Arts. They were on special display in the fall of 1994.

11. Of course, Montagu is misrepresenting the Levant, screening her sight-seeing and commentary through her own imaginary. Even as she proposes the greater freedom of Levantine women, that freedom is accorded only to women of the aristocratic classes with whom she identifies. In fact, Montagu's claim of greater freedom "misrepresents and appropriates," according to Lisa Lowe, "Turkish female experience for the purpose of defending English feminism" (44).

12. Transporting these women away from the constraints of home and the identity it forced on women and extracting them from what Pratt calls the "heterosexist and matrimonialist structures of bourgeois society" (*Eyes* 240 n. 10), travel promised to effect the shift from an unenlightened dependence to an enlightened autonomy. It is not surprising, then, that the majority of these new travelers tended to be "spinster adventurers," single women whose orphanhood

and/or inheritance released them from dependence upon patriarchal authorities (Pratt, *Eyes* 115).

13. As Denise Riley argues of the emergence of "the social" in the nineteenth century, "If woman's sphere was to be the domestic, then let the social world become a great arena for domesticated intervention, where the empathies supposedly peculiar to the sex might flourish on a broad and visible scale. If 'women' were a separate species, then let them make a separate contribution to the world, and let their efforts humanise the public" (46–47).

14. Caren Kaplan looks specifically at the original narrative and the movie versions of the story of Anna and the king of Siam to explore the individualist feminism of the Englishwoman and the racial politics it supports.

15. As Dea Birkett has noted of the intrepid Victorian travelers, the racial positioning of travelers vis-à-vis the people with whom they came into contact mediated the "un-becoming" aspects of their identities as traveling women. "As women travellers frequently pointed to the continuities and similarities with earlier European male travellers," she suggests, "the supremacy of distinctions of race above those of sex allowed them to take little account of their one obvious difference from these forebears—the fact they were female" (125).

16. Pratt notes certain of these adjustments in two texts from the early nineteenth century. She observes that Anna Maria Falconbridge, in her *Narrative of Two Voyages to the River Sierra Leone* (1802), refuses to present herself as actively seeing and doing things: "As a woman she is not to see but be seen, or at least she is not to be seen seeing" (*Eyes* 104). If Falconbridge masks her "I" and her eyes, Sarah Lee, in her *Stories of Strange Lands and Fragments from the Notes of a Traveller* (1835), confines her "I" to the margins of her text. She places conventional travel-narrative material in the footnotes and asides, thereby stuffing the stuff of her seeing into footnotes. It is as if she becomes a footnote to history, a ghostly narrator only too aware of the difficulties in avoiding self-promotion: "The number of I's that I have scratched out, the sentences that have been turned and twisted, to avoid this provoking monosyllable, almost surpass belief," she confesses to her reader (qtd. in Pratt, *Eyes* 107). But in the confession of her dutiful self-erasure, she gestures to the very self-promotion (there have been so many "I"s struck out!) she would stifle. She reminds her reader of excess even as she resists it.

17. Some women travel narrators even proffered their own "feminine" version of the sentimental journey, which, Pratt observes, turns upon the celebration of feminocentric social organizations (*Eyes* 166–69).

18. See also Catherine Barnes Stevenson, Shirley Foster, and Sara Mills for discussions of the personal stakes in women's travel writing.

19. Women travelers became persons who "read widely about the lands and cultures that they visited, and compared their findings to those of reputable historians, geologists, anthropologists, and explorers"; they became persons who "wrote letters, essays, articles, and books about their experiences abroad, and . . . gave lectures about what they learned to audiences at home" (Frawley 24).

20. For a fascinating analysis of the interrelationships of new technologies, cultural practices, artistic movements, and notions of human consciousness between 1880 and the end of World War I, see Stephen Kern.

## 2. On Foot

1. I am indebted for aspects of my analysis of Isabelle Eberhardt to students in a course on travel literature I taught in the spring of 1992, specifically Christine Bucher, Dianne Fallon, Vicki Ramirez, and Steve Krempa.

2. Eberhardt's home in Europe was an illegitimate home, literally as well as figuratively. Eberhardt's mother, also illegitimate, joined by her children's tutor, ran away from Russia and her husband. In Geneva, where she lived as an expatriate member of the Russian aristocracy, she and the tutor maintained their masquerade. He remained the avuncular "tutor" even though he was in fact the father of Eberhardt and her brother. Born an illegitimate daughter of an illegitimate daughter, Eberhardt can claim no "proper" name (nor a "proper" nation or national identity, as she both is and is not Russian, Swiss, and French; more properly, then, she is a "European" transnational). She is born, in effect, in exile and remains an exile within Europe. If literally and metaphorically her European self is what Hedi Abdel-Jaouad calls the *heizatlose*, or "statusless," self, then the "nomad" self—that "other" to the European self—becomes for her the legitimate self, proper, authentic, and real (95).

3. This identification with normative masculinity and with a masculine code of behavior had a long history for Eberhardt. As her biographer Annette Kobak notes, her father-tutor "kept her hair cropped, dressed her like a boy, and brought her up like a boy, in keeping with Bakunin's dictum that 'every child of either sex should be prepared as much for a life of the mind as for a life of work, so that all may grow up equally into complete men'" (16).

4. In assuming the proper name of Mahmoud Saadi, Isabelle Eberhardt rejects the name of the mother, given that, as an illegitimate child, she carries her mother's name (itself taken from Eberhardt's grandmother).

5. See the discussion of Eberhardt's friendship with and respect for Lalla Zaynab, an Algerian saint and mystic who served as her religious mentor, in Julia Clancy-Smith (69).

6. Only once in the journal (that we have as translated) does Eberhardt identify herself specifically as female. Into the text of the diary she incorporates the two letters she wrote for the public in response to an attempt on her life. In a letter written after the verdict of the trial that followed, she admits: "Abdallah [the assailant] has a wife and children. I am a woman and can only feel bottomless pity for the widow and orphans" (62). But this is not the journal so much as a letter for public consumption, an explanatory epistle through which she seeks to put the record straight about the attempted assassination and the trial. Although she incorporates this letter in her journal, its purpose is significantly different from that of the journal. She would "normalize" herself in this letter, positioning herself not as a freak but as someone who shares common, and rather more conventional, values with her reader.

7. "The very idea of the couple," Malek Alloula writes, "is an imported one which is applied to a society that operates on the basis of formations that are greater than simple twoness, such as the extended family, the clan, or the tribe. The couple, in the Western sense, is an aberration, a historical error, an unthinkable possibility in Algerian society" (38).

8. Eberhardt's personal history, her roots in an aristocratic family that had lost its wealth, catapulted her into a position of homelessness, although her failure to act in her own interest continued a poverty that was hers to avoid.

9. The paths of Eberhardt and David-Neel might literally have crossed. David-Neel lived in Tunisia from 1901 to 1904 and traveled to Bône, Algeria (the city where Eberhardt's mother died), where her husband, Philip Neel, was chief engineering officer of the railroad line between Bône and Guelma, in Algeria.

10. There was a trace of David-Neel's youthful anarchism in her desire to thwart these prohibitions, to defy at once the British Raj, the Chinese army, and the Tibetan authorities in order to pursue her desire for a clandestine pilgrimage to the capital city of Tibet. For David-Neel's probable youthful involvement in the anarchist movement in Paris, see Barbara Foster and Michael Foster (chap. 4).

11. The performance of peasant identity gives David-Neel a certain kind of freedom on the road. "I felt really safe as to my disguise, after having passed these huge mountain ranges," she notes. "No one would ever think that a foreign woman had dared to venture on that road. No one would ever suspect the pilgrim tramping over these distant tracks on which a white traveller was never seen.

This feeling of security was a great comfort and allowed me to enjoy the charm of my adventure more freely" (177).

12. Annie Taylor had also worn this disguise in her unsuccessful attempt to reach Lhasa in 1892–1893.

13. For a discussion of the travelers who attempted to journey through Tibet, see Foster and Foster (178–83).

14. David-Neel thus participates in what Edward Said describes as the "unrelenting Eurocentrism" at the heart of the imperial enterprise (72).

15. Sara Mills catalogs these tropes as follows: the courageous and resilient traveler, the westerner in disguise, the westerner who never loses face, the westerner in control of the situation, and the knowledgeable westerner (139–49).

16. Foster and Foster note the disjunction between David-Neel's presentation of herself as hardy in the narrative and her confession of continual pain in letters written to her husband (189).

17. This doubled rhetoric is a pattern in travel narrative that stretches back to the sixteenth and seventeenth centuries, as Mary Louise Pratt argues ("Fieldwork" 33–50).

18. Peter Bishop reads the humor in narratives of Tibetan travel in the early twentieth century as a sign that Western travelers no longer felt authorized to travel anywhere they wanted; they had begun to appear strange to themselves as they were reflected in the gaze of the Tibetans (228). But the success of David-Neel's imposture means that she did not appear strange in the eyes of the Tibetans.

19. The paradox behind David-Neel's travels is that she inserted herself into the heterosexist contract by marrying a distant cousin and benefited from her husband's unflagging support of her adventures. She could be so independent because she had married.

20. Bishop notes that in the twentieth century more and more travelers to Tibet sought such confirmations, because they wanted "to believe literally in such an apparent acceptance, with its associated sense of belonging" (229). But he argues that such confirmations functioned as Tibetan social tactics to incorporate alien influences. Such interactional tactics "neutralize[d]" various influences, "sustain[ed] the coherence of [Tibetans'] social world [,and] ma[d]e sense of and incorporate[d] any intrusions" (229). Thus, David-Neel's is a scripted narrative of acceptance.

21. In fact, David-Neel insinuates her desire to become a legend: "Nevertheless, it is always presumptuous to rejoice too soon about one's good luck or success. I had not finished with the Popas. But they, too, were to see more of the first foreign woman who walked through their beautiful country, and while their acts were to be quite commonplace and not in the least surprising, mine will probably live long in the memory of those who witnessed them. Maybe a legend will arise out of it all; and who knows if, in the future, a learned student of folklore will not offer some interesting commentary on the story, being far from suspecting the truth of it" (220). Ironically, she is constituted as a legend in the summary postscript at the back of the Beacon Press edition of *My Journey to Lhasa:* "A legend in her own time, she died just before her 101st birthday, in 1969."

22. Throughout Australian history, such discourses have positioned Aboriginal peoples on the lowest rung of the ladder of racial groups and thus as the least civilized of human beings. From this assignment of a degraded humanity all kinds of practices have followed: genocide in the early decades of settlement; the civilizing mission of the state and the church in the late nineteenth and early twentieth centuries; the official call for assimilation during the mid-twentieth century; and the forced removal of mixed-race children from their mothers and traditional communities.

23. Perhaps it is illuminating to unpack the relationship between identity and subjectivity in David-Neel's masquerade as the common *arjopa*. Her external bodily coverings mark the identity of the *arjopa*, or peasant mother; the surface of her body signals the body of the Western woman; her interiorized identity is that of the lama, marked culturally as both masculine and feminine; and her interiorized subjectivity is that of a universal (Western) subject (scholar and individual) who would erase any differentiating identity markings, whether those of gender or nationality.

## 3. In the Air

1. This abstracted mode of seeing linked the aviators in the air to certain avant-garde artists on the ground. Identifying with the future that flight augured and with its energy, vibrancy, and promise of unboundedness, the painter Robert Delaunay, for instance, used the airplane as a generative image in his canvases. Delaunay's propellers slash the space of the canvas, shattering color into patches of vibrating light, rearranging and redefining the space of representation in ways analogical to the ways in which flight redefined the aviator's relation to physical

space. For the Russian formalist Kazimir Malevich, as Robert Wohl suggests, "flight became a metaphor for the transformation of consciousness, its liberation from the constraints of normal day-to-day existence, and the redefinition of time and space" (161).

2. Before these women came the earlier aeronauts or balloonists: Madeléine-Sophie Blanchard, chief of air service for Napoleon; Elisa Garnerin; and Margaret Graham.

3. Yet the history of these aviators has been all but erased, except for the story of Amelia Earhart, the aviator who garnered the most publicity.

4. In *Queering the Moderns: Poses/Portraits/Performances* (New York: Palgrave, 2000), Anne Herrmann also explores the "queer" figure of the aviatrix, of Earhart as "dandy" and Markham as "tomboy." Herrmann's book came out as this book was in press, precluding my sustained engagement with her provocative disscussion.

5. As Joseph J. Corn argues, the women aviators of the late 1920s and 1930s "self-consciously conformed to feminine norms for the cause of flight" (566). They designed proper feminine attire for the airplane, they identified themselves with the realm of domesticity, and they socialized while on tour and during races.

6. Susan Ware sees this contradiction in discursive strategies as integral to Earhart's modern feminism. "In order to get women into the air as passengers," Ware notes, "she was forced to rely on traditional gender stereotypes that exaggerated the differences between women and men. This strategy was a very different approach from that of hers for getting women into the air as pilots, which downplayed such differences" (71).

7. For a discussion of the machine aesthetic and the fashionable female body in the 1920s and 1930s, see Christine Moneera Laennec.

8. The controversy over authorship of *West with the Night* has continued throughout the 1980s and 1990s. Out of print since its initial publication in 1942, the book gained an avid readership with the release of a new edition in 1983. Yet the question of authorship plagued the text and affected the sales. Was Markham the author, or was her husband, Raoul Schumacher, the author? A biographer of Markham in 1987 came down unequivocally on the side of Markham as author (Lovell 330–33). But a more recent biography, by Errol Trzebinski in 1993, unsettled the question once again. Trzebinski argues vigorously for the authorship of Schumacher (238–41). It is not my intent to make a definitive statement

about authorship. Robert Viking O'Brien, invoking Mikhail Bakhtin's discussion of "biographical value," argues that the text may well be a hybrid of autobiography and biography, a kind of jointly authored text through which "order [is brought] out of memory" in answer to Markham's opening epigraph.

9. I am indebted to O'Brien for this analysis of the multiple significations of the scene at the crossroads.

## 4. By Rail

1. In *The Races of Man and Their Geographical Distribution* (1894), Oscar Peschel wrote that "the opening of the great western railroads to California will greatly accelerate the extinction of the Bison tribe and the other remnants of the Indian race, and the next century will not find any Redskins in the United States, or at most as domesticated curiosities they may drag on a miserable existence for a few years. This process by which the beings of a past age pass away ought to be no mystery to us" (150).

2. For a complex discussion of the ways in which tourist sites are sacralized, see Dean MacCannell.

3. See Julia Kristeva for a discussion of the abject.

4. See Wolfgang Schivelbusch (77) for a discussion of Freud's representation of the attraction little boys feel for trains.

5. See Michel de Certeau on "the ('melancholy') pleasure of seeing what one is separated from" (114).

## 5. On the Road

1. Judy Wajcman notes how, in the 1930s, tire and oil interests bought out the electric rail franchises in order to convert them to buses, "which were manufactured and fuelled by members of the holding company" (128).

2. "Cars have long been a metaphor for sex and something wild in the already tamed urban environment" (Wajcman 134).

3. I am indebted in this reading of Donofrio's (auto)education to a paper by Jennifer Drake, a former student at the State University of New York at Binghamton. The paper was presented in a course on travel narratives in May 1992.

4. Car styling, David Gartman notes, has always combined the "themes of aeronautics and escapism" (163).

5. This photograph was part of an exhibition in Soho in 1997 entitled *Car Culture*.

# Works Cited

Abdel-Jaouad, Hedi. "Isabelle Eberhardt: Portrait of the Artist as a Young Nomad." *Yale French Studies* 83 (1993): 93–117.

Adas, Michael. *Machines as the Measure of Men: Science, Technology, and Ideologies of Western Dominance*. Ithaca, N.Y.: Cornell University Press, 1989.

Alloula, Malek. *The Colonial Harem*. Translated by Myrna Godzich and Wlad Godzich. Minneapolis: University of Minnesota Press, 1986.

Angelou, Maya. *I Know Why the Caged Bird Sings*. New York: Random House, 1970.

Apollonio, Umbra, ed. *Futurist Manifestos*. London: Thames & Hudson, 1973.

Baedeker, Karl. *Italy: Handbook for Travellers*. Leipzig: K. Baedeker, 1895–1897.

Baker, Houston A., Jr. *Blues, Ideology, and Afro-American Literature: A Vernacular Theory*. Chicago: University of Chicago Press, 1984.

Balsamo, Anne. "Feminism for the Incurably Informed." *South Atlantic Quarterly* 92 (fall 1993): 681–712.

———. *Technologies of the Gendered Body: Reading Cyborg Women*. Durham, N.C.: Duke University Press, 1996.

Bartkowski, Frances. *Travelers, Immigrants, Inmates: Essays in Estrangement*. Minneapolis: University of Minnesota Press, 1995.

Beer, Gillian. "The Island and the Aeroplane: The Case of Virginia Woolf." In *Nation and Narration*, edited by Homi K. Bhabha. New York: Routledge, 1990. 265–90.

Bialostosky, Don. "Liberal Education, Writing, and the Dialogic Self." In *Contending with Words: Composition and Rhetoric in a Postmodern Age*, edited by

Patricia Harkin and John Schilb. New York: Modern Language Association of America, 1991. 11–22.

Birkett, Dea. *Spinsters Abroad: Victorian Lady Explorers*. London: Victor Gollancz, 1991.

Bishop, Peter. *The Myth of Shangri-la: Tibet, Travel Writing, and the Western Creation of Sacred Landscape*. Berkeley and Los Angeles: University of California Press, 1989.

Bodichon, Barbara Leigh Smith. *An American Diary, 1857–58*. Edited by Joseph W. Reed Jr. London: Routledge & Kegan Paul, 1972.

Bongie, Chris. *Exotic Memories: Literature, Colonialism, and the Fin de Siècle*. Stanford, Calif.: Stanford University Press, 1991.

Bowlby, Rachel. "Breakfast in America: Uncle Tom's Cultural Histories." In *Nation and Narration*, edited by Homi K. Bhabha. New York: Routledge, 1990. 197–212.

Box-Car Bertha [pseud.], as told to Ben L. Reitman. *An Autobiography*. New York: AMOK Press, 1988.

Busia, Abena. "Silencing Sycorax: On African Colonial Discourse and the Unvoiced Female." *Cultural Critique* (winter 1989–1990): 81–104.

Butler, Judith. *Bodies That Matter: On the Discursive Limits of "Sex."* New York: Routledge, 1993.

———. *Gender Trouble: Feminism and the Subversion of Identity*. New York: Routledge, 1990.

Campbell, Mary B. *The Witness and the Other World: Exotic European Travel Writing, 400–1600*. Ithaca, N.Y.: Cornell University Press, 1988.

Carden, Mary Paniccia. "The Hobo as National Hero: Models for American Manhood." *a/b: Auto/Biography Studies* 11.1: 93–108.

Cassady, Carolyn. *Off the Road: My Years with Cassady, Kerouac, and Ginsberg*. New York: Morrow, 1990.

Chard, Chloe. *Pleasure and Guilt on the Grand Tour: Travel Writing and Imaginative Geography, 1600–1830*. Manchester, England: Manchester University Press, 1999.

*Christopher Strong*. Directed by Dorothy Arzner. Produced by David O. Selznick. RKO Radio Pictures, 1932.

Cixous, Hélène. "The Laugh of the Medusa." Translated by Keith Cohen and Paula Cohen. In *New French Feminisms: An Anthology*, edited by Elaine Marks and Isabelle de Courtivron. New York: Schocken, 1981. 245–64.

Clancy-Smith, Julia. "The 'Passionate Nomad' Reconsidered: A European Woman in L'Algerie Francaise (Isabelle Eberhardt, 1877–1904)." In *Western Women and Imperialism: Complicity and Resistance*, edited by Nupur Chaudhuri and Margaret Strobel. Bloomington: Indiana University Press, 1992. 61–78.

Clarsen, Georgine. Letter on women and motoring to Dr. Kay Schaffer, University of Adelaide, Adelaide, South Australia, April 1998.

Claudy, C. H. "The Lady and the Electric." *Country Life in America*, July 15, 1912, 36, 44, 46, 48.

Comaroff, Jean, and John Comaroff. *Of Revelation and Revolution: Christianity, Colonialism, and Consciousness in South Africa*. Chicago: University of Chicago Press, 1991.

Conneau, Jean [Andre Beaumont]. *Mes trois grandes courses*. Paris: Hachette et cie, 1912.

Corn, Joseph J. "Making Flying 'Thinkable': Women Pilots and the Selling of Aviation." *American Quarterly* 31.4 (autumn 1979): 556–81.

Craft, William. *Running a Thousand Miles for Freedom; or, The Escape of William and Ellen Craft from Slavery*. 1860. Miami: Mnemosyne, 1969.

D'Annunzio, Gabriele. *Forse she si forse che no*. Milan: Treves, 1910.

David-Neel, Alexandra. *Magic and Mystery in Tibet*. 1932. New York: University Books, 1965.

———. *My Journey to Lhasa*. 1927. Boston: Beacon, 1983.

Davidson, Lillias Campbell. *Hints to Lady Travellers at Home and Abroad*. 1889.

Davidson, Robyn. *Tracks*. New York: Pantheon, 1980.

Davis, Angela. *Blues Legacies and Black Feminism*. New York: Pantheon, 1998.

de Certeau, Michel. *The Practice of Everyday Life*. Translated by Steven Rendall. Berkeley and Los Angeles: University of California Press, 1984. 111–14.

Dekobra, Maurice. *The Madonna of the Sleeping Cars*. Translated by Neal Wainwright. New York: Payson & Clarke, 1927.

de Lauretis, Teresa. *Technologies of Gender: Essays on Theory, Film, and Fiction*. Bloomington: Indiana University Press, 1987.

Donofrio, Beverly. *Riding in Cars with Boys: Confessions of a Bad Girl Who Makes Good*. New York: Penguin, 1990.

Duras, Marguerite. *The Lover*. Translated by Barbara Bray. London: Flamingo, 1986.

Earhart, Amelia. *The Fun of It*. New York: Putnam, 1932.

————. *Twenty Hrs. Forty Mins.: Our Flight in the "Friendship": The American Girl, First Across the Atlantic by Air, Tells Her Story*. New York: Putnam, 1928.

Eberhardt, Isabelle. *The Passionate Nomad: The Diary of Isabelle Eberhardt*. Translated by Nina de Voogd. Edited by Rana Kabbani. Boston: Beacon, 1988.

Faith, Nicolas. *Locomotion: The Railway Revolution*. London: BBC Books, 1993.

Falconbridge, Anna Maria. *Narrative of Two Voyages to the River Sierra Leone during the Years 1791–1793*. 2d ed. 1802. London: Cass, 1967.

Flink, James J. *The Car Culture*. Cambridge: MIT Press, 1975.

Foster, Barbara, and Michael Foster. *Forbidden Journey: The Life of Alexandra David-Neel*. San Francisco: Harper, 1987.

Foster, Shirley. *Across New Worlds: Nineteenth-Century Women Travellers and Their Writings*. New York: Harvester Wheatsheaf, 1990.

Frawley, Maria H. *A Wider Range: Travel Writing by Women in Victorian England*. Rutherford, N.J.: Fairleigh Dickinson University Press, 1994.

Freeman, Judi. *The Fauve Landscape*. Los Angeles: Los Angeles County Museum of Art; New York: Abbeville, 1990.

Gagnier, Regenia. "The Literary Standard, Working-Class Autobiography, and Gender." In *Revealing Lives: Autobiography, Biography, and Gender*, edited by Susan Broag Bell and Marilyn Yalom. Albany: State University of New York Press, 1990. 93–114.

Gartman, David. *Auto Opium: A Social History of American Automobile Design*. New York: Routledge, 1994.

Giles, Paulette. *Sitting in the Club Car Drinking Rum and Karma-Kola: A Manual of Etiquette for Ladies Crossing Canada by Train*. Winlaw, British Columbia: Polestar, 1986.

Gilmore, Leigh, and Marcia Aldrich. "Writing Home: 'Home' and Lesbian Representation in Minnie Bruce Pratt." *Genre* 15 (spring 1992): 25–46.

Goldstein, Lawrence. *The Flying Machine and Modern Literature*. Bloomington: Indiana University Press, 1986.

Graham, Maury "Steam Train," and Robert J. Hemming. *Tales of the Iron Road: My Life as King of the Hobos*. New York: Paragon, 1990.

Green, Barbara. *Spectacular Confessions: Autobiography, Performative Activism, and the Sites of Suffrage, 1905–1938*. New York: St. Martin's, 1997.

Gregg, Lyndall Schreiner. *Memories of Olive Schreiner*. London: W. & R. Chambers, 1957.

Grewal, Inderpal. *Home and Harem: Nation, Gender, Empire, and the Cultures of Travel.* Durham, N.C.: Duke University Press, 1996.

Gusdorf, Georges. "Conditions and Limits of Autobiography." In *Autobiography: Essays Theoretical and Critical,* edited by James Olney. Princeton, N.J.: Princeton University Press, 1980. 28–48.

Haizlip, Shirlee Taylor. *The Sweeter the Juice.* New York: Simon & Schuster, 1994.

Hansen, Miriam. "The Mass Production of the Senses: Classical Cinema as Popular Modernism." Paper delivered at the University of Michigan, Ann Arbor, Michigan, March 26, 1997.

Haraway, Donna. *Simians, Cyborgs, and Women: The Re-invention of Nature.* London: Free Association, 1991.

Herrmann, Anne. "On Amelia Earhart: The Aviatrix as American Dandy." *Michigan Quarterly Review* 39.1 (winter 2000): 76–107.

Holden, Henry M. *Her Mentor Was an Albatross: The Autobiography of Pioneer Pilot Harriet Quimby.* Mt. Freedom, N.J.: Black Hawk, 1993.

Holland, Patrick, and Graham Huggan. *Tourists with Typewriters: Critical Reflections on Contemporary Travel Writing.* Ann Arbor: University of Michigan Press, 1998.

hooks, bell. "Representing Whiteness in the Black Imagination." In *Cultural Studies,* edited by Lawrence Grossberg, Cary Nelson, and Paula Treichler. New York: Routledge, 1992. 338–46.

Hulme, Peter. *Colonial Encounters: Europe and the Native Caribbean, 1492–1797.* London. 1986.

Irigaray, Luce. *This Sex Which Is Not One.* Translated by Catherine Porter with Carolyn Burke. Ithaca, N.Y.: Cornell University Press, 1985.

Jay, Karla. "No Bumps, No Excrescences: Amelia Earhart's Failed Flight into Fashions." In *On Fashions,* edited by Shari Benstock and Suzanne Ferriss. New Brunswick, N.J.: Rutgers University Press, 1994. 76–94.

Johnson, Joyce. *Minor Characters.* London: Picador, 1983.

Kabbani, Rana. Introduction to *The Passionate Nomad: The Diary of Isabelle Eberhardt,* by Isabelle Eberhardt. Translated by Nina de Voogd. Edited by Rana Kabbani. Boston: Beacon, 1988. iii–xii.

Kaplan, Caren. "'Getting to Know You': Travel, Gender, and the Politics of Representation in *Anna and the King of Siam* and *The King and I.*" In *Late Imperial Culture,* edited by Román de la Campa, E. Ann Kaplan, and Michael Sprinker. London: Verso, 1995. 33–52.

Kempe, Margery. *The Book of Margery Kempe*. 1436. London: Penguin, 1994.

Kern, Stephen. *The Culture of Time and Space, 1880–1918*. Cambridge: Harvard University Press, 1983.

Kerouac, Jack. *On the Road*. New York: Viking, 1957.

Kimmel, Michael S. "Consuming Manhood: The Feminization of American Culture and the Recreation of the Male Body, 1832–1920." *Michigan Quarterly Review* 23.1 (1996): 7–36.

Kobak, Annette. *The Life of Isabelle Eberhardt*. New York: Knopf, 1989.

Kristeva, Julia. *The Powers of Horror: An Essay on Abjection*. New York: Columbia University Press, 1982.

Kurtz, Irma. *The Great American Bus Ride*. New York: Simon & Schuster, 1993.

Lackey, Kris. *RoadFrames: The American Highway Narrative*. Lincoln: University of Nebraska Press, 1997.

Laennec, Christine Moneera. "The 'Assembly-Line Love Goddess': Women and the Machine Aesthetic in Fashion Photography, 1918–1940." In *Bodily Discursions: Genders, Representations, Technologies*, edited by Deborah S. Wilson and Christine Moneera Laennec. Albany: State University of New York Press, 1997. 81–102.

Laffrado, Laura. "Postings from Hoochie Mama: Erika Lopez, Graphic Art and Female Subjectivity." In *Interfaces: Women's Visual and Perfomance Autobiography*, edited by Sidonie Smith and Julia Watson. Ann Arbor: University of Michigan Press, forthcoming.

Lawrence, Karen. *Penelope Voyages: Women and Travel in the British Literary Tradition*. Ithaca, N.Y.: Cornell University Press, 1994.

Lee, Mrs. R. [Sarah]. *Stories of Strange Lands and Fragments from the Notes of a Traveller.* London: Edward Moxon, 1835.

Leed, Eric J. *The Mind of the Traveler: From "Gilgamesh" to Global Tourism*. New York: Basic Books, 1991.

Lindbergh, Anne Morrow. *North to the Orient*. New York: Harcourt Brace, 1935.

Lionnet, Françoise. "Logiques Métisses: Interpretation and Appropriation in Cross-Cultural Representation." Paper presented at the annual meeting of the American Comparative Literature Association, San Diego, Calif., April 1991.

*Locomotion: Magic Machines and Mobile People*. Special Broadcasting Service (Australia), May 22, 1994.

Lopez, Erika. *Flaming Iguanas: An Illustrated All-Girl Road Novel Thing.* New York: Simon & Schuster, 1997.

Lovell, Mary S. *Straight On till Morning: The Biography of Beryl Markham.* New York: St. Martin's, 1987.

Lowe, Lisa. *Critical Terrains: French and British Orientalisms.* Ithaca, N.Y.: Cornell University Press, 1991.

MacCannell, Dean. *The Tourist: A New Theory of the Leisure Class.* New York: Schocken, 1976.

Marinetti, F. T. "The Aeropainting of the Italian Futurists." Translated by Samuel Putnam. *New Review* 1. 4 (winter 1931–1932): 295–97.

———. "The Founding and Manifesto of Futurism." 1909. In *Marinetti: Selected Writings*, edited by R. W. Flint, translated by R. W. Flint and Arthur A. Coppotelli. New York: Farrar, Straus & Giroux, 1972. 39–44.

———. *Poupées électriques: Drame en trois actes* (Electric puppets). Paris: E. Sansot, 1909.

Markham, Beryl. *West with the Night.* 1942. San Francisco: North Point, 1983.

Marlatt, Daphne, and Betsy Warland. *Double Negative.* Charlottetown, Calif.: Gynergy Books, 1988.

Marvingt, Marie. "The Intoxication of Flight." *Colliers*, September 30, 1911, 15.

Mayne, Judith. *Directed by Dorothy Arzner.* Bloomington: Indiana University Press, 1994.

McGrath, Melanie. *Hard, Soft, and Wet: The Digital Generation Comes of Age.* New York: HarperCollins, 1997.

McPherson, James Allen. *Railroad: Trains and Train People in American Culture.* New York: Random House, 1976.

Merian, Maria Sibylla. *Mariae Sibillae Merian Dissertatio de Generatione et Metamorphosibus Insectorum Surinamensium* (A Dissertation on Insect Generation and Metamorphoses in Surinam). Amsterdam: J. Oosterwyk, 1719.

———. *Metamporphosis Insectorum Surinamensium: Ofte Verandering der Surinaamsche Insecten* (Metamorhposis of the Insects of Surinam). 1705. Zutphen, Netherlands: Walburg Pers, 1982.

Mills, Sara. *Discourses of Difference: An Analysis of Women's Travel Writing and Colonialism.* London: Routledge, 1991.

Montagu, Mary Wortley. *The Letters and Works of Lady Mary Wortley Montagu.* 3d ed. 1861. Edited by James Wharncliffe. New York: AMS, 1970.

Moretti, Franco. *Signs Taken for Wonders: Essays in the Sociology of Literary Forms.* Translated by Susan Fischer, David Forgacs, and David Miller. London: Verso, 1988.

Morris, Mary. *Nothing to Declare: Memoirs of a Woman Traveling Alone.* Boston: Houghton Mifflin, 1988.

———. *Wall to Wall: From Beijing to Berlin by Rail.* New York: Penguin, 1992.

Morris, Meaghan. "At the Henry Parkes Motel." *Cultural Studies* 2 (January 1988): 3–25.

Mouffe, Chantal. "Feminism, Citizenship, and Radical Democratic Politics." In *Feminists Theorize the Political,* edited by Judith Butler and Joan W. Scott. New York: Routledge, 1992. 369–84.

Mulvey, Laura. "Visual Pleasure and Narrative Cinema." In *Visual and Other Pleasures.* Bloomington: Indiana University Press, 1989. 14–26.

Niemann, Linda. *Boomer: Railroad Memoirs.* Berkeley and Los Angeles: University of California Press, 1990.

Nussbaum, Felicity A. "Eighteenth-Century Women's Autobiographical Commonplaces." In *The Private Self: Theory and Practice of Women's Autobiographical Writings,* edited by Shari Benstock. Chapel Hill: University of North Carolina Press, 1988. 147–71.

O'Brien, Robert Viking. "Teaching Beryl Markham's *West with the Night.*" Paper delivered at the annual meeting of the Modern Language Association, December 1995.

Paterson, William. *A Narrative of Four Journeys into the Country of the Hottentots, and Caffraria.* 1789. Ann Arbor, Mich.: University Microfilms, 1960.

Pelz, Annegret. *Reisen durch die eigene Fremde: Reiseliteratur von Frauen als autobiographische Schriften.* Cologne: Böhlau, 1993.

Pendo, Stephen. *Aviation in the Cinema.* Metuchen, N.J.: Scarecrow, 1985.

Peschel, Oscar. *The Races of Man and Their Geographical Distribution.* New York: Appleton, 1894.

Poling-Kempes, Lesley. *The Harvey Girls: Women Who Opened the West.* New York: Paragon, 1989.

Porter, Dennis. *Haunted Journeys: Desire and Transgression in European Travel Writing.* Princeton, N.J.: Princeton University Press, 1991.

Pratt, Mary Louise. "Fieldwork in Common Places." In *Writing Culture: The Poetics and Politics of Ethnography,* edited by James Clifford and George E. Marcus. Berkeley and Los Angeles: University of California Press, 1986. 27–50.

———. *Imperial Eyes.* New York: Routledge, 1992.

———. "Scratches on the Face of the Country; or What Mr. Barrow Saw in the Land of the Bushman." In *"Race," Writing, and Difference*, edited by Henry Louis Gates Jr. Chicago: University of Chicago Press, 1986. 130–62.

Pudney, John. *The Thomas Cook Story*. London: M. Joseph, 1953.

Pykett, Lyn. *Engendering Fictions: The English Novel in the Early Twentieth Century*. London: E. Arnold, 1995.

Quimby, Harriet. "How I Made My First Big Flight Abroad." *Fly*, June 1912, 9.

Rice, Laura. "'Nomad Thought': Isabelle Eberhardt and the Colonial Project." *Cultural Critique* 17 (winter 1990–1991): 151–76.

Richards, Jeffrey, and John M. MacKenzie. *The Railway Station: A Social History*. Oxford: Oxford University Press, 1986.

Riley, Denise. *"Am I That Name?": Feminism and the Category of "Women" in History*. Minneapolis: University of Minnesota Press, 1988.

Robertson, George, et al., eds. *Travellers' Tales: Narratives of Home and Displacement*. London: Routledge, 1994.

Robinson, Lillian. *Sex, Class, and Culture*. New York: Methuen, 1986.

Ross, Kristin. *Fast Cars, Clean Bodies: Decolonization and the Reordering of French Culture*. Cambridge: MIT Press, 1995.

Rowlandson, Mary White. "The Sovereignty and Goodness of God." 1682. In *American Captivity Narratives*, edited by Gordon M. Sayre. Boston: Houghton Mifflin, 2000. 137–82.

Sachs, Wolfgang. *For Love of the Automobile: Looking Back into the History of Our Desires*. Translated by Don Reneau. Berkeley and Los Angeles: University of California Press, 1992.

Said, Edward W. "Yeats and Decolonization." In *Nationalism, Colonialism, and Literature*, edited by Terry Eagleton, Fredric Jameson and Edward W. Said. Minneapolis: University of Minnesota Press, 1990. 69–95.

Scharff, Virginia. *Taking the Wheel: Women and the Coming of the Motor Age*. Albuquerque: University of New Mexico Press, 1992.

Schivelbusch, Wolfgang. *The Railway Journey: The Industrialization of Time and Space in the Nineteenth Century*. Berkeley and Los Angeles: University of California Press, 1986.

Schriber, Mary Suzanne. *Writing Home: American Women Abroad, 1830–1902*. Charlottesville: University Press of Virginia, 1997.

Silk, Gerald. *Automobile and Culture*. Los Angeles: Museum of Contemporary Art; New York: Abrams, 1984.

Silko, Leslie Marmon. "Fences against Freedom." *Hungry Mind Review*, fall 1994, 9, 20, 58–59.

Silverman, Kaja. *The Acoustic Mirror: The Female Voice in Psychoanalysis and Cinema.* Bloomington: Indiana University Press, 1988.

Singer, Bayla. "Automobiles and Femininity." In *Research in Philosophy and Technology.* Vol. 13, *Technology and Feminism.* Greenwich, Conn.: JAI Press, 1993. 31–42.

Slotkin, Richard. *Regeneration through Violence: The Mythology of the American Frontier, 1600–1860.* Middletown, Conn.: Wesleyan University Press, 1973.

Smith, Sidonie. "Cheesecake, Nymphs, and 'We the People': About 1900 in America." *Prose Studies* (fall 1994): 120–40.

———. "Memory, Narrative, and the Discourses of Identity in *Abeng* and *No Telephone to Heaven.*" In *Postcolonialism and Autobiography*, edited by Alfred Hornung and Ernstpeter Ruhe. Amsterdam: Rodopi, 1998. 37–59.

———. *A Poetics of Women's Autobiography: Marginality and the Fictions of Self-Representation.* Bloomington: Indiana University Press, 1987.

———. "Re-citing, Re-siting, and Re-sighting Likeness: Reading the Family Archive in Drucilla Modjeska's *Poppy*, Donna Williams' *Nobody Nowhere*, and Sally Morgan's *My Place.*" *mfs* 40 (Fall 1994): 509–42.

———. *Subjectivity, Identity, and the Body: Women's Autobiographical Practices in the Twentieth Century.* Bloomington: Indiana University Press, 1993.

———. *Where I'm Bound: Patterns of Slavery and Freedom in Black American Autobiography.* Westport, Conn.: Greenwood, 1974.

Smith-Rosenberg, Carroll. *Disorderly Conduct: Visions of Gender in Victorian America.* New York: Knopf, 1985.

Smolan, Rick, and Robyn Davidson. *From Alice to Ocean: Alone across the Outback.* Against All Odds Productions, 1993. Book and CD-ROM.

Stallybrass, Peter, and Allon White. *The Politics and Poetics of Transgression.* Ithaca, N.Y.: Cornell University Press, 1986.

Stedman, John Gabriel. *Narrative of a Five Years' Expedition against the Revolted Negroes of Surinam.* 2 vols. 1796. Edited by Richard Price and Sally Price. Baltimore: Johns Hopkins University Press, 1971.

Stein, Gertrude. *The Autobiography of Alice B. Toklas.* New York: Harcourt, Brace & Co., 1933.

Stevenson, Catherine Barnes. *Victorian Women Travel Writers in Africa.* Boston: Twayne, 1982.

Stone, Allucquère Rosanne. *The War of Desire and Technology at the Close of the Mechanical Age.* Cambridge: MIT Press, 1995.

Torgovnick, Marianna. *Gone Primitive: Savage Intellects, Modern Lives*. Chicago: University of Chicago Press, 1990.

Tractenberg, Alan. Foreword to *The Railway Journey*, by Wolfgang Schivelbusch. Berkeley and Los Angeles: University of California Press, 1986. xiii–xvi.

Trzebinski, Errol. *The Lives of Beryl Markham*. New York: Norton, 1995.

Turkle, Sherry. "Constructions and Reconstructions of the Self in Virtual Reality." In *Electronic Culture: Technology and Visual Representation*, edited by Timothy Druckrey. New York: Aperture, 1996. 354–65.

Van Den Abbeele, Georges. *Travel as Metaphor: From Montaigne to Rousseau*. Minneapolis: University of Minnesota Press, 1992.

Wajcman, Judy. *Feminism Confronts Technology*. Cambridge, England: Polity Press, 1991.

Ware, Susan. *Still Missing: Amelia Earhart and the Search for Modern Feminism*. New York: Norton, 1993.

Warhol, Robyn, and Helena Michie. "Twelve-Step Teleology: Narratives of Recovery/Recovery as Narrative." In *Getting a Life: Everyday Uses of Autobiography*, edited by Sidonie Smith and Julia Watson. Minneapolis: University of Minnesota Press, 1996. 327–50.

Watson, Julia. "Unspeakable Differences: The Politics of Gender in Lesbian and Heterosexual Women's Autobiographies." In *De/Colonizing the Subject: Gender and the Politics of Women's Autobiography*, edited by Sidonie Smith and Julia Watson. Minneapolis: University of Minnesota Press, 1992. 139–68.

Wharton, Edith. *A Motor-Flight through France*. New York: Scribner, 1908.

Wohl, Robert. *A Passion for Wings: Aviation and the Western Imagination*. New Haven, Conn.: Yale University Press, 1994.

Wolff, Janet. "On the Road Again: Metaphors of Travel in Cultural Criticism." *Cultural Studies* 7.2 (May 1993): 224–39.

Woolf, Virginia. *Between the Acts*. New York: Harcourt Brace, 1941.

———. "Mr. Bennett and Mrs. Brown." London: L. and V. Woolf, 1924.

———. *Mrs. Dalloway*. New York: Harcourt Brace, 1925.

———. *The Voyage Out*. London: Duckworth, 1915.

———. *The Years*. New York: Harcourt Brace, 1937.

Zitkala-Ša [Gertrude Bonnin]. "Four Autobiographical Narratives." 1900, 1902. In *Classic American Autobiographies*, edited by William L. Andrews. New York: Mentor, 1992. 413–62.

**Sidonie Smith** is currently director of women's studies and professor of English and women's studies at the University of Michigan. Her books include *A Poetics of Women's Autobiography* and *Subjectivity, Identity, and the Body: Women's Twentieth-Century Autobiographical Practices*. She has co-edited, with Julia Watson, *De/Colonizing the Subject: The Politics of Gender in Women's Autobiography* (Minnesota, 1992), *Getting a Life: Everyday Uses of Autobiography* (Minnesota, 1996), and *Women, Autobiography, Theory: A Reader*. Her book *Reading Autobiography*, coauthored with Julia Watson, is forthcoming from the University of Minnesota Press.

# Index

Adams, Henry, 73
Adas, Michael, 121
adventure: associations with, 9
African women: agency and cross-cultural identification, 68; as defined by travel, ix; forced transport of, 12–13
airplane: as masculine prosthesis, 76
air travel, 73–120; conclusions about, 115–19; versus cyberspace travel, 204; Earhart's domestication of, 93–94; Earhart's narrative of, 87–95; Lindbergh's narrative of, 95–106; Markham's narrative of, 106–19; masculinization of, 75, 79–80; narratives of, 78–80. *See also* individual writers
Alcoholics Anonymous, self-recovery through, 150–53, 164
alcoholism: identity through, 150–53
Alloula, Malek, 40–41, 213n.7
Angelou, Maya, xiv, 200–201

Anzaldúa, Gloria, xiv
Arzner, Dorothy, 82, 83, 86, 115–16
Australia: indigenous people, 62–67, 215n.22
automobile: electric versus gasoline-driven, 174; female access to, 188–90; gender and, 171–76, 183, 185–87; identity and, 188–89; male sexual prowess and, 183; perception and, 169–71; as prosthetic device, 170; social change and, 168–69; social relations and, 199; suburbanization and, 24; women as market for, 173–74
automobiling: bad girls and, 182–90; Donofrio's narrative of, 182–90; flight as metaphor for, 179; masculine versus feminine, 174–75; versus rail travel, 179–80; and romance of travel, 199
automobility: deconstructing myths